The Survival of English

BOOKS BY IAN ROBINSON

Chaucer's Prosody (1971)

Chaucer and the English Tradition (1972)

Edited by Ian Robinson

The Human World, a quarterly review of English letters
The Brynmill Publishing Co.
130 Bryn Road, Brynmill, Swansea SA2 0AT

The Survival of English

English

essays in criticism of language

Ian Robinson

Lecturer in English Language in the
University College of Swansea

O gentile Engleterre, a toi j'escrits
Pour remembrer ta joie q'est novelle

Cambridge
at the University Press
1973

Published by the Syndics of the Cambridge University Press
Bentley House, 200 Euston Road, London NW1 2DB
American Branch: 32 East 57th Street, New York, N.Y.10022

Library of Congress Catalogue Card Number: 72–96680

ISBN: 0 521 20191 8

Printed in Great Britain by
Western Printing Services Ltd, Bristol

Language games are played by men who have lives to live: lives involving a wide variety of different interests, which have all kinds of different bearings on each other. Because of this what a man says or does may make a difference not merely to the performance of the activity he is at present engaged on, but to his *life* and to the lives of other people. Whether a man sees point in what he is doing will then depend on whether he is able to see any unity in his multifarious interests, activities and relations with other men; what sort of sense he sees in his life will depend on the nature of this unity. The ability to see this sort of sense in life depends not merely on the individual concerned, though this is not to say that it does not depend on him at all; it depends also on the possibilities for making such sense which the culture in which he lives does, or does not, provide.

Peter Winch

Und eine Sprache vorstellen heißt, sich eine Lebensform vorstellen.

Wittgenstein

What desperately needs to be emphasized in the present plight of mankind is the essential human creativity that is human responsibility.

F. R. Leavis

To Hilary Berrow

Contents

Acknowledgments

This book does not pretend to be a work of philosophy, but it could fail if its philosophical bearings are hopeless; and so I am grateful to Professor D. Z. Phillips for having warned me of some of the things wrong with a draft of the first chapter. Any absurdities that remain after drastic rewriting cannot be laid to Professor Phillips's charge. I gratefully acknowledge the sabbatical term, arranged by the English Department of the University College of Swansea and permitted by the College Council, which enabled me to finish the book. I am obliged to the editors of *The Cambridge Quarterly* for permission to reprint in chapter 2 some fragments of an essay from their volume ii, no. 4 (1967). A first version of chapter 3 appeared in the excellent and unfortunately defunct *Oxford Review*, Hilary, 1968. I am also grateful to the following for giving me permission to reprint the texts of complete poems in copyright. Jonathan Cape Ltd for 'All Fools' Day' by Adrian Mitchell from *Poems*; Faber and Faber Ltd for 'Talking in Bed' by Philip Larkin from *The Whitsun Weddings*; Hart-Davis Ltd and Ronald Duncan for 'Words are a Net' from *Collected Poems*; Deborah Rogers Ltd, London, and Adrian Henri for 'Remember' Copyright © 1967 by Adrian Henri, from *Love, Love, Love* (Corgi).

Things here and there throughout the book, in particular in chapters 4 and 5, derive from work published in *The Human World*, and it is in them that the influence of Mr David Sims, strong throughout, is most direct. Some few of the phrases in these passages and in chapter 6 are in fact his – the best ones, I suspect. My substantial debts to other contributors to *The Human World* are acknowledged at the places where they are incurred.

The dedication commemorates some conversations in the summer of 1967 during which I realized I was trying to define a subject which, to be properly treated, would need a book; since then, though parts have appeared piecemeal, I have always thought of them as deriving from a whole.

Swansea, 1961–72   I.R.

I

Introductory: Language and Life

In the beginning was language . . . That was the true light, which lighteth every man that cometh into the world.

'Everything exists, nothing has value.' Mrs Moore in *A Passage to India* learns this from the god of the Marabar caves, and it is the end of her. As far as we are concerned – and beyond that 'what we cannot speak about we must pass over in silence' – we have to be able to rewrite the sentence and say everything has value, nothing merely 'exists'. With her values, her sense of the difference between marriage and rape, Mrs Moore has lost what F. R. Leavis calls a 'grasp of a real', as well as her will to go on living. Her death, merely reported later in the novel, only confirms, without much emphasizing it, that anything truly to be called 'her life' has ended.

'Value' is not always the same as 'significance', but I do not wish to distinguish them yet. To say, though, that nothing exists without significance offends our commonsense, for one of our central beliefs in the modern world, when we are not merely taking it for granted, is that things exist whether they mean anything or not. I don't want to join the ranks of the flightier descendants of Bishop Berkeley who airily deny the existence of things, or to contend that we create the universe unaided, merely by looking at it. Yet things can only exist for 'the human race, to which so many of my readers belong' as what they mean to it, no more and no less. Knowledge organizes the meaning of things, and the specialist academic disciplines are specially developed styles of organized meaning, in which the existence of things is especially cultivated in one way or another.

'But,' a friend objects with the voice of commonsense, 'I find it restful to think that some things exist without significance, especially when you and I aren't watching.' So do I. That way of imagining things is one way of giving them significance, as well as of reminding oneself that there are in the world things other than oneself. But what of the same things when nobody is imagining them? What of the unimaginable things not yet discovered? –

America before Columbus, say, or Australia before Cook? They begin to exist, as far as we're concerned, as they are discovered – when they can be given the place in life that their discovery entails. What difference could it make to say they existed before that? Yet we *do* like to believe in a creation myth that has the things first lying about in a calmly untrammelled way, a complete world waiting ready-made for Adam, who invents language by giving names to the creatures and later, perhaps, begins asking what all these existent things mean in his life. (This wouldn't do even as an account of the Book of Genesis, where Adam has a conversation with God before naming anything – he comes to the creatures, that is to say, with a ready-made language within which the names can make their sense and in the absence of which it would make no sense to talk of 'naming'.) Even D. H. Lawrence used to comfort himself with the thought that the world would get on quite well without us, handed over to the rabbits – a very human imagination quite beyond a rabbit. Modern science, we are comparably told in popular histories of ideas, has displaced the earth from the centre of the universe, which is seen as a large collection of objects with, presumably, some geometric centre. This, however, is another human vision: it presupposes a point of view.

If things exist as meaning, the context where they do so can only be our lives. We are the people to whom things signify. The centre of the universe is therefore where it always has been, in all the human lives on earth.

Sometimes we can change the meaning of a thing by seeing it in a different aspect (cf. L. Wittgenstein, *Philosophical Investigations*, 2nd edn (1958), section IIxi) and in those cases the meaning of a thing will depend upon the exercise of the individual will within the bounds of the trained human imagination. Some things and experiences do change as we look back on them (or *we* change, which is here the same thing). I am not asserting, though, that in general we simply *decide* what things mean, any more than we simply decide that the world exists. Yet I would say we are all responsible for our world. That problem – how we can be said to will the existence of a world to which there is no alternative for us but madness or death – is one of the themes of the following discussions, suggesting the underlying question: what it can be, in the context of such concerns, to will the good. Things are, at any rate, whatever they mean to an individual.

Events, like things, are always the same as their significance.

Even in common speech, to be an event in one's life what happens must mean something. Imagine being hit on the head and losing consciousness. What the blow means, its real existence, is certainly the blow in itself – but in your life. The meaning depends on the circumstances, your character, etc., as well as on whatever is physically measurable about it. As you recover and think about what happened you may give the event any number of different meanings as you understand it differently. (If the blow is a rock falling from a cliff, that in itself will make the event different from your wife or husband dropping it on you with precisely the same physical force.) Moreover, the way you create the event by understanding it may affect the pace and style of recovery. (I introduce the ideas of discussion and response, by which I mean criticism, so early into the argument because they are central to my theme.) But nobody who has ever been hit hard on the head will want to deny that that is something unalterable which has happened to the body.

'The same' event is different for different people. I leave my wallet in a telephone box, go back five minutes later and, as the saying goes, 'find it gone'. Anyone else at that moment looking into the box would see the same interior, but nobody else would see the wallet missing. (Someone else during the previous five minutes, unfortunately from my point of view but not theirs, saw the missing wallet, but that is different.) This same event was different in the experience of the local constabulary – almost, one might say, a non-event. It consisted in a bored but sympathetic policeman filling up two forms which thereupon disappeared from his life and (one can say) from existence, until summoned back to their present ghostly imaginative being or momentarily glimpsed during some clearance of files. For some undiscovered third party the same event was a lucky find, possibly accompanied by pangs of conscience. The interesting thing from the point of view of the present discussion is our capacity to make 'the same' event of these different experiences and describe it in such a simple sentence as 'I left my wallet in a telephone box and it was stolen.'

So far, much of what I have written would apply to all forms of life that achieve consciousness. Remove a hen's chickens and the event, for the hen, is the emotions and instincts she then experiences, which it would not be stretching the word too far to call the 'meaning' of the event.

3

For a hen her young are not a source of torment. She does for them what it is natural and pleasurable for her to do ... When a chick falls ill her duties are quite definite: she warms and feeds it. And doing this she knows that she is doing all that is necessary. If her chick dies she does not have to ask herself why it died, or where it has gone to; she cackles for a while, and then leaves off and goes on living as before.

Tolstoy, *The Kreutzer Sonata*, transl. Aylmer Maude, chapter 16

The hen's experience is limited by her nature of a hen, a proper study of zoology. But if *our* experience is comparably limited, the nature in question must be human nature, which is not determinable by zoology. Something an onlooker might call the same event might be experienced very differently by different hens (if it is one pecking another or one getting to the corn-trough before another, for instance). The difference between hens and humans relevant to this discussion is that for us things and events vary coherently in ways they can't for hens.

Think of an old photograph of, let us say, your Victorian great-great-grandmother. Imagine it to be in an excellent state of preservation, so that for the sake of argument we can assume it to be as good as new. It is, nevertheless, not the same photograph as when it was new. It is different according to each viewer: one may recognize the subject, another may see the dress as foreign, one may note the different finish made by a technique of which others know nothing. Nobody can see a photograph without seeing, individually, things of this sort; but the interesting thing here is that some of the variations are general within a culture. All modern viewers who know what 'Victorian' means will see this as an old photograph with the look of an old photograph; and that phrase will be understood by almost anyone able to read it. The photograph has generally changed because it now has the sense of an old photograph.

The last movement of J. C. Bach's first keyboard concerto sounds extremely odd, in one particular way, to all British listeners, but not to anyone else in quite the same way, for it consists of a set of variations on the theme of what is now our national anthem. We cannot not notice that; it is inevitably part of listening to the work, for us. But there must be many listeners to 'the same' music for whom it hasn't that sense at all. The reality there varies with different cultures.

The fact that we all see things from a unique individual point of view does not mean, then, that there are no connections between our different individualities; and I argue so obvious a point only because there is something in the present climate of the West that makes it hard for people to accept. The more important step is to bring out the even less well-recognized truth that unless we could communicate – unless there were phrases like 'an old photograph' we can all understand – we would not be able to develop our unique differences.

If I had to tell in this context the difference between us and hens, I would answer either that we are the creatures with souls, or that we are the creatures who talk. I would not mean that the two things are always the same, but that the connection between them, the way that a common view of the world may grant the individual the possibility of his own unique view, does differentiate us from the animal kingdom.

Our view of the world, the way the individual sees things, is also the way we put things together. We call ourselves *homo sapiens* and think that a kind of knowing, or thinking, or reasoning, unique in the natural creation, distinguishes our humanity. The power to make sense, to put things together, to compose, that I am referring to, is what at widest one means by 'thought'. We think when we make connections or comparisons between meanings. And what could be more individual and unfettered than to make a comparison? We are quite free to make any sense – any connection between things and events and experiences – which inspiration may suggest to us, and we do so, for instance, in dreams.

It wouldn't be stretching the word far to call this composing activity itself language; St John seems to be doing so in my epigraph. It must be in our beginning. If dreaming is a language of the soul it is because the soul is the agent for connecting the meanings. Our perceptions and experiences signify to us in a vast variety of ways, and our world is the sum of the connections we make between them.

We think, dream, make the connections, see the bearings which come to us by pure inspiration. But it is also true that we make connections and see bearings every time we use a common noun; and words, though they may come to us as inspirationally as dreams, are limited by ordinary verbal language: this table is like other tables within the limits of our use of the word.

My subject is the connection of the primitive human shaping activity with verbal language, the human reason as it lives in words. The book is all about different examples of the interplay between language and life, and I take up the general discussion at the beginning of chapter 5 and in the last chapter. At present I will only record my belief that without the common systems of sense, the natural languages, human beings could not put their nature as *homo sapiens* into practice and could not know that they were rational creatures.

I introduced the blow on the head and the lost wallet because I did not want to prejudice my issues by using examples of 'things' which obviously have no home outside verbal language, and I agree with D. H. Lawrence's doctrine in *Psychoanalysis and the Unconscious*:

> We know the sun. But we cannot conceive the sun, unless we are willing to accept some theory of burning gases, some cause-and-effect nonsense. And even if we do have a mental conception of the sun as a sphere of blazing gas – which it certainly isn't – we are just as far from knowing what *blaze* is. Knowledge is always a matter of the whole experience, what St Paul calls knowing in full, and never a matter of mental conception merely.
>
> (chapter 2)

I shall nevertheless try to argue – and I don't think it is inconsistent – that our knowledge is dependent on language, in the ordinary sense of the words we use. 'Knowing what "blaze" is' is, as Lawrence says, a matter of the whole experience; but equally it is a knowledge of words. It is also 'knowing that this is "blaze"' – a word not exactly translatable into French. That is to say that for the French the whole experience of knowing what 'blaze' is must be different from ours, even though *any* burnt child fears the fire. There are many areas of experience and feeling where dependence on verbal language is more obvious. 'It doesn't feel like Saturday today.' But it couldn't, without that particular way of organizing the week. (Would it follow that Saturday is unnatural?) 'I felt like a millionaire.' Among the necessary constituents of the feeling is a knowledge of what 'a million' means, which is impossible outside a language with a number-system. I talk about the 'feeling' of these bits of language in order to register agreement with R. G. Collingwood's doctrine[1] that language permits a vastly greater range of emotions than can be experienced by the brute creation.

Partly the difficulty in thinking about the question of individuality and speech is that our individuality isn't quite of the

[1] See *The Principles of Art* (1938), pp. 266ff.

kind we like to believe. From the fact that we are all unique
it does not follow that our uniqueness always expresses itself
(as we may fall into assuming) as difference from other human
beings. 'When she knew that: $x^2 - y^2 = (x+y)(x-y)$ then she
felt that she had grasped something, that she was liberated into
an intoxicating air, rare and unconditioned.'[2] Ursula's knowledge is here an intensely individual experience which depends,
however, on precisely the same knowledge being available to
other individuals.

Further, our individuality itself has to develop within a common verbal language which we share with others (however individually we use it) and which differs from other languages in ways
not explicable by individual whim on the one hand or the prescribed physical limits of human beings on the other.

Children cannot be taught language. They are corrected and
guided once they begin to speak, but the primitive activity of
making connections and comparisons cannot be taught, nor the
possibility of doing it in words. Before the child begins to speak
all the parents can do is surround it with humanity and wait for it
to latch on. 'When did he say his first word?' mothers ask each
other, and any answer implies that before that date the baby was
not only *homunculus sapiens*, a rational creature, but capable of
understanding (at one level) verbal language, in which the 'first
word' alone makes sense. It doesn't follow that if a child repeats
syllables after its mother it has begun to speak, any more than
when a parrot imitates us. There is more sense than there may
seem in saying that children begin to talk when they want to.
(And talking is always a *commitment* to a world.)

D. H. Lawrence and R. G. Collingwood give a surprisingly
similar answer to the question *when* a child leaves behind him
that mysterious infant state and begins to come to a human
consciousness.

At first the child cleaves back to the old source. It clings and adheres.
The sympathetic centre of unification, or at least unison, alone seems
awake. The child wails with the strange desolation of severance, wails
for the old connection. With joy and peace it returns to the breast, almost
as to the womb.

But not quite. Even in sucking it discovers its new identity and *power*.
Its own new, separate *power*. It draws itself back suddenly; it waits. It has
heard something? No. But another centre has flashed awake. The child

[2] D. H. Lawrence, *The Rainbow*, chapter 10.

stiffens itself and holds back. What is it, wind? Stomach-ache? Not at all. Listen to some of the screams. The ears can hear deeper than eyes can see. The first scream of the ego. The scream of asserted isolation. The scream of revolt from connection, the revolt from union. There is a violent anti-maternal motion, anti-everything. There is a refractory, bad-tempered negation of everything, a hurricane of temper. What then? After such tremendous unison as the womb implies, no wonder there are storms of rage and separation. The child is screaming itself rid of the old womb, kicking itself in a blind paroxysm into freedom, into separate, negative independence.

Lawrence, Psychoanalysis and the Unconscious, chapter 3

Every one who is accustomed to looking after small children, in addition to distinguishing the cry of pain from the cry of hunger and so forth – various kinds of psychical expression – learns to distinguish the automatic cry of uncontrolled emotion from the self-conscious cry which seems (through a certain exaggeration on the listener's part) deliberately uttered in order to call attention to its needs and to scold the person to whom it seems addressed for not attending to them. The second cry is still a mere cry; it is not yet speech, but it is language. It stands in a new relation to the child's experience as a whole. It is the cry of a child aware of itself and asserting itself. With that utterance, language is born; its articulation into fully developed speech in English or French or some other vernacular is only a matter of detail.[3]

Collingwood, Principles of Art, p. 236

This voluntary assertion of conscious individuality is itself the beginning of the child's re-creation of a world he shares with others. Collingwood says a little later:

The discovery of myself as a person is the discovery that I can speak, and am thus a *persona* or speaker; in speaking, I am both speaker and hearer; and since the discovery of myself as a person is also the discovery of other persons around me, it is the discovery of speakers and hearers other than myself.

(Ibid. p. 248)

The child's 'first word' is often 'Mama' or something similar; and no child, obviously, will get far in life in an ordinary family until it begins to recognize mother. Children and mothers are notoriously free to make an infinite variety of different relationships, according to their characters and desires – but limited by their opportunities. Calling her 'mother' is an important part of the child's recognition. But the role of mothers varies with (*inter*

---

[3] It is plain from the rest of the chapter that Collingwood doesn't, as this brilliant sentence alone might suggest, think the 'matter of detail' unimportant.

alia) the culture they inhabit, the language they are named in. Mothers cannot be the same in matriarchal and patriarchal societies; the corresponding words for 'mother' express the differences to native speakers. The child begins the path towards naturally seeing his mother in one of the particular ways of the language he speaks as soon as he begins to recognize her with the word. This is not an alternative to knowing his individual mother, but part of it.

'We know we have freewill and there's an end on't,' said Johnson, thus offering a definition of human nature which differs from mine less than may appear (if, at least, I can get this paragraph anything like as comprehensible as the arguments of Mr Rush Rhees, and of Wittgenstein in *On Certainty*, on which I base it). But it is a little odd to say we *know* we have freewill, because freewill (like being able to talk) is a precondition of anything we usually call knowledge. (I am writing these words voluntarily. But how do I *know* that? Perhaps I don't. Not that I suspect some mysterious involuntary force, or someone else, of pushing the pen; but questions about knowing – by what evidence? and so on – just don't arise: which is why I can't say, either, that I do know 'infallibly' that I *am* writing. I say so to limit a later use of that dangerous word.) There's nothing odd in saying things like 'I intend to finish this this evening', nothing odd about human beings stating their individual intentions, in time; indeed, if we couldn't make suchlike voluntary, temporal statements *we* wouldn't exist, though other creatures of similar physique might, naked apes or the like. But there can be no freedom of the will and no time without their respective 'grammars'. 'I'll do so-and-so soon' is so natural, so deep down among our foundations, that it is hard for us to see that things like will or time are language-dependent and that they can indeed vary from language to language.

'Second nature' is therefore often a misleading phrase. We say that so-and-so has become second nature to us, supposing that really it is something added to the basic us who remain unchanged somewhere beneath it: people often classify language, the ordinary first language we begin to speak, as second nature in this sense. But if our language is our second nature where is the first? Must it be confined to our physical constitution (even if that can be imagined somehow unmodified in life)? People think so. For instance ' [Chomsky] has claimed that the principles underlying the structure of language are so specific and so highly articulated that they must be regarded as being biologically determined; that is to say, as constituting part of what we call "human nature" and as being genetically transmitted from parents to their children.'[4] That restricts human nature to the genetic foundation of life. Similarly Mr Gore Vidal on the roles of the sexes: 'By the age of four or five boys are acting in a very different manner from girls. Since there is no hormonal explanation for this, the answer is plainly one of indoctrination.'[5] Nature would make boys and girls exactly alike at five, he thinks, and if they aren't, then there is something unnatural.

But higher systems organize lower. Faces are, in some cases, physical, but the physical does not explain what it is about a face that allows us to call it so. The face's expression explains the physicality of the face; or rather the physicality is expressed, made meaningful, *in* the face, by being seen as a face. It is the nature of a face to be a face, and that is what organizes the physical constituency of the face, not *vice versa.*[6] It is *our* nature to think and to talk, and if we didn't we wouldn't be somehow pristinely natural, we'd be sub-human. 'Commanding, questioning, recounting, chatting, are as much a part of our natural history as walking, eating, drinking, playing.'[7]

Speaking a language is then part of the natural individuality of every human being and we become ourselves in it; but language is also something each individual creates in common with others. Surely this is the sense (however it was originally intended) in the old Greek tag 'man is a social animal'. I don't think it can be argued that we cease to be human if we avoid our fellows: hermits are not social animals in the obvious sense but are as human as the rest of us. But like ours their human individuality is only developed through and in the common possession, language.

---

[4] John Lyons, *Chomsky* (1970), p. 11.
[5] *The New York Review of Books*, 22 July 1971.
[6] The obvious case of a thing's existing as meaning is, of course, a linguistic utterance. A sentence is obviously itself only in the understanding of what it means. In a totally unknown language written in what look like sentences that appearance of being sentences is the extent of the existence of the sentences of the language. But sentences have their physical realization, too, in sound or writing, and a whole generation of linguisticians (as they then were) drove themselves to or beyond the limits of sanity by trying to restrict the study of language to this physical level, uncontrolled by the higher level of meaning, which does really control it.
[7] Wittgenstein, *Philosophical Investigations*, p. 12e.

Introductory: Language and Life

The normal child develops his power to talk, and the entry it gives him into the vast freedom of humanity, from what Chomsky calls the 'degenerate data'[8] furnished by his parents' 'language performance'. The world thus entered is not restricted to the child's family (since the parents' language is their version of the common language) but it *is* restricted to one language, and his individuality normally becomes one that can express itself in that language. The possibilities into which a child grows therefore vary (in ways it is my task to exemplify) with his language.

> O body swayed to music, O brightening glance,
> How can we know the dancer from the dance?

II

If things are what they mean, languages are shared systems for organizing what things mean, which is the same both as allowing them to exist and knowing them. A language is a form of the possibilities of a common sense, including the possibilities of change in a common sense. But how to discuss the form, the whole language? The ways people have attempted are notoriously difficult and various. (The bearings of my discussion upon the most widely respected contemporary way, the 'science of language', linguistics, are interesting, but I must reserve my attempt to treat them for another occasion.) I put the impossible-looking effort to see a language as a whole beside another: the two may seem more possible, though not much less formidable, if they can be seen as the same thing.

One responsibility of us all is to think about and try to understand the way civilization is going. But how to do that? How is so vague a phrase to become meaningful?

One way of coming at the unity of a civilization is to ask how many cultures there are. One? Two? Sixty-three? The question might be made to make sense if you re-phrase it to ask how many styles of a language there are and how they might bear upon one another to form a whole language. I suggest that the number of styles is infinite, but that they are all seen to be themselves, and defined, by their connections and contrasts with one another which form the whole. I use 'style' here in a wide sense, the sense I intended when I said that specialist academic disciplines are different styles of organizing knowledge. But it also is true enough

[8] N. Chomsky, *Language and Mind* (1968), p. 68.

to take 'style' in the ordinary sense of (leaving aside for a moment the difficulties in the phrase) 'the way of saying a thing'.

Linguists of the school of J. R. Firth sometimes write of 'register', by which they mean a style appropriate to a particular situation. (I do not say a 'given' situation, because I think it is often the 'register' that 'gives'.) It makes sense to think of a register's selecting words and rhythms from the total possibility of the language. One modern fallacy I discuss in chapter 2 is that there is a simple, uniform, easily recognizable thing called 'ordinary language' (at which the great writers of our century, progressively abandoning style, are sometimes thought to have aimed). 'Ordinary speech' covers a range of styles only less numerous than those of the whole language. I am likely to speak in different styles to my mother, my doctor and my butcher, and in different styles to each on different occasions, though some styles will be usable to all on yet other occasions.

The *vast* range of styles in a language, quite beyond the reach of the traditional discipline of grammar even as developed by Chomsky, was one of the truths that dawned on Wittgenstein between the *Tractatus Logico-Philosophicus* and the *Philosophical Investigations*.

Think of exclamations alone, with their completely different functions.

> Water!
> Away!
> Ow!
> Help!
> Fine!
> No!

Are you still inclined to call these words 'names of objects'?

Wittgenstein, *Philosophical Investigations*, p. 13e

Speakers of the language know when to use which, and in what sense. This knowing what to say makes a unity of the very different parts of language by making sense of their contrasts and connections.

The recognition of the richness of the ordinary heritage of language is J. L. Austin's contribution to language-criticism (I won't say 'to philosophy', since he seems more interested in what English actually does than in philosophical questions about the possibility of language). 'Our common stock of words', he says, 'embodies all the distinctions that men have found worth drawing, and the connections they have found worth marking, in the lifetime of many generations.'[9] Austin is particularly good at showing how finely ordinary language can distinguish between the different situations of life – which is here the same as saying what fineness of life ordinary language makes possible, the fineness of the connections between things by which we make a world in common.

Written English like spoken English varies in the same writer from context to context as well as varying between different writers. (Think of the different ways of beginning and ending letters to business firms, family, newspapers, friends, lovers.)

Shaw, stumbling on the idea of the appropriateness of style to situation, rose far above himself in the one marvellously funny scene in *Pygmalion* (act III) where Liza, in her perfect upper-class accent, treats Mrs Higgins's At Home to gossip in the style that Shaw takes for the working-classes'. So, similarly, the best part of Mrs Muriel Spark's novel, *The Prime of Miss Jean Brodie*, is the chapter where two schoolgirls try to write a love story but have only the language of the divorce courts as reported in the popular press to do it in.

The complete range of styles available to the literate English, defined in their connections and contrasts, constitutes standard English. And a sense of the way standard English as a whole is going might emerge from comment on well-chosen examples of different styles.

A style carries with it the sense of what is proper to it (as I discuss further in the last chapter) and so does a whole language. There can be what I shall call 'common-language' judgments.

Take the following propositions:

(1) Murder is right and proper.
(2) All they that love not tobacco and boys are fools.
(3) Muck is beautiful.

These can all be said (so can those other well-formed English sentences 'Black is white', and 'Colourless green ideas sleep furiously'). Melville comes close to arguing (1) in *White Jacket*; Shakespeare's witches in *Macbeth* hold (3) together with its moral consequences; if Marlowe didn't say (2) it was at least rather convincingly attributed to him. The weight of the language is nevertheless against these expressions, the weight of the common values we create merely by speaking English. Setting aside the tobacco

[9] 'A Plea for Excuses'.

(2) would not have been offensive in classical Greek except in its attempted inclusiveness, but at the end of the sixteenth century the effort was not to *refute* the sentiment, only to establish that Marlowe had said it, which would in itself have established his guilt. If it is less offensive now, that says something about the changed values of the whole language. It is, of course, possible to go against the language. In one way the poet does so, stretching it, at least, further than one could have thought possible, and becoming within it a self one might not have supposed it could permit. In the extreme cases of going against language we have defined madness or tragedy, the latter being a man finding himself whole, the former unwhole, but 'at daggers drawn with the very forces of life itself' as they are made present to his own life through his language. (Marlowe wasn't tragic, only offensive.)

If we can see changes in the weightings of words, changes in the style of their use, we are seeing changes in the sense we all make; and if we can link the observations of change we might suggest things about the whole language. And that in itself will be saying things about the lives we lead, for it will define some of the common context in which alone we can be ourselves.

This is a possiblility the current talk of 'pluralism' would destroy, at least when it is used to say that it doesn't matter if members of the same society speak quite different and disconnected languages. It is possible to believe that genuine pluralism, a society of groups with nothing in common, can lead to a high civilization (India): my objection is to the casualness of the assumption that the Indianization of this country will be an improvement, the failure to see the importance in our life of a common language.

I believe in the morality of pluralism and compassion. Those who talk of 'life' should acknowledge that there are human beings of infinite complexity and variety who cannot be measured by a single moral yardstick. They cannot be so measured because there are many good ends; and these ends conflict. Mercy conflicts with justice, reverence with gaiety, change with order, stability with spontaneity, liberty with equality.

Lord Annan in *T.L.S.*, 30 April 1970, pp. 455–6

Leaving aside what might elsewhere be the important retorts that neither gaiety, change nor order are good ends in themselves, and that there are some moral yardsticks we do apply universally (calling murder 'múrder', for instance), I agree that *of course* our lives are made up of infinite complexity and differences, but object that the battles Lord Annan mentions must take place in the same war.

'Mercy' may perhaps conflict with 'justice', but the prior truth is that the former makes no sense without the latter: you can have no idea of mercy except in a language which shows it to conflict with justice. Lord Annan's 'yardstick', which he doesn't recognize as such, is the term 'human being'. I do not commit myself to the belief that we are all the same if I say that the possibility of using the phrase 'human being' precludes Lord Annan's pluralism.

In various ways, then, I shall be discussing aspects of what it is to be human in our time and place, by looking at the Wittgensteinian 'grammar' of words.

British universities, to take an obvious example, seem to me to have changed their nature in the last fifteen years. This could be established in various ways – by a history, for instance, or an appeal to introspection. A change in the idea of a university currently held can equally if not better be shown by an examination of the way the word is used. Its 'scatter' and 'collocability' have altered. The one phrase 'technological university', not applicable fifteen years since to any British degree-granting body, itself says a good deal. And it is now commonplace to talk of a university's 'output', of its 'producing' graduates. For instance a letter to *The Times*[10] urged universities to increase the 'production' of an 'out-turn' of graduates and referred to students as 'the young material'. That was a straightforward, and now more commonplace, application to universities of the language used of manufacturing industry; years later the only oddity is probably that anyone should think the use worth remark. It would nevertheless have been very surprising indeed in 1950 to find anyone writing of universities as if they were factories. To point this out is a final demonstration of the change, if you agree that the language now does work like that and that twenty years since it didn't, though it is possible in this case to resist the change: cf. below, p. 114. 'Industry' itself has changed. Things are now industries which twenty years ago would have been trades or professions. Farming used not to be thought of as an industry (it was just farming) nor even used publishing, but the latter is now officially described as an industry on the forms publishers are compelled by law to fill up under the Statistics of Trade Act 1947. (It would now surely have been called something more like 'The Statistics of Industry (Progress and Development) Act'.)

[10] 5 May 1966.

In much the same period 'military' (adjective) has been largely replaced by 'defence' (cf. the transformation of what used to be called 'para-military police' into 'security forces') so that the most purely offensive weapons in human history are budgeted for under a heading universally called 'defence spending'. This use of 'defence' began to come in with the Cold War: we were organizing *defence* against the Russians, who were increasing their military spending. The phrase 'defence spending' has now, however sunk so far into the ordinary that it is applied to the Russians as well, and there is nothing odd in thinking of their 'defence spending' that allowed them, for instance, to occupy Czechoslovakia at a moment's notice. So, too, we call our nuclear weapons 'the Deterrent', as if they were not weapons of mass-destruction but a kind of knight in shining armour. (The French are not so mealy-mouthed and talk, with a different magic, of their '*force de frappe*'.)

'Friendship' is one of the most important words. If the Rev. Chad Varah and his friends succeed in making friendship a commodity available anonymously to people who need distraction from their troubles, they will have altered the nature at once of friendship and of our language, and not, in my view, for the better. 'We've got about 14,000 Samaritans now ... The thing they offer is Instant Friendship to those in need. That's what being a Samaritan is all about – befriending people ... Most people just want to talk to anyone at the end of the phone.'[11] Friendships used not to be made like that in English. Here the voice of one style of commonsense will make itself heard (not one of the impressive kinds of commonsense, but not one I can afford to ignore) making some such complaint as: 'How academic and pettifogging! You sit in your armchair excoriating a group of people who do good to others in real need, just because of some verbal infelicity. Grammarians should leave life alone.' But I'm afraid I don't believe the 'Samaritans' do do any good, except by lucky chance. 'Samaritans' seem to be trying, as an essential part of their idea, to relieve people of the necessary (if intolerable) human responsibility for one's own life. It *is* wearing to be a human soul, but the soul is not to be saved (though life may be made more comfortable) by being given away.

I am not, then, making a gratuitous academic attack upon the Rev. Chad Varah, but pointing out what this modern develop-

[11] *Radio Times* interview, 17 February 1972.

ment of the grammar of 'friendship' says about our life. I am
offering this as an example of that 'criticism of style' which 'becomes, as it follows down into analysis, criticism of the thought,
the essence, the pretentions'.[12] So I can add that I feel no surprise
when a Prime Minister contemporary with the modern 'Samaritans' can misuse friendship in a very comparable way. The word
has a political use, the lineal descendant of the Middle English
idea by which one's friends were the people who at a pinch would
turn up on the right side on the battlefield; politicians may therefore be forgiven for making friends where the rest of us would
think of acquaintances: the lobby must have its due. But it really
wasn't the great compliment Mr Harold Macmillan intended
when he wrote:

Perhaps the clue to her success was that she treated everybody exactly the
same; whatever their rank or station, they were all to be regarded as
friends and as people in whom she took a deep personal interest. Of course,
it would have been better if they had all been children, for it was with
children of all ages that she was supremely at her ease. If they must be
adults it was just too bad; and the best thing to do was to treat them also
more or less like children.

Pointing the Way (1972), pp. 27–8

Being the friend of everybody is exactly the same as being the
friend of nobody: to treat everybody the same is to fail to distinguish between people, and in that case you may indeed just as
well treat everybody as children – or as dogs or cats, though even
in those cases there would be a certain insult to the animals'
identity. The vacuity of this idea of friendship is, in other words,
an emptiness at once of language and of life.

It seems to me a comforting sign of the congruity of things
that *Vanity Fair*'s 'Guide to the New Sexual Etiquette' (mentioned in chapter 5, below) should offer the same doctrine, more
explicitly. 'Friends are to be used. Use is not a dirty word' (p. 22).
Oh yes it is, there, if anybody is going to be a friend of anybody
else in English. For though we *do* use our friends, and a friend in
need is a friend indeed, the belief that friends are *to be* used
demolishes friendship. But if we make friends *in order* to use
them, or believe that use alone justifies 'friendship', the Samaritans can indeed provide friendship as a social service.

Even the layers of language mentioned above (p. 9) that we
take utterly for granted do alter and are sometimes attacked. If the

[12] F. R. Leavis, *Nor Shall My Sword* (1972), p. 44.

older American school of structural linguistics were to get its way and impose on us a 'grammar' in which language was a system of cause-and-effect, or stimulus-and-response, they would to the extent of the acceptance of their view have demolished human nature (the sense, for instance, of the personal pronouns and of all expressions of intention) for they would have got rid of the freedom of the will.

We could make the crude beginnings of a suggestion about how English as a whole has gone since the fifties by putting together such notes on the new styles of use of important words.

The connections between rationality, the way an individual connects the things and events that make sense in life, and language, in the narrower sense of the words he speaks, span a very wide range. I am anxious not to suggest the absurdity that our verbal language is a set of shackles, forcing us into one set of opinions or beliefs, and I might say so by commending part of Chomsky's basic doctrine, that any language is an *infinite* set of sentences. All the same another part, that not all imaginable sentences belong to a language, is also true. I am not here restricting the discussion to Chomsky's grammatical criteria but am interested in other ways a language may decide that something makes a sense proper to it, of which the above 'common-language judgment' is one.

There are, of course, many cases where a sense is language-defined and where no individual (unless a cataclysmic poet or scientist, and only then by a kind of conversion of other users) can vary it. It is not open to the individual arithmetician to say that two plus two is five; for though the sentence is in fact frequently used in English and is 'well formed', as a proposition it is ruled out of arithmetic. That rule isn't of grammar in Chomsky's sense; it is, so to speak, a rule of meaning. All languages have a great multiplicity of different kinds of such rules which are applied in a great multiplicity of ways.

At another extreme one might think that language can sometimes be purely an implement with the help of which we express what on earth we like, unaffected by the language. This looks suspicious to me (freedom to say *anything* makes me think rather of the creative effort, *within* the rules of common speech, of Shakespeare) but perhaps there are cases. For instance, to express sudden pain or dismay or fury you might make an appropriate noise or you might utter words – almost any words, so that sometimes we hear 'Ow!' and sometimes 'My God!' with the same meaning. The latter has no connection with the rules of theology and little with the language of religion; the meaning depends on what feeling is put into it, not on any dictionary definition. (Yet even here the feeling, to be intelligible, has to be expressed in the rhythms and intonations of your language.)

My concern in this book is with a vast central area between the two extremes, an area where language may sometimes be seen shaping individual lives in various ways (but always in co-operation with the individual) sometimes only influencing the individual – who may, then, resist the push it gives him .

Political English, I argue in chapter 3, is an orthodoxy that can be resisted, though with difficulty, from within the modern common language. The language of sex, on the other hand, has many layers, and one may use the deeper ones to evaluate the shallower. But with the subject of my first discussion, the language of religion, it seems to me that we have a change in language which directly affects everyone, whether we will or no (because it is a loss of possibility), and on which we can gain a perspective only by including the language of former times in our own language.

Is 'love' just a label like (in some cases) 'moon', for something we can't help seeing in the world and which is there whether we name it or not? It is tempting to say so, and I don't want to argue that 'love' would make any sense unless there were something answering to it really present in the world which one can sometimes see without using the word. It is also true that love is far from being kept in bounds by language or anything else, in some cases. I shall argue all the same that there *is* an interaction between the thing and the word which makes the word more than a label, that the use of the word affects the sense of the thing, and that since the sense (by my earlier argument) is the real existence of the thing, even here word affects thing and love as we really know it in life varies with the way we use 'love'.

My effort in the succeeding chapters is to conduct the argument in such a way as to show what is the connection between the language and the individual life in each different case.

I am not offering a method, only, I hope, an occasional illumination. Such as it is, however, any light thrown is infallible, for the meaning of language is our criterion of truth. I used the quotation from the fourth gospel as an epigraph not for its doctrine of Christ as the Word but because of its convincing and quite general statement of the place of language in every individual life. If the true light lighteth every man that cometh into the world one is not required to subscribe to Christian doctrine to see in that light. On the contrary, John is there offering a definition of the human: we are those individuals whose lives are illuminated by the *logos*. We can make mistakes in language and let us hope that we live and learn. But to be *generally* mistaken in our use of language would be to be incorrigibly mad. We can know that our language works as surely as (though not more surely than) that we are alive and sane. If you agree with me when I say 'This is so, isn't it?' about some of the things we do to language and *vice versa*, or if you want to continue the discussion, we have demonstrated at least, with the substantiality of human life, that some final truth lies between us – final because it is our life, the kind of reality that Mrs Moore loses. It can't be a *mistake* to know one is alive.

We suffer deeply, in an age when scientific method is venerated outside science, from the confusion represented by the words 'subjective' and 'objective'. As we ordinarily use the word, an objective view or opinion is something superior and reliable which excludes mere individual irrelevance. So far, perhaps, so good: disinterested and informed opinion certainly is a need and something to be respected. But the usual corollary is to deny that real knowledge is 'subjective' – to deny that it belongs in individual experience. And that is to confuse the kind of intellectual reliability we may hope for. The individual does master different styles of looking and thinking which are appropriate to different parts of life: there are different rules for different studies, and when we do experiments with lights we refrain (unless we're Goethe) from saying how beautiful the colours are. But doing physics is not less subjective than seeing beauty; both activities belong to the individual. The 'objective' view of physics is simply that style of looking which is appropriate to the study. The use of 'subjective'/'objective' ought instead to be to remind ourselves of the way we create a reliable common world from our different individual viewpoints – and *vice versa*. When the dentist pulls out my tooth that is an intense subjective experience for me, but objectively I see the dentist being a dentist. From his point of view he is subjectively doing his job and objectively looking at me cowering in the chair. A man feels subjectively angry but we

objectively see him turn red. Eyes objectively speak but subjectively look. Add the two up and you get in one case a visit
to the dentist, in the second an idea of anger, in the third of looking – and my point is that those descriptive terms are as reliable
and sure as the experiences they refer to. It is as More makes
the dying Edward IV say: 'My Lordes, my dere kinsmenne and
alies, in what plighte I lye you see, and I feele.' Apart from the
obvious pathological conditions, I can't be mistaken in saying I
have been to the dentist's unless I can also be mistaken that he is
pulling my tooth out. My language there is as unfailing as the
experience. This book is about some of the ways in which the
two are interdependent.

> Love thy country, wish it well,
>   Not with too intense a care;
> Be content that when it fell
>   Thou its ruin didst not share.

But if the country's fate touches its language it touches the lives
of all the people. We cannot escape the ruin of our country if
that is how it occurs rather than by conquest. Decline of language
is the decline of the life of the people who use it, which is why
I began with Mrs Moore. If her plight were general, if it were
how the English language ordinarily worked, instead of being
recognizable as such within the language (in this case E. M.
Forster's), there would be no possibility of sense in our lives; and
homo sapiens could no longer apply to us even if anybody were
left to try to do so. Conversely, great creativity in language, if it
is recognized, can only deepen life. (I discuss in the last chapters
how that might be seen as an improvement, which is a much
harder question than it looks.)

These thoughts may begin to suggest my theme: how judgments
on a whole style of life might be made, and with what limitations,
by comment on different styles of language – how, that is, Leavis's
remark, bolder even than Wittgenstein's in my epigraph, might be
true: 'A language *is* a life . . .'[13]

[13] *The Human World*, no. 2 (1971), p. 28.

2

Religious English

Thy testimonies have I claimed as mine heritage for ever: and why? they are the very joy of my heart.

(Psalm 119: 111; 1611 Version)

I

We all try to see signs of the times. In 1961 the publication of the New English Bible (N.E.B.) version of the New Testament and its enthusiastic reception (one year after the trial and publication of *Lady Chatterley's Lover*) presented itself to me as unmistakably a sign of the times. The final outcome was that I wrote this book. Immediately, however, I did an odder thing; I wrote a letter to the *Guardian*, from which they printed the following passage.

The new New Testament is a dismaying document. How well known, from Moffatt down, is that uneasy but confident mixture of prim colloquiality, timid daring, and old-fashioned literariness; and what a shock to the hopes of those, after so many years of publicity in depth, who hoped for something better! The effect of 'But now that this son of yours turns up, after running through your money with his women, you kill the fatted calf for him' is typical: it is ludicrous – the imitation contemporary jargon (so up-to-date, you know, 'his women'), but the biblical fatted calf still there. This is in no known language; but then, anyone who thinks that 'you scoundrel!' is contemporary English will also probably think that 'fatted calf' is . . .

This noncontemporary piece of work aims all over the place. It has to be modern and up-to-date ('be quick about it' for 'quickly') and it has to be dignified ('the arrogant of heart and mind' for 'the proud'); it must be scholarly and yet easily understood; it must be accurate and yet in concise current English. It tries to be faithful to the Greek – yet it cannot wholly ignore the five hundred years of English experience.

The one aim it appears to have consistently is to be journalistic; and its one consistent effect is that it cheapens. 'It will' (as you yourself say) 'make Christian teaching easier. It will reach new generations more readily. That is its purpose.' But it is not *easy* to read the truth about God: one cannot expect to read about God in the same sort of language as one reads, even in the great liberal daily, about Mr Macmillan: and though this version is certainly more 'ready' than the Authorized Version, its language is apparently rather more journalistic than that of your leaders.

It is *easier* to read 'Tell out, my soul, the greatness of the Lord', than 'My soul doth magnify the Lord' primarily because the former has less

22

meaning. What *does* 'the greatness of the Lord' mean? And the apostrophic form – presumably in the simple Greek? – and easy pentameter serve their usual function of distracting the attention from the meaning.

The naïve overconfidence of the translators is well echoed by your two reviewers. 'The Bible,' says the Bishop of Middleton, 'comes from a pre-scientific age; its thought-forms belong to a "mythological" world-view . . . [which] has become blurred if not erased.' Yet he seems cheerfully to share the assumption of the translators that all it needs to get over this difficulty is an essay in nice, polite, donnish journalese! It would be much more convincing if he told us to go on using the great English translation which was not made into either a scientific or a journalistic language. 'Theological students,' as your other reviewer says, 'must still learn Greek' (though there are better reasons for learning Greek) but the rest of us who are not theological students will go on using the Authorized Version.

This brought forth a crop of answers, including the only threatening or anonymous letters I had then received. (One correspondent explained that expert advice had been taken in Smithfield Market and that 'fatted calf' *is* still current English – later in the decade the well of English was thought to flow more undefil'd from Billingsgate.) Why did both I and my anonymous and other correspondents feel that an outrage had been committed? This essay is an attempt to answer the question. Looking back, I still think that the N.E.B. New Testament was portentous, and that my immediate attempt to define the portent is a good enough introduction to the discussion, which I hope, however, can now be taken further.

Later in the sixties a drastic revision of the Prayer Book was undertaken; the Church of Rome abandoned Latin in favour of what may or may not rightly be called English (since the new services were composed by Americans in accordance with a Vatican desire that they should be uniform throughout the Anglo-Saxon world, and called by a word unknown to the English language, 'the New English Missalette'); and the new Roman Catholic version, the Jerusalem Bible, appeared and seemed to me not much better than the N.E.B. Finally the latter was completed in 1970 by versions of the Old Testament and Apocrypha and a revised version of the New Testament. The complete version was saluted by what one very favourable reviewer[1] called 'a fanfare unusually shrill and orchestrated'.

I found myself pondering the simple but difficult question why it is now so hard for even much-praised translators to render the

[1] *The Times*, 25 February 1970.

Word of God in English and for liturgists to provide language for the worship of God.

In the case of the N.E.B., however, that was not the most immediate question. One first naturally asked why the translators can't write English at all (and why so glaringly obvious a fact was generally missed by the literary critics who reviewed the version). 'What are we to make of the fact that, when we sample the translation, we find it written in an English which is muted, certainly, but also compact, clear, elegant and dignified?' asked Professor Donald Davie, an expert on the style of syntax, in the *Spectator*.[2] I can't answer his question. For it seems to me that many passages are so badly written, in a way any intelligent sixth-former and any editor would notice, as to be a kind of attack on the idea of modern English prose.

Now in this same district there were shepherds out in the fields, keeping watch through the night over their flock, when suddenly there stood before them an angel of the Lord, and the splendour of the Lord shone round them. They were terror-struck, but the angel said, 'Do not be afraid; I have good news for you: there is great joy coming to the whole people. Today in the city of David a deliverer has been born to you – the Messiah, the Lord. And this is your sign: you will find a baby lying all wrapped up, in a manger.' All at once there was with the angel a great company of the heavenly host, singing the praises of God:
'Glory to God in highest heaven,
And on earth his peace for men on whom his favour rests.'
Luke 2: 8–14 (1961)
(N.E.B. (1970), N.T. p. 71, reinstates the 'swaddling clothes')

This goes wrong with its first word, 'Now'. Is it 'now' a mere conjunction or has it some adverbial sense of 'at this time'? It turns out to be the former; but any competent writer of English knows that if 'now' equals 'and' it is confusing to have that sort of 'when'-clause later in the same sentence. Here, at the 'when' we have to go back and wonder if the 'now' wasn't temporal: it is almost as if the sentence is designed to confuse its deep grammar. 'Keeping watch through the night over their flock' abandons standard English word order for no reason, and so suggests that the shepherds are peering through the darkness over the top of the sheep and failing to see them. The next quoted sentence is a model misuse of syntax and rhythm. 'They were terror-struck, but . . .' – the suggestion is that if the sentence were clarified it would read, 'Though they were terror-struck, the angel

[2] 17 March 1961.

24

said . . .' The failure at this elementary level reminds one that there is no alternative to expressing ourselves through sentence shape and rhythm, and that unless the meaning controls them they will attack it. Again in the next sentence the clauses make no expressive shape, and the most important thing comes in the most unimportant place (so near to and so far from the 1611 version discussed below) tacked on by a dash, and having the effect of an afterthought when the sentence proper is over – 'the Messiah, the Lord'. 'Sign' is obscure; if I say 'This is your sign' there is no reason why you should know what I mean. 'Host' is archaic (it should have been 'army', but perhaps it would have been too unfashionable to associate God and an army) and 'singing the praises' is unfortunate cliché in which these translators seem more at home than elsewhere. 'All wrapped up' is a similar ridiculous descent into the wrong brand of colloquiality. But the worst thing is the attempt at poetry. 'Glory to God in highest heaven' is traditional cliché and nothing worse, but the next line is impossible: 'And on earth his peace for men on whom his favour rests.' This seems to be an acephalous long line of a poulter's measure, with all the rigidity of the form. It could not imaginably be sung; it is stiffly and unalterably prosaic. And the connection between stylistic and syntactic failure is clear in the line because the angels are singing so ambiguously that they seem to be trying to mislead or trap the shepherds. Do they mean that peace is for all men because God's favour rests on them, or that peace is for those God's favour happens to rest on? There is no knowing.

The passage is typical of the linguistic chaos of the version, which seems to carry us back to the ages before the development of English prose. There is something pre-Dryden in its amorphousness. Is it an exaggeration to call the passage an attack on the idea of prose? Try instead beginning the complete N.E.B. at the beginning and you find:

THE CREATION OF THE WORLD

In the beginning of creation, when God made heaven and earth, the earth was without form and void, with darkness over the face of the abyss, and a mighty wind that swept over the surface of the waters. God said, 'Let there be light,' and there was light; and God saw that the light was good, and he separated light from darkness.   Genesis 1: 1–4

The creation of earth is put into a temporal clause at two removes subordinated to a main clause saying that the earth was without form and void; that is sheer incompetence of expression in English. The 'and's' later in the passage are equally bad; they make the tone trivial and commonplace. Perhaps this is contemporary English speech – of a kind you might overhear in a bus queue, 'And I says put on the light and he puts on the light and that was all right and that was better than being in the dark and . . .' But I don't see that that improves matters.

The N.E.B. is as bad as this all the way through. I haven't *read* it all the way through, but make the judgment confidently: those committees were incapable of doing any better. I defy anyone to find two consecutive well-written pages in the whole thing.

The 1611 version is so good here because its translators command the style for the subject. The slow, measured rhythmic sentences, one for each step in creation, convince one in a poetic way as well as being, I am told, closer to the procedure of the Hebrew.

In the beginning God created the heaven and the earth.
    And the earth was without form, and void; and darkness was upon the face of the deep. And the Spirit of God moved upon the face of the waters.
    And God said, Let there be light: and there was light.
    And God saw the light, that it was good, and God divided the light from the darkness.

Look at the different use of 'and' – the difference made to the rhythm of the passage, its pace, phrasing and stressing. That was, at least, done by people who were masters of the craft of writing English. Professor J. C. Maxwell was therefore incomprehensible when he gave the N.E.B. New Testament 'an overwhelmingly favourable verdict from the literary point of view' and said that 'the present committee need have no great sense of inferiority side by side with King James's often injudiciously praised committee of 350 years ago'.[3] If not, we have lost all sense of what is well and badly written, all standards of literacy. And that is not a merely stylistic matter; I shall show that it directly affects every reader of the Bible.

Yet what has been lost in the new versions was, only a few years ago, it seems, pretty generally recognized. The strength of the English Bible's language was not a particularly contentious matter. The greatness of the 1611 Bible style was rightly seen to lie in its weight, definiteness, irresistible rightness of rhythm, and its power

[3] *The Spectator*, 17 March 1961.

to draw on Shakespearean ranges of meaning – which last is why its boldness is so far from French *clarté* and why its style can be seen as essentially English, making the language, at one central place, fully itself. The language of the English Bible is also, of course, one of great beauty. I place beauty so low in my first list of attributes not because I despise it but because of that tendency of modern Christians to see *only* beauty in the style, and only rolling cadences in its rhythms, which is part of the history of the collapse of religious English. The English Bible's beauty proceeds from its other qualities. At its best it is as functional as the beauty of the new Forth Bridge: it is first and foremost a style for getting something said, and for getting it said in the right way, because without the right way, as I shall argue, there cannot be the 'thing'.

And there were in the same country shepherds, abiding in the field, keeping watch over their flock by night.

And, lo, the angel of the Lord came upon them, and the glory of the Lord shone round about them: and they were sore afraid.

And the angel said unto them, Fear not: for, behold, I bring you good tidings of great joy, which shall be to all people.

For unto you is born this day in the City of David a Saviour, which is Christ the Lord.

And this shall be a sign unto you; Ye shall find the babe wrapped in swaddling clothes, lying in a manger.

And suddenly there was with the angel a multitude of the heavenly host praising God, and saying,

Glory to God in the highest, and on earth peace, good will toward men.

Luke 2: 8–14

The passage contains a few archaic words whose dictionary meaning the modern general reader may not know, but it is far easier to read than the N.E.B. version, for it carries its meaning so deeply within it. The passage is a model of rhythmic expression ('and thus', as Professor Gifford says, in the best thing I have seen on the N.E.B., 'of the passions and sensibility that were expressed through that rhythm'[4]). This is a very real compliment to pay; the rhythm, so far from being a kind of rhetorical optional extra, is the shape of the meaning. It tells the reader how to connect and stress, and makes the point of its sense in that connecting and stressing. The rhythmic climaxes are the climaxes of sense: 'a Saviour, which is Christ the Lord' is rightly the central focus of the whole passage, made so by the accumulation of

[4] Henry Gifford, 'English Ought to be Kept Down', *Essays in Criticism*, vol. XI (1961), pp. 466–70.

rhythmic phrases leading up to it. One may note, too, the human rightness of the second quoted verse: how right that the first response of the shepherds should be great fear, and how convincingly the words express that! The genuineness is not at all diminished by the fact that these shepherds speak, as much as the modern ones, a dialect never heard in any English county. They speak a variety of Bible style (not 'ordinary speech') like everyone else in the Bible. I shall argue that that is no disadvantage at all – quite the contrary. As for the poetic life of the passage: how does 'glory' work? Is it a thing? It shines, and surely only things can shine? But to take it in the medieval sense, 'a halo', is to restrict the 'suggestibility' of the passage, to misconceive the way language works there.

That degree of rightness of style is never (as Professor Matthew Hodgart called it, reviewing the Jerusalem Bible in *The New York Review of Books*, 9 February 1967) 'a peculiar historical accident', and it can never be *only* a question of style. Such rightness of language can only be the result, and the medium, of a great creative effort in life, in this case the collaborative effort of King James's committee. It was a collaboration, too, between the translators and the language they found, inside and outside the Bible – itself the outcome of earlier collaborative effort. The result is a language of religion in which God can be spoken of; a language, as Professor Gifford says, which 'only yesterday ... controlled our speech, and provided a measure for high seriousness'.

The new Roman Catholic version, the Jerusalem Bible (1966) is less simply incompetent than the N.E.B., but comes decisively from the same moment of history. Like the Douai Version's, some of its oddities spring from a failure to translate at all. This is most obvious in some of the nouns: 'Yahweh' is not an English word (the preface apologizes for it on the grounds that like the 'still stranger form *Yah*' it preserves the flavour and meaning of the originals – a variety of a fallacy discussed below, for in the originals the form is not strange); but the phrasing is often not English either: 'acquired a man' is not English if it has to mean 'borne a male child'. 'The man had intercourse with his wife Eve, and she conceived and gave birth to Cain. "I have acquired a man with the help of Yahweh," she said' (p. 18). She couldn't say so if she was speaking English. I don't know in this case whether the idiom is Hebrew or French.

But the main feeling one gets from the Jerusalem Bible is its protracted flatness. The Old Testament histories are peculiarly prosaic.

The Philistines made war on Israel and the men of Israel fled from the Philistines and were slaughtered on Mount Gilboa. The Philistines pressed Saul and his sons hard and killed Jonathan, Abinadab and Malchishua, the sons of Saul. The fighting grew heavy about Saul; the bowmen took him off his guard, so that he fell wounded by the bowmen. Then Saul said to his armour-bearer, 'Draw your sword and run me through with it; I do not want these uncircumcised men to come and gloat over me.' But his armour-bearer was afraid and would not do it. So Saul took his own sword and fell on it. (p. 382)

This prose is so simply neutral that one could imagine an effective reading of it, a reading that would bring out the significance of this tragic moment. But the work would all have to be done by the reader; it is not in the language of the passage. In bulk this flat tone wears down the reader's efforts and neutralizes the sense; everything becomes flatly non-committal. Saul and his sons die. So what? The 1611 version does make something tragic of the same passage – something very unShakespearean but which might remind one that Shakespeare was a contemporary of the version.

Now the Philistines fought against Israel: and the men of Israel fled from before the Philistines, and fell down slain in Mount Gilboa.

And the Philistines followed hard upon Saul and upon his sons; and the Philistines slew Jonathan, and Abinadab, and Melchi-shua, Saul's sons.

And the battle went sore against Saul, and the archers hit him; and he was sore wounded of the archers.

Then said Saul unto his armour-bearer, Draw thy sword, and thrust me through therewith; lest these uncircumcised come and thrust me through, and abuse me. But his armour-bearer would not; for he was sore afraid. Therefore Saul took a sword, and fell upon it.

1 Samuel 31: 1–4

Are these passages the same? Perhaps it begins to be clear that the sense of the Bible depends upon its translators' command of right style.

As might be expected, the Jerusalem Bible comes to final grief with the Psalms. Everything seems prosaically goody-goody.

THE TWO WAYS

Happy the man
who never follows the advice of the wicked,
or loiters on the way that sinners take,
or sits about with the scoffers,

but finds his pleasure in the Law of Yahweh,
and murmurs his law day and night
(p. 786)

If these are the alternatives, I would certainly rather sit about with the scoffers.

So with the N.E.B.: if plain prose is beyond the N.E.B. translators it is scarcely surprising that their attempts at verse are hopeless. In poetry the version keeps launching off into the sidetracks of metre before bumping back on to the motorway of journalistic prose: the effect is stiffly comic.

> Happy is the man
>   who does not take the wicked for his guide
>   [iambic pentameter]
>   nor walk the road that sinners tread
>   [iambic tetrameter]
>   nor take his seat among the scornful;
>   [ditto]
>   the law of the LORD is his delight,
>   [anapaestic rollicking tetrameter imitated from 'The Lincolnshire
>   Poacher']
>   the law his meditation night and day.
>   [pentameter]
>
>   He is like a tree
>   planted beside a watercourse,
>   which yields its fruit in season.
>
>   Psalm 1

By the seventh line we are so used to metre that we probably go on in it and read '*He* is *like* a *tree*' etc. If so we get a fittingly bathetic last line:

> but the *way* of the *wicked* is *doomed*.

In the beautifully-produced little book put out by the Cambridge University Press in triumphant celebration of the completion of the N.E.B., Mr Geoffrey Hunt's *About the New English Bible* (1970), it is explained that they write like this on purpose:

In longer poetic passages and in poetic books, the form of the Hebrew is represented, as far as can be done in translation, by the arrangement of the lines. Those containing four beats or accents in the original are set furthest to the left, and those containing three and two respectively are indented, or set in to the right, by one or two steps... As the N.E.B. is often not a line-for-line translation, this system does not represent the Hebrew precisely, but it is intended to give the English-speaking reader a reasonable idea of the structure of the original. (pp. 54–5)

This intention could not be successfully achieved in this way, for the translators are here committed to the belief that the forms of one language can be reproduced in another. (As if ablative absolutes have the same effect in English as Latin. 'With which things having been accomplished, Caesar went into winter quarters . . .') We shall recur to this confusion. It is hardly surprising that the results are unlike the original in being risibly inept.

'LORD, how my enemies have multiplied!' (Psalm 3). Lord! what a way of putting it! 'Save me, O God; for the waters have risen up to my neck!' (Psalm 69 N.E.B.) I object not that this is more immediate than the old versions, and not even that it is comic (with its derivation from the cliché 'up to the neck in it') but that the comedy is uncontrolled and unintentional. One is in no doubt about the degree and kind of seriousness of the 1611 version: 'Save me, O God; for the waters are come in unto my soul.'

Noah, a man of the soil, began the planting of vineyards. He drank some of the wine, became drunk and lay naked inside his tent. When Ham, father of Canaan, saw his father naked, he told his two brothers outside. So Shem and Japheth took a cloak, put it on their shoulders and walked backwards, and so covered their father's naked body; their faces were turned the other way, so that they did not see their father naked. When Noah woke from his drunken sleep, he learnt what his youngest son had done to him and said:

> 'Cursed be Canaan,
> slave of slaves
> shall he be to his brothers'

And he continued:

> 'Bless, O LORD,
> the tents of Shem;
> may Canaan be his slave.
> May God extend Japheth's bounds,
> let him dwell in the tents of Shem,
> may Canaan be their slave.'

After the flood Noah lived for three hundred and fifty years, and he was nine hundred and fifty years old when he died.

Genesis 9: 20–9

The comicality here derives from the translators' failure to worry about the changed world. The style seems appropriate to a quite wrong reaction. The modern viewer of television comedy is likely to ask something like 'Why is Noah to touchy about being seen in the nude? And what is he up to when he begins carrying

on about Canaan?' The story is quite senseless. And if one is
baffled by it the only help available is likely to be scholarly notes
about the father in patriarchal societies, blessing and cursing,
taboos on nakedness and so on. They won't adequately replace
a translation which would give us this strange and savage sense
in our own language.

The complementary fault is to make the Bible homely, to remove its strangeness. The decisive instance is the Song of Songs,
which it is now not easy to believe is Solomon's.

> *Bridegroom*
>> How beautiful you are, my dearest,
>> O how beautiful,
>> your eyes are like doves!
>
> *Bride*
>> How beautiful you are, O my love,
>> and how pleasant!
>
>> (1: 15–16)

'Pleasant' is so nice, so sweet, and so ordinary. 'My dearest among
girls' he calls her in the next speech but one: almost they might
be leaving the register office *en route* for their new semi. We are
assured (see below) that a literary panel inspected the N.E.B.
closely. Could not these 'dozing brothers of the craft' (as Professor
Gifford called them) at least have saved their translating colleagues from the suggestion of a *Waste Land* pub scene in these
two lines?

> When my beloved slipped his hand through the latch-hole,
>> my bowels stirred within me.   (5: 4)

The life of the old versions has given place to a wistful charming-
ness varied by vulgar lapses, as of the popular songs of the thirties,
the era of the youth of most of these translators. 'Faint with love',
she calls herself (5: 8) – how Tennysonian and charming! In the
English Bible the girl was 'sick'. The Jerusalem Bible retains the
word, but unsuccessfully, for its rather complicated 'grammar'
has now changed this side the Atlantic (the difference between
'do you feel sick?' and 'do you feel ill?'), so that 'sick with love'
suggests specifically vomiting. The word should have been 'ill'.
The woman is ill with love. She has what was called in the Middle
Ages the lover's malady of Eros; and that is something you would
never get out of the new versions. The Jerusalem Bible does it
better than the N.E.B.; it does make some parts of the book more

readily available. But there is still something – and I think it is the one vital thing – missing. The version is comparatively shallow, smooth and watery.

> My Beloved thrust his hand
> through the hole in the door;
> I trembled to the core of my being.
> Then I rose
> to open to my Beloved,
> myrrh ran off my hands,
> pure myrrh off my fingers,
> on to the handle of the bolt.
>
> I opened to my Beloved,
> but he had turned his back and gone!
> My soul failed at his flight.
> I sought him but I could not find him,
> I called to him but he did not answer.
> The watchmen came upon me
> As they made their rounds in the City. [*sic*]
> They beat me, they wounded me,
> they took away my cloak,
> they who guard the ramparts.
>
> I charge you,
> daughters of Jerusalem,
> if you should find my Beloved,
> what must you tell him . . .?
> That I am sick with love.

That isn't a bad piece of work. But 'the core of my being' – so coy and stiff, and 'failed at his flight' – so literary. The one needful thing missing which it took the old translators to supply – those stern Protestants who might have been expected to take any available cover afforded by the idea that the work is an allegory – is a most authentic note of passionate abandon.

I sleep, but my heart waketh: it is the voice of my beloved that knocketh, saying, Open to me, my sister, my love, my dove, my undefiled: for my head is filled with dew, and my locks with the drops of the night . . .

My beloved put in his hand by the hole of the door, and my bowels were moved for him.

I rose up to open to my beloved; and my hands dropped with myrrh, and my fingers with sweet smelling myrrh, upon the handles of the lock.

I opened to my beloved: but my beloved had withdrawn himself, and was gone: my soul failed when he spake: I sought him, but I could not find him; I called him, but he gave me no answer.

The watchmen that went about the city found me, they smote me, they wounded me; the keepers of the walls took away my veil from me.

33

I charge you, O daughters of Jerusalem, if ye find my beloved, that ye tell him, that I am sick of love.

Song of Solomon: 5: 2–8

'Rise up, my darling, my fairest,' he now says (N.E.B.). The old versions, in which 'fairest' was not archaic, and meant 'most beautiful', dared to say, 'my love'.

Both the new versions have even tampered with the text, with the same effect of making it nice and pleasant. At least the old allegorical interpretation used to be restricted to the running title: the text was left alone. Now the N.E.B. inserts tendentious cross-heads and saves the poem's moral orthodoxy by attributing the speeches to 'the Bride' and 'the Bridegroom'. The poet didn't choose to settle the question whether they were married; from the situation, so well done in the 1611 version, of the girl's throwing respectability to the winds and turning herself into a night-walker, rightly apprehended by the watchmen, it seems not very probable. At all events she isn't behaving like the mature adult the new versions want to make her. The Song of Songs is a great love poem, and that is what emerges so strongly from the old versions, and not at all from the new.

So I think I got it right when I said that the word for the N.E.B.'s style is 'journalism'. (It does not follow that the journalism is competent: useful journalism is written by journalists, not a committee of Protestant divines.) And that does seem to me disastrous, not because there is anything wrong with journalism in its place, but because its place could not be in the Bible and in public reading in church. A similar point was well and copiously made by Professor Gifford:

St Paul in the Authorised Version is an impressive though difficult writer (a Carlyle with a literary sense). 'Be not deceived; God is not mocked...' Today he rattles this out on the keys of his typewriter: 'Make no mistake about this: God is not to be fooled...' 'Go to now, ye rich men, weep and howl for your miseries that shall come upon you.' 'Next a word to you who have great possessions. Weep and wail over the miserable fate descending on you.' The Apostle was a busy man, clearly; and like other busy men he is driven to use clichés. 'Weep and howl' has the force of medieval wall-painting; 'weep and wail' is the language of sedentary men who have lost the capacity to see and touch. 'Are not two sparrows sold for a farthing?' Christ asks in the Authorised Version (which follows Tyndale). 'Are not sparrows two a penny?' is wrong, because 'two a penny' is cliché; like the pennies that drop, and are offered for thoughts, the coin has no existence.

'English Ought to be Kept Down', pp. 468–9

Are not those good examples of one of the ways 'style' affects 'content'? (I use the inverted commas because without them one is committed, as we must discuss, to misleading categories.) And the point is that the failure of style in the new versions makes the book insignificant and incredible.

The N.E.B. version of the New Testament records a mean, insignificant religious movement. My predominant impression on reading it is surprise that any scholar could have thought the original worth respectful attention. The N.E.B. consistently conveys the impression that the New Testament was the work of a clique of credulous and ignorant fanatics. The book, one infers, comes from the worst moment of Christianity, when the second generation was codifying the wild new impulse of the first. The moment of writing down is a dangerous one for any cult and the Church, we gather from the N.E.B., really made no better job of it than the angel who produced the Book of Mormon. John passes off his modish Greek ideas with the self-advertisement that he was the favourite of Jesus. Paul is a recognizable and unattractive figure, of a type to be found rising rapidly in many prosperous organizations: he compensates himself for his loss of status in the old religion with an unscrupulous ascendancy in the new, which he maintains by a mixture of soft soap and stage thunder.

In the N.E.B. Satan tries to establish a feudal system with Jesus as a vassal, but Jesus says, after the manner of the Victorian damsel rebuking the importunate villain, 'Begone Satan! Scripture says . . .' (Matthew 4: 10). A similar girlish gush ends the first chapter of the Sermon on the Mount: 'You must therefore be all goodness, just as your heavenly Father is all good'[5] (Matthew 5: 48). There is also something very Victorian-governessy here: 'Then I will tell them to their face, "I never knew you: out of my sight, you and your wicked ways!"' (Matthew 7: 23). The

---

[5] This phrase was altered in the 1970 edition to 'There must be no limit to your goodness, as your heavenly Father's goodness knows no bounds.' Mr Hunt (*About the New English Bible*, p. 37) says the change was made 'for stylistic reasons'. If so the translators must have been under the impression that the two versions mean the same. The later is either a *non-sequitur* or nonsense, but is different in any case from the earlier. If the 'as' now means 'since' the consequence just doesn't follow, for why should my goodness be unlimited because God's is? unless I think myself to be God. Yet that is better than the other possible meaning, that our goodness must be as infinite as God's, which is not possible to a finite creature. The awful 1961 text yet refrained from such nonsense.

version is even, not infrequently, more straightforwardly obscure
than the 1611 version. The passage about sex in Matthew 19 is so
vague as to defy interpretation. 'Let those accept it who can' –
or who can understand it. And as part of the Lord's Prayer we are
made to say (in the Jerusalem Bible, too) 'Do not bring us to the
test.' What does that mean? One might find out by consulting
a commentary; but that suggests the failure of the translation as
translation. The Revelation of St John the Divine becomes the
woolly rhapsody of a thwarted peasant: 'Then I saw a new
heaven and a new earth, for the first heaven and the first earth
had *vanished* . . .' (Revelation 21: 1, my italics). There one word
makes the difference between a vision and a conjuring-trick. If
this earth can vanish so easily how real is the next? The Jerusalem Bible varies the mistake: 'Then I saw a new heaven and a
new earth; the first heaven and the first earth had *disappeared*
now . . .' (my italics). The Revised Version of 1885, the last version this side the Atlantic to maintain the traditional Bible style,
simply gets it right: 'And I saw a new heaven and a new earth:
for the first heaven and the first earth are passed away . . .'

Then he who sat on the throne said, 'Behold! I am making all things new!'
And he said to me, 'Write this down; for these words are trustworthy and
true. Indeed,' he said, 'they are already fulfilled . . .'   Revelation 21: 5–6
                    (N.E.B. (1970), N.T. p. 334, deletes second 'he said')

One cannot believe this, because of its journalistic style. The pro-
phetic pretension of 'Behold!' collapses with the instruction to the
scribe, which seems to place us at a press-conference. Then comes
the slipping of the choice titbit of information to the favourite
correspondent. No wonder the *Guardian* liked the version so
much, for the feeling of a *Guardian* interview is prevalent in it.
'Then the angel said to me, "Write this: 'Happy are those who are
invited to the wedding-supper of the Lamb!' " And he added,
"These are the very words of God." ' (Revelation 19:9). *Added!*
(The Jerusalem Bible makes the same blunder, if that is the name
for it, and goes on, 'Then I knelt at his feet to worship him, but he
said to me, "Don't do that . . ."' (Revised Version: 'See thou do it
not.') If those are the very words of God (his very words! not the
'true words' which is the sense of the phrase in the old versions)
one inevitably thinks 'So much for God'. If God and angels are to
speak it must be somehow like the way they speak in the Revised
Version: 'And he saith to me, Write, Blessed are they which are

bidden to the marriage supper of the Lamb. And he saith to me, These are true words of God.'

The N.E.B. miracles all seem gross impostures, superstitions as reported by the modern journalist. Whatever it is in Christ that has inspired so many generations of Christians is effectively hidden by these gospels, which present a cheap miracle-worker and dispenser of pretentious half-truths. Matthew's miracles are about as cheap as his sparrows. It is the casualness of style that destroys them as miracles: one can get no sense of the miraculous. '"Why are you such cowards?" he said; "how little faith you have!" Then he stood up and rebuked the wind and the sea, and there was a dead calm. The men were astonished at what had happened . . .' (Matthew 8: 26–7). Only astonished! The word could only work if it were an archaism, not in the world of such phrases as 'You astonish me!' And, as Professor Gifford observed, 'dead' for the old 'great' kills the wonder, in the interests of accuracy to cliché. The Jerusalem Bible is little better: '"Why are you so frightened, you men of little faith?" And with that he stood up and rebuked the winds and the sea; and all was calm again. The men were astounded . . .' This calming is like turning off a tap. And again one could say simply that, in comparison, the Revised Version gets it right: 'And he saith unto them, Why are ye fearful, O ye of little faith? Then he arose, and rebuked the winds and the sea; and there was a great calm. And the men marvelled . . .'

I don't intend to rush in here with a doctrine of miracles; that would be beyond both my scope and my theological capacities. I only observe that the new versions make nonsense of the miracles by placing the centre of truth outside religion. If the only possible world is our world of newspapers and commonsense, then the miracles are not merely impossible; they are mischievous impostures. Of course any modern writer who asks us to believe in miracles is in deep trouble, because we know as part of living in our world and speaking our language that miracles don't and can't happen. I am not sure that anyone in the pre-scientific world thought differently, or that any sane human being has ever believed, for instance, that death is curable (a line of Sophocles deserves its fame for the weightiness of its assertion of the contrary as something we all know); but the belief of the early Christians was strong enough for Tertullian to be able to say (what was too much even for Charles Wesley, who weakened it to "'Tis certain though impossible'), 'certum est quia impossibile est'. For the first

Christians the belief was the centre, triumphing, perhaps a little madly, over what everybody knows. It is this anti-commonsense (and potentially evil as well as potentially good) power of the Bible that is present in the old versions and quite missing from the new.

In the N.E.B. the story of the resurrection, the central miracle of Christianity, is simple nonsense.

The angel then addressed the women: 'You,' he said, 'have nothing to fear. I know you are looking for Jesus who was crucified. He is not here; he has been raised again, as he said he would be. Come and see the place where he was laid, and then go quickly and tell his disciples: "He has been raised from the dead and is going on before you into Galilee; there you will see him." That is what I had to tell you.'

Matthew 28: 5–7

The angel is obviously an impostor: he speaks far too much like a usually reliable source, flustered by an impossible brief. To take a miracle so much as a matter of course ('He has been raised from the dead and is going...') is a sign either of extraordinary stupidity or a wide credibility gap. So it is hardly surprising that Matthew's continuation of the story would convince no dispassionate reader.

After meeting with the elders and conferring together, the chief priests offered the soldiers a substantial bribe and told them to say, 'His disciples came by night and stole the body while we were asleep.' They added, 'If this should reach the Governor's ears, we will put matters right with him and see that you do not suffer.'

(vv. 12–15)

A likely tale! Roman soldiers expected to put out the story that they had been asleep on duty but yet knew what happened. Even so, in this version some sort of body-snatching seems the most likely solution to a question which almost puts the book into the *genre* of detective novel.

The Jerusalem Bible's angel is similarly unangelic and even chatty. The 1885 version is again the only one of the three I could in any sense believe in:

And the angel answered and said unto the women, Fear not ye: for I know that ye seek Jesus, which hath been crucified. He is not here; for he is risen, even as he said. Come, see the place where the Lord lay. And go quickly and tell his disciples, He is risen from the dead; and lo, he goeth before you into Galilee.

The failure of style here *is* a failure of belief. How can the new translators have felt right, in those words? How can they have felt they have said what the Bible says? By satisfying themselves with incompetent journalism they have branded their own religion as shallow and chaotic. In that sense they have published work that is not sincere.

This question of sincerity, which will have to recur in these pages, is so important (connected as it is with what counts as truth everywhere outside the exact sciences) and so generally misunderstood that I must go out of my way to make it clear that I am not accusing anybody of deception or deliberate hypocrisy. But with that last word the difficulty and the importance of the subject may appear, for did Christ accuse the Pharisees of deception or deliberate hypocrisy? It is possible to be a whited sepulchre with one kind of sincerity, believing in one's own whitewash and unconsciously suppressing knowledge of the rottenness within. I am writing not about trickery but the difference between the real and the sham – 'sham' too, here, implying nothing for which anybody could be held responsible in a court of law (though on the day of judgment matters may be different, and it may perhaps then not count as an excuse to say we knew no better). The exploration of the idea of 'sincerity' is one of F. R. Leavis's major contributions to thought, one of the places where literary criticism may offer general illumination.[6] Perhaps the problems come clearer if one thinks of music. With music the question of ordinary deception can hardly arise, for, even more obviously than the poet, the composer 'nothing affirmes, and therefore neuer lyeth'. But music may certainly be sincere or insincere, real or sham, and in that way true or false. Brahms (I instance someone whose stature is real and whose talent genuine enough to invite consideration) is to my mind an insincere composer, though I wouldn't want to rebuke him for deceiving his admirers, even himself. He is, when he seems most serious, insincere because sentimental.

Sentimentalism is the working off on yourself of feelings you haven't really got. We all *want* to have certain feelings: feelings of love, of passionate sex, of kindliness and so forth. Very few people really feel love, or sex passion, or kindliness, or anything else that goes at all deep. So the mass just fake these feelings inside themselves. Faked feelings! The world is all gummy with them.

D. H. Lawrence, 'John Galsworthy', *Phoenix* (1936), p. 545

By this argument all real insincerity is self-deceiving rather than

[6] See, for instance, 'Reality and Sincerity', *Scrutiny*, vol. XIX (1952–3).

trickery. In the fourth movement of his first symphony Brahms seems to me to be working off on himself feelings of affirmation and serenity he hadn't really got. The contrary, the sincerity that discovers the real, is what one looks for in art or in religion: truth to life or to God. In that sense there could be point in saying that Mozart cannot tell a lie.

The modern Bible translators, honest, learned and painstaking men and women as by their own light one can imagine them to be, are yet insincere in this more important sense, Mark Rutherford's sense when he writes 'He was as sincere as he could be, and yet no religious expression of his was ever so sincere as the most ordinary expression of the most trifling pleasure or pain.'[7]

Translators who cannot show the Bible to be the word of God cannot produce a sincere translation. It is surely a sign of the times when a group of earnest Protestant scholars bent on furthering what they take to be the Kingdom of Heaven produce between them the Atheists' Bible.

II

It may be worth returning to one of my first questions and asking what the new translators *thought* they were doing. To find out from the N.E.B. prefaces is a bibliographically complicated task, for different ones were issued in 1970 in the library and ordinary editions (and for all I know in the later popular, illustrated and Penguin editions) and parts of the 1961 New Testament preface turn up, a little modified, in one general preface of 1970. The general outlines of intent and fallacy are, however, clear enough.

As their first effort the N.E.B. translators said this in the preface to their 1961 New Testament:

---

[7] *Autobiography*, original edn, p. 28. It is in this poetic sense that Dr J. A. T. Robinson can be justly accused of insincerity. It wasn't particularly difficult for Alasdair MacIntyre to demonstrate that Robinson's position is atheistical (*Against the Self-Images of the Age* (1971)) but I don't suppose anyone would say that the atheism is deliberate or that Dr Robinson would confess it. He is, indeed, more earnest than most Christians, trying hard to make something of an institution for which, in the absence of God, it is certainly hard to discover a *raison d'être*. Dr Robinson is nonetheless insincere because he tries to discuss religion in a language where God can have no place. Whatever else his book is honest to, it can't be God.

In doing our work, we have constantly striven to follow our instructions and render the Greek, as we understood it, into the English of the present day, that is, into the natural vocabulary, constructions and rhythms of contemporary speech ... Since sound scholarship does not always carry with it a delicate sense of style, the Committee appointed a panel of literary advisers, to whom all the work of the translating panel has been submitted.

(Penguin edn, p. x)

I have tried to show that one of the version's failings is a lack of any secure sense of contemporary English, natural or otherwise. The more important objection is that the belief that *the English of the present day* is the same as *contemporary speech* shows a blank unawareness that different modes of discourse need different styles which here even tends to deny the existence of prose. For prose is *not* the same as speech, and the relations of prose and speech are a highly subtle and controversial knot of problems. This unawareness is not removed by the later explanation (even if in view of the evidence of the text, one can believe that the 'literary panel' ever met) that the literary panel 'took pains to secure the tone and level of language appropriate to the different kinds of writing'. For the literary panel is itself further evidence of a misunderstanding of the nature both of religious language and of translation. It is another sign that for these translators style is a decorative addition, not essentially concerned with the meaning, and makes me reiterate that a failure of style is not some separate failure. If the style fails the sense fails. So one can contradict their statement that sound scholarship does not always carry with it a delicate sense of style, for sound scholarship in this case *is* the saying in English, with all possible delicacy and precision, what the original says in Greek. If the scholarship does not emerge in the translation itself, where is it? According to these translators, it is in reading the original. 'The next step was the effort to understand the original as accurately as possible, as a preliminary to turning it into English.'

But in what language did the discussions, questionings, tryings out and so forth that are part of reading a classical text, take place? Were they all in New Testament Greek? The translator's understanding of the original simply *is* – like the evidence of his sound scholarship – his translation, the relation he has made between the text and the life of the language he is translating into. The 'literary panel' is a trap (the acknowledgments in the Jerusalem Bible identically separate 'translation' from 'literary revision') which the committee of 1611 did not fall into. They knew far too much about language and were far too devoted to their task to risk having their meanings altered by mere literary men: in fact their preface makes them sound altogether more businesslike and canny: 'not too many, lest one should trouble another; and yet many, lest many things haply might escape them. Neither did we disdain . . . to bring back to the anvil that which we had hammered . . .' I don't think it is irrelevant to observe that their good sense went hand in hand with a belief – consistent with necessary scholarship – one does not find in the N.E.B. prefaces.

And in what sort did these assemble? In the trust of their own knowledge, of their sharpness of wit, or deepness of judgment, as it were in an arm of flesh? At no hand. They trusted in him that hath the key of *David*, opening, and no man shutting; they prayed to the Lord . . .

The complete N.E.B. does on the contrary suffer from those kinds of *hubris*, which are at once unscholarly and a kind of unbelief. For in 1970 the earlier humility gave place, in the preface to the library edition of the Old Testament, to a most ill-timed sense of superiority:

the language of the Revised Version tended to be several centuries out of date when it appeared; it even contained Latinisms which had come down from the Vulgate through a succession of English translations and which had long gone out of use. The present translators, therefore, were instructed to keep their language as close to current usage as possible . . . This task they have tried to perform to the best of their ability. (p. xix)

Cf. 'Today that language [of the old versions] is even more definitely archaic, and less generally understood, than it was eighty years ago, for the rate of change in English usage has accelerated' (N.E.B. N.T. (Penguin, 1961), p. viii). This last is simply untrue. New styles of English do develop, and old ones fade, but it is not true that received standard English usage changes rapidly. We do not need a translation of George Eliot (as the Norwegians do of Ibsen). It is probably true that fewer people are now familiar with the language of the Bible and the Prayer Book than eighty years ago, but that is not because of some mysteriously inevitable process of linguistic development, it is because fewer people use that language. The sense survives if the book is read. But if it is read, the Bible is no more unusable than Shakespeare. (And it is a corollary of the argument that Shakespeare ought to be performed

in modern translation.)[8] Therefore the language of the Revised
Version was not 'several centuries out of date' when it appeared:
it was the living expression of a religious English, and in that sense
was 'current usage' though not ordinary speech. The Latinisms
had not gone out of use; they were used in the Bible: the 'succession of English translations' gives the N.E.B.'s case away.

Even if the N.E.B. translators were right, however, to display
such confident superiority to their predecessors, their 'therefore'
would still be a *non sequitur*. It doesn't follow that the alternative
to the old style is 'current usage' if by current usage is meant the
language of the slangy crib we are in fact offered. The real alternative would have to be a language that does for us something
comparable with what the Bible English did for its readers: a
modern religious English. How could that be? These translators at
any rate did not see that the question is one whose inordinate difficulty is proportionate to its importance; and it didn't dawn on
them that a rejection of the only possible exemplar was not a good
beginning.

The N.E.B. translators seem to have had two ambitions: on
the one hand to produce a scholarly version that takes into
account all the recent advances in textual, historical and archaeo-
logical knowledge, and on the other hand to do so in language
that is easy and natural to the man in the street in his less serious
mood.

> They are well aware that a precise equivalent for a Hebrew word can
> only rarely be found in another language, and that complete success in
> such an undertaking is unattainable; but they had in mind not only the
> importance of making sense, which is not always apparent in previous trans-
> lations, but also the needs of ordinary readers with no special knowledge of
> the Ancient East . . .   Library edn O. T., pp. xix–xx

These ambitions, though self-contradictory, are *both* equally far
from the ambition to translate the Bible into English. Finding
exactly equivalent words is not translation. On the other hand the
needs of ordinary readers seem to be in the eyes of these scholars

---

[8] This has been attempted, too. 'We invited a very distinguished poet,
Ted Hughes, to collaborate with us, gave him the text of *Lear* (slightly
cut, from our first version) and suggested that he "translate" it, treating
it exactly as if it were a foreign classic; Goethe, Racine, or Dante perhaps.' (Lord Birkett on Peter Brook's *Lear*, quoted in Roger Manvell,
Shakespeare and the Film (1971), p. 137.) Mr Hughes obliged, 'But by
and large, in spite of this very interesting experiment – some remarkable
work by Ted Hughes – we decided to stick to the original language.'

for a popularized version – which, however, they think a scholarly possibility. 'The translators . . . have made every effort to avoid the introduction of anachronisms and words reflecting an entirely different social background' (*ibid.*, pp. xviii–xix) – an effort which displays a quite stupendous failure to see that *all* our words reflect an entirely different social background from that of the Old Testament, which has, nevertheless, before now been successfully translated into English. The language of the Greek New Testament, they say, 'is indeed more flexible and easy-going than the Revisers were ready to allow, and invites the translator to use a larger freedom' (*ibid.*, p. xii). Only if he is radically confused about the purpose of his translation, which is in this case to produce a New English Bible, not a modern replica of an easy-going first-century text. The intended fidelity is *not* to whatever it is that allowed the text to become the Bible.

There is all the difference in the world between making the Bible available and making it easy. (I do stand by my words to the *Guardian* at this point.) Fr Baker suggested 'calling NEB the "fireside" Bible, in recognition of its readability . . . NEB is a concession to modern man, who wants a book in the evening that he can read'.[9] But is that how a Bible can be read? The old Protestant insistence that reading the Bible is a central part of the Christian life is not at all like tempting people into reading their Bible. It is their duty to read it, which they neglect at peril to the soul – that was the feeling that drove Tyndale and his successors. And so Bibles were chained in churches, to give people a chance to read and understand them. 'But we desire,' said the 1611 translators in their preface, 'that the Scripture may speak like itself, as in the language of *Canaan*, that it may be understood even of the very vulgar.' The essential demand is that the Bible be itself in our language, not that it be easy; and in 1611 (but not 1970) that went well with the mission to save souls. The N.E.B. people said nothing like 'But now what piety without truth? What truth, what saving truth, without the word of God? What word of God, whereof we may be sure, without the Scripture?'

And so the other half of the N.E.B.'s ambition, to be scholarly, is the other aspect of a misconception of the nature of the English Bible. (How scholarly was it, in any case, to insert cross-heads like 'The Purpose of God in History' (Romans 9) or 'The Christian in a Pagan Society' (1 Corinthians 7: 13) or even 'A Collection

9 Review by Aelred Baker, *New Blackfriars* (1970), pp. 218–22.

of Wise Sayings', 'Another Collection of Wise Sayings' (*ad lib.*, Proverbs)?) Bunyan's treatment of the Bible was not scholarly; he had little knowledge of the ancient East, and isolated texts seem to fight a war in his mind. Yet it is a holy war, and the Bible was God's word in his life. Bunyan's dread of the text 'For ye know how that afterward, when he would have inherited the blessing, he was rejected; for he found no place of repentance, though he sought it carefully with tears' proves, as he tells it so really in *Grace Abounding to the Chief of Sinners*, the terrible power the Bible had for him. That has not much to do with readability, ordinary speech, or scholarly knowledge. 'Oh what stings did I find in all these sentences!' he says, with truth to his own account of what they did in his life.

Of course it is right that scholars should devote themselves to the study of the text, and the sense a translator makes must be found in, not imposed upon, the text. But a translation that restricts itself to accuracy to the original leaves too much of the real work, the relating the original to the life of the translated language, to the reader and the scholar. It is not the duty of a translator of the Bible to be accurate in the way that a translation of a scientific paper out of Russian into American must be accurate. There 'translation' is hardly the word, for the style of thought is the same in both languages. (The obvious case is 'translating' mathematics.) Tyndale's earnest effort to be true to the meaning of the original was different; it was inseparable from his urgent knowledge of his mission to speak the word of God in English, so that he who seeks may find. Without that sense, the only one that makes the book worth translating, the sense that spoke to Bunyan, questions of accuracy are only intelligible as a kind of academic frivolity.

The Jerusalem Bible is even worse in its misunderstanding of why English needed to evolve a religious style:

Still less must it be supposed that there should be throughout a kind of hieratic language, a uniform 'biblical' English, dictated by a tradition however venerable. There is no doubt that in forfeiting this we lose something very precious, but one hopes that the gain outweighs the loss.

(p. vi)

But the 'something very precious' turns out to be the 'rhetorical quality' mentioned a little lower down:

The Psalms present a special problem for translators since, unlike other

45

parts of the Bible, the psalter is not only a book to be read but a collection of verse which is sung or chanted. Moreover, many of them are so familiar in their sixteenth-century form that any change may seem to be an impertinence. Nevertheless, here too the first duty of a translator is to convey as clearly as he can what the original author wrote. He should not try to inject a rhetorical quality and an orotundity of cadence which belong more truly to the first Elizabethan age in England than to the Hebrew originals. He must avoid the pure bathos of prosy flatness, of course, but he will be aware that there is no longer an accepted 'poetic language' which can be used to give artificial dignity to plain statements. It would certainly be dangerous to give the form of the translation precedence over the meaning.

The muddle here is so complicated as to be worth unravelling. Firstly, why is the old style something very precious if it is only an orotundity of cadence (or, as Fr Baker described the style of the Revised Version, a 'resonant opacity') which injects a rhetorical quality into plain statements? If so it is just a nuisance and should be got rid of. Secondly, the only way to convey as clearly as possible what the original author wrote is to copy it: their formulation abandons the idea of translation altogether. The remarks on the rhetoric of the first Elizabethan age are a way of avoiding the question what a modern equivalent of Elizabethan rhetoric might be. And so it isn't clear from the passage why 'prosy flatness' should 'of course' be avoided, especially if the Psalms are 'plain statements'. (And, of course, it isn't.) But if flatness has to be avoided the alternative is some kind of poetic style; and if there is no longer an accepted poetic language the translator must either develop one or abandon his task. The misunderstanding running through the passage is one we have met before, the unawareness that the way 'things' are said affects the 'things'. Where, in the case of the Psalms, and separate from style, is the 'thing' said? Therefore, although the last quoted sentence may look unexceptionable it is proposing a false dichotomy: for what would the alternative be, to give the meaning precedence over the form? The one only exists in the other.

The result of these attitudes is that the Bible becomes a very foreign book, needing copious notes and introductions about such matters as the Spiritual Value of the Psalms (which if the reader cannot read he can hardly be told) or the allegory in the Song of Songs (which one agrees is not there in the poem to be read). If the twenty-third Psalm is to begin 'Yahweh is my shepherd, I lack nothing', the Psalter is a foreign text, not part of the English Bible.

III

> *Sweeney:* Birth, and copulation and death.
> That's all, that's all, that's all, that's all,
> Birth, and copulation, and death.
> *Doris:* I'd be bored.

'Birth, and copulation and death' is such an inadequate summary of human life, even without considering the things it omits, because in birth, copulation and death there is nothing specifically human. Cows, too, are born, copulate and die, and elephants, and mice. But animals do not marry, they mate; and when an animal is buried there is only a funeral if it is organized by human beings.

The move from birth, copulation and death to initiation, marriage and burial is from an animal to a specifically human world. We may reduce the human realities represented by words like *marriage* and *burial* to nonsense; but without the possibilities they express there is no human life.

It is a universal characteristic of human societies to make a solemn event of a funeral (or a comic event, for 'jesting in the presence of death' is almost as widespread a recognition of the majesty of death). It is true of all human groups that they make of a funeral something quite other than and more serious than disposing of a corpse by putting it into the earth or burning it. The seriousness of funerals is as widespread as language – no more and no less.

When one considers the more public and ceremonial aspects of religion it is very clear that without a language for the occasions the occasions cannot be what we at present call them. A funeral is a funeral only within the shared assumptions, associations and ways of talking that permit it to be so: and the seriousness of any public ritual must be enacted in language, whether the language be of words or gestures. In English the verbal part of this language has been traditionally supplied since the Reformation by a style closely associated with the style of the English Bible, the style above all of the Book of Common Prayer.

Wilt thou have this woman to thy wedded wife, to live together after God's ordinance in the holy estate of Matrimony? Wilt thou love her, comfort her, honour, and keep her, in sickness and in health; and, forsaking all other, keep thee only unto her, so long as ye both shall live?

We are granted in such language the capacity to see our marriages as something other than the mating of beasts and our burials as something more important than waste-disposal; without this common human possession we would all die the death of dogs.

The way the 1662 Prayer Book creates the idea of marriage or burial makes available a possibility of living humanly. Can anything similar be said for the efforts of the liturgical revisers who are currently trying to offer a more modern religious English?

This is not a bibliographical study and I shall offer no detailed account of the complicated steps by which the Church of England Prayer Book is being revised.[10] I am only concerned to discuss a few examples and what they suggest about religious English in the late sixties and early seventies.

In the 1965 series of Alternative Services there was no consistent attempt to rewrite the Prayer Book in journalese; at a surface level they are more competent than the new versions of the Bible. But in the end they show me a similar loss of seriousness.

When the new version of the Burial Service appeared, the *Times* report said that it struck 'a less sombre note' than the 1662 text. The new service *is* less sombre – but also less joyful. It insists even more than the old service on Christian hopes of personal immortality; but it is both less adequate to the occasion, not confronting us so simply with the fact that a corpse is being put into the ground, and less hopeful in that it fails to build anything so profoundly serious on the event. The aims of the Liturgical Commission are on the whole well stated:

What ought we to be doing at a burial service? ... the Commission puts forward the following fivefold answer:

(a) To secure the reverent disposal of the corpse.
[This may be misleading unless they mean 'to secure that the disposal of the corpse is reverent', which seems to me to cover their other headings. For disposing of the corpse is not what we should be but what we are doing, and *qua* disposal, reverence is unnecessary. What the reverence does is to turn the disposal of the corpse into a funeral.]

(b) To commend the deceased to the care of our heavenly Father.
(c) To proclaim the glory of our risen life in Christ here and hereafter.
(d) To remind us of the awful certainty of our own coming death and judgment.

10 I shall quote from The Church of England Liturgical Commission, Alternative Services, Second Series (1965); ditto, Morning and Evening Prayer, Second Series (revised, 1970); ditto, An Order for Holy Communion, Alternative Services Series 3 (1971). I shall also refer to the New English Missalette, International Committee on English in the Liturgy Inc., etc., n.d.

(e) To make plain the eternal unity of Christian people, living and departed, in the risen and ascended Christ.

(Second Series, p. 105)

This is a specifically Christian statement of what, generally, a funeral can do. But the revisers suppose that because the old service emphasized the misery of human life it cannot perform these functions. They imply that the old service expresses a 'denigration of a life that God has created' (p. 110) and say:

the Commission believes that, although protests against worldliness are necessary in every generation, it is unfortunate that the only reference in the Burial Service to the earthly life of the deceased should be in terms of the miseries of this sinful world. (p. 117)

The 1662 Burial Service begins with one of the most challengingly hopeful assertions in the world. I am surely not the only person to have been struck dumb with wonder as the minister, advancing into church followed by the very coffin, shouts 'I am the resurrection and the life, saith the Lord...'[11] The tension between this statement and the presence of the corpse (unequivocally so called in the rubric of the 1662 book) is at the heart of the old service. A funeral is the occasion for asserting in the act of burying a corpse the possibility of making something of a life whose natural end is the grave. The Lord hath given and the Lord hath taken away, blessed be the name of the Lord. The Commission understand this in their different language, and echo Joyce's words[12] in saying that 'the message of the New Testament is rather "In the midst of death we are in life" than the reverse' (p. 118). What they seem not to have realized is the effort it needs to say so. The old service, in its very insistence on transience, connects death significantly with life in the way the revisers wish to do. It does not follow at all that if misery and mortality are emphasized life is denigrated.

One of the pieces the new service alters and partly cuts is the

---

[11] This remains optionally in the new service in a weaker form, 'Jesus said, I am the resurrection and the life...' but the introductory sentences in the new service, all optional, are now all from the New Testament, which means the exclusion of the best version of all of the wonderful passage from Job: 'I know that my Redeemer liveth, and that he shall stand at the latter day upon the earth. And though after my skin worms destroy this body, yet in my flesh shall I see God: whom I shall see for myself, and mine eyes shall behold, and not another.'

[12] *Ulysses* (1960), p. 136.

passage that provides the text for the anthems in Purcell's *Music for the Funeral of Queen Mary*:

Man that is born of a woman hath but a short time to live, and is full of misery. He cometh up, and is cut down, like a flower; he fleeth as it were a shadow, and never continueth in one stay ...

Thou knowest, Lord, the secrets of our hearts; shut not thy merciful ears to our prayer; but spare us, Lord most holy, O God most mighty, O holy and merciful Saviour, thou most worthy Judge eternal, suffer us not, at our last hour, for any pains of death, to fall from thee.

I mention Purcell because most of all in his music it becomes very clear that this is not simply a miserable passage. We have but a short time – a short time, though, to *live*. And if we come up and are cut down like a flower, a flower is hardly an emblem of misery. Would life be saved from denigration if it were asserted that we are creatures who do 'continue in one stay'? Purcell shows the poignancy and greatness of what is mortal, the necessary connection between greatness and transience which is the subject of a funeral service of whatever religion. As for the prayer, I, who am not a Christian, feel that it expresses exactly the truth I would like to find at that moment.

Similarly the 'sure and certain hope of the resurrection' (which now becomes 'having our whole trust and confidence in the mercy of our heavenly Father' – surely too much like a chancellor of the exchequer announcing his whole trust and confidence in the exchange-rate of the pound the month before a devaluation?) is made tense by its position immediately after that dramatic moment when the beat of *dust to dust, ashes to ashes* is marked by the first earth dropping on to the coffin, or, in the old days, straight on to the shrouded corpse.

The new burial service is comfortable in the modern sense; the old one was comfortable in *its* sense. The new belongs to a world where the action will usually be a mechanized cremation, where the waste-disposal is well organized and the significance minimal as, to a faint hum and, as often as not, canned music, the coffin slides genteelly through a trapdoor to be consumed offstage in the fires of an electric Gehenna.

Since the 1965 series the revisions seem to have gone in two different directions. Morning and Evening Prayer have undergone a kind of streamlining which yet leaves much of the old language at least optionally intact. The parts that have been thoroughly rewritten tend to leave the work to the reader rather than doing it in the language. The 1965 services had made the General Confession (now optional in Morning and Evening Prayer) vague and expansive, though so much shorter than the old versions:

> Almighty God, our heavenly Father,
> We have sinned against thee,
> Through our own fault,
> In thought, and word, and deed,
> And in what we have left undone.
>
> (p. 26)

This has the air of being an expansion of 'God, we have sinned' which the Commissioners perhaps thought too bald and striking. The 1970 text varies the phrasing, bringing in our fellow men and thereby confusing the point that sin against our fellows *is* sin against God, but leading up to a baldness of another kind:

> Almighty God, our heavenly Father,
> We have sinned against thee and against our fellow men.
> We have sinned in thought and word and deed,
> in what we have done,
> and in what we have failed to do.
> We are heartily sorry and repent.
>
> (Pew edition, pp. 8–9)

There is nothing very expressive about that last line. It *could* be the expression of sincere penitence, but there is no stylistic reason why it naturally *should*. There is nothing of the progress of the old text where, by the time we get to the phrase that draws the rest together, we have been taken through a thorough exploration of our condition which it would need much more of a positive effort to ignore:

Almighty and most merciful Father, We have erred and strayed from thy ways like lost sheep, We have followed too much the devices and desires of our own hearts, We have offended against thy holy laws, We have left undone those things which we ought to have done, And we have done those things which we ought not to have done, And there is no health in us:

so that the turn to hope is much more powerful: 'But thou, O Lord, have mercy upon us miserable offenders...' The new version postpones the cry for mercy and makes it sound much less urgent, much more like an application for a permit through the usual channels:

> We are heartily sorry and repent.
> For the sake of thy Son Jesus Christ

who died for our sins,
forgive us all that is past,
and raise us to newness of life. Amen.

There is a similar toning-down of the Gloria in the 1971 Holy Communion (p. 28):

Holy, holy, holy Lord,
God of power and might,
Heaven and earth are full of your glory.
Hosanna in the highest.

The ending is oddly snappy and unglorious compared with the old rhythms, 'Holy, holy, holy, Lord God of hosts, heaven and earth are full of thy glory: Glory be to thee, O Lord most high.' The new people would never risk that repeated 'glory', and the natural result is that the glory has departed. The reforms of Morning and Evening Prayer are, however, conservative and could imaginably be successful (even though one of the alternatives of the former does seem to have been reduced to a few psalms and lessons strung together on no observable principle and eked out with a very meagre portion of prayer). By contrast the new service of Holy Communion is radically transformed in a way that seems to me likely to prevent anyone experiencing the grace of God by its means, as far, anyway, as I am able to track it through the maze of alternatives.

At the beginning 'the minister' (who later becomes transmogrified into 'the president') may say 'The Lord be with you', to which the people reply 'And also with you', a form also much in vogue in the New English Missalette. It reduces this exchange to polite greeting. Of course it *is* polite greeting, but now it is no more. The response might as well have been 'The same to you!' If the old form had to be replaced it should have read 'The Lord be with thee also.'

The second person singular is, however, abolished, with occasional dubiously grammatical results. 'Thou that takest away the sin of the world' becomes not 'you who take . . .' but 'Lord God, Lamb of God, you take away the sin of the world,' which could be either an order or a piece of ridiculously gratuitous information like the following 'you are seated at the right hand of the Father'. ('Are seated' is actually stuffier than the 1662 version which did use the verb 'to sit'.)

The old second singular was, of course, a special use, in which religious English differed from the rest of the standard language. But in standard English it was and is the natural and proper way to address God: it was not, I think, embarrassing to Christians and did not stand out as odd, which the new 'you' certainly does to anyone who has used the old service. However that may be, the phrases 'lamb of God', 'sin of the world' and so on, retained in the new version, are equally special to the religious style. Can the style be deliberately replaced piecemeal without doing damage to the whole? Won't 'Lamb of God' come to seem ridiculous (as it does to Anna Lensky in *The Rainbow*) more readily if the Lamb is to be addressed like any more ordinary person?

The worst sign, however, of the loss of conviction is the insertion of modern ungodly prayers and explanations, which follow a pattern we shall be meeting throughout this book, of disintegrating one system of value and replacing it by another lower one which offers itself not as a system of value but the merest unobjectionable commonsense. The (now optional) ten commandments are now justified by unBiblical explanations of why it is a good thing to obey them. 'You shall not commit adultery. Know that your body is a temple of the Holy Spirit.' I might commit adultery although I know that; further, I might commit adultery *because* I know my body is a temple of the Holy Spirit. The commandment is, however, perfectly clear and not dependent upon the gloss. Thou shalt not commit adultery (whatever the state of your beliefs and opinions). Why not? To offer explanations is to judge the commandment by some other system of value: the only Christian answer to the 'why not?' is something like 'For the mouth of the Lord hath spoken it.' And the right thing for a Prayer Book to do is to follow a commandment not by something to buttress it but by the old prayer 'Lord, have mercy upon us, and incline our hearts to keep this law.' I am discussing religion not morality; but of course the two belong closely together in the Christian tradition and it goes with my argument that there is nothing surprising when the absence of God from religion is accompanied in morality, even amongst Christians, by attempts to judge moral questions according to commonsense or utility rather than according to Christian or any other absolute standards. (Cf. Cardinal Heenan quoted on p. 162, below.) The Durham Report on Religious Education (1970), for instance, a very respectable attempt to make the case for something of that name, tried to persuade teachers to offer reasons for morality. 'We are as sure as we possibly can be that it is wrong to kill people for fun, or to lie whenever it pleases us . . . But the teacher is not therefore precluded from helping [children] to understand for themselves why it would be wrong to do these things' (pp. 79–80). The 'reason' lies in the proper perception of the things themselves: murder just is, absolutely, wrong, and there is no further reason. It is this sort of example that might give sense to a commentary, not *vice versa*. Thou shalt do no murder, and that's that. Anyone who can't see it needs conversion rather than argument. If we don't take the force of 'thou shalt . . .' we are losing the sense that anything can be absolutely right or wrong. 'Thou shalt not commit adultery.' And if we nevertheless do? Then the commandment carries its own punishment as the explanation cannot: we are then adulterers; and that remains true, whatever the mitigating circumstances or explanations, as long as we understand the language.

The new series of commandments also warns us that 'You shall not steal. You shall do honest work that you may be able to give to those in need.' There are good reasons for doing honest work, of which the one given is one of the least. None of them, however, either adds to or explains the commandment. Children, pregnant women, the old and infirm can do no honest work but are not therefore permitted to steal. It is possible, of course, to hold that the commandment is justified by some such reasoning, but that isn't the view of the Bible or of historic Christianity.

Though it repeats the unintelligible 'Do not bring us to the test' this service does at least refrain from *explaining* the Lord's Prayer, which is more than can be said for the Roman Catholic Missalette, where 'the words our Saviour gave us' include:

> Deliver us, Lord, from every evil,
> and grant us peace in our day.
> In your mercy keep us free from sin
> and protect us from all anxiety.

I can't imagine a more irreligious wish than to be protected from all anxiety, about, for instance, one's salvation: it is a prayer to be delivered from religious life into hebetude. (Christ did indeed offer rest, but only to those who labour and are heavy laden; and the blessed who shall be filled are not those who wish to be protected from all anxiety, but those who hunger and thirst after righteousness.) You might as well pray 'let everything be nice' which, on the tenth Sunday after Pentecost, the hapless R.C.'s pretty nearly have to do: 'Grant us such full measure of your grace that we

54

may hasten towards the good things you have promised.' What could such good things be, in Mr Heath's England or President Nixon's America, but an easy life and an automatic annual wage-increase? (Something like that is, after all, the basis of the image in the Magnificat.) 'Good things' is a phrase better used of his financial pickings by Dickens's Mr Merdle.

> Blessed are you, Lord, God of all creation.
> Through your goodness we have this wine to offer,
> fruit of the vine and work of human hands.
> It will become our spiritual drink.

> (Missalette)

The trouble is that in this language it seems very unlikely that any drink will thus transcend the material.

The weakness of the new services will be particularly felt by congregations as a lack of command of rhythm and pace. The new Anglican Holy Communion gives far less than the old form a sense of trying to conduct a congregation through a series of necessary steps, at the speed for allowing them to realize what is happening. By contrast the old burial service was superbly dramatic, bringing out of the act of burial a significance only an enactment could enforce. The people who made the 1662 Prayer Book had nothing to learn from the dramatists about how to enact a story.

Seeing the loss in the new services we are once again willy-nilly discussing sincerity. Is it possible to attend to the Missalette with any depth of concentration? When the new services are most themselves they lull us into the pleasant Sunday slumber of churchiness. How can one wait on God in such words? And unless a service allows for the fear of the Lord (not, as Lady Beatty wrote to *The Times*, 25 September 1971, 'comfort and pleasure') how can it be sincere?

Perhaps even this is possible, for God moves in a mysterious way, and perhaps the grace of God will be found to have flowed even through these channels. But that would be a kind of miracle, and not the same as the kind that allows us to find sense in language.

IV

Religious English is the style of our common language that makes religion possible (or not, as the case may be). Religious English can only make religious seriousness possible to the individual, in whom any religion is not restricted or standardized but perpetually new, unique and his own; it could not do so, however, without the many generations whose lives have expressed themselves in our language, in its context of the many Christian languages, in *their* context of history and human nature.

The generation that impinges most perceptibly on a child beginning to understand a language of religion is, of course, that of his parents, and by talking of language in the present way I am not trying to suggest that if the parents' lives are wholly godless anything religious will happen when the children are made to speak the words of religion. ('That word "grace" in an ungracious mouth is but profane.') Language is found only in use, and unless a child knows some people who use seriously the religious styles of English, he will not be able to use them himself, unless he grows up to do historical research. That is why it is so important that (what? – it used to be called 'Scripture' and is now sometimes misleadingly known as 'R.I.') should be taught in schools by people who have, at least, some reverence for God. Miss Brigid Brophy's Fabian pamphlet *Religious Education in State Schools* therefore misses the point of religious education. 'Our children have the right to stop being indoctrinated with belief in one religion and to start being told, in a factual way, the content of the myths and doctrines of as many religions and objections to all religions as the teacher's general knowledge will run to' (p. 17). The objection is that though belief can't be forced upon anyone, as must be surely proved by the present plight of Christianity if that is what nearly universal religious education is supposed to do, belief can yet be made impossible by the atrophy of its language. In the name of freedom Miss Brophy is advocating that children be deprived of the possibility of either practising or understanding religion. For of course myths factually recounted, doctrines separate from their home in religious life, will be simple nonsense by the standards of the language of materialism, or freedom-and-democracy, or the pursuit of happiness, in which they will be told; and that will itself be a kind of indoctrination in the belief that religion is necessarily senseless. A language of religion can always be destroyed in one generation.

Yet the other truth, that religious styles of a language are not created by one generation, and that they are certainly not the exclusive property of contemporary churchgoers, ought also to be considered. Miss Brophy wants to deny children the possibility of understanding one of the most important styles of English, which cost the best effort of many of the best minds from Anglo-Saxon times on.

The prose of the 1611 and 1885 Bible is traditional not only in its use of the sixteenth-century versions, but also in its deep rhythmic modes, which go right back to the prose of the *Ancrene Riwle* and to Anglo-Saxon alliterative poetry. I have already joined the consensus that praises the Bible's prose as prose; but it is very different from the post-Dryden prose of periodic structure, and also from the non-prose generally written in 1611.[13] The Bible works not by the elegant progress of the Augustan sentence through its main and subordinate clauses, a prose which, though it reads well aloud, is somehow logically written before spoken: the Bible depends on the rhythmic two-beat speech-phrases that were the staple of the verse tradition of Anglo-Saxon and Middle English.

The repetitive phrases of the Prayer Book are often enough rhythmically regular Anglo-Saxon half-lines:

> to have and to hold · from this day forward
> for better or for worse · for richer for poorer
> in sickness and in health · to love and to cherish
> till death us do part . . .

[13] The Epistle Dedicatory makes an instructive contrast to the language of the Bible itself. When not translating, King James's committee wrote the usual rambling sub-latinate prose of the contemporary learned, in which clauses follow each other in no particular order and a sentence may wander on, as it frequently does in Milton, for a page or two between full stops. 'And this their contentment doth not diminish or decay, but every day increaseth and taketh strength, when they observe, that the zeal of Your Majesty towards the house of God doth not slack or go backward, but is more and more kindled, manifested itself abroad in the farthest parts of *Christendom*, by writing in defence of the Truth, (which hath given such a blow unto that man of sin, as will not be healed,) and every day at home, by religious and learned discourse, by frequenting the house of God, by hearing the Word preached, by cherishing the Teachers thereof, by caring for the Church, as a most tender and loving nursing Father.' This has the same elements as the Bible – the duplications, the strong, bold use of nouns, the rhythmic phrases – but with no principle of organization. Who would have thought the same people would be responsible for the Book of Proverbs? – or for this: 'Be not rash with thy mouth, and let not thine heart be hasty to utter any thing before God: for God is in heaven, and thou upon earth: therefore let thy words be few. For a dream cometh through the multitude of business; and a fool's voice is known by multitude of words' (Ecclesiastes 5: 2–3).

To say that the Bible's mastery of language is primarily a question of rhythm, the careful and strong rhythms of the individual phrase controlled by the tempo of a whole passage, is not to reduce it to 'orotundity' or 'resonant opacity', but to discuss the meaning and the credibility of what is said. That is why it was insufficient, though true, to say that the 1611 opening of Genesis was done by masters of the craft of writing. The old translators were religious artists, the truth of whose utterance depended on their grasp of their language. The steps of creation in the first chapter of Genesis ón which I commented are controlled from within by their rhythm, and that is what enables the translators to say what they have to say. The alternative is not a weaker or more prosaic version of the same thing, but a failure to say what is to be said. 'To express it badly is not one way of expressing it (not, for example, expressing it, but not *selon les règles*), it is failing to express it.'[14]

This rhythmic rightness, this power to say what has to be said, is shared by all the sixteenth- and seventeenth-century versions – but not to the same extent, and I am not saying that any such power was automatically inherited by any translator. On the contrary, the state of the language permitted widely different religious expressions each of which was the accurate measure of the degree of devotion and intelligence of the translator. It is not true that all the old versions are as good as each other. (Tyndale is, and is generally agreed to be, the best of all the New Testament translators, though patchy: he takes risks which sometimes wonderfully succeed, and he is less concerned to achieve a good sound in church than, especially, the Bishops' Bible, the forerunner of the 1611 version, which tends somewhat to propriety and the Church Voice. The Douai Version is usually inferior.) Yet with all the variety of the old versions, they are varieties of the stylistic power of a common religious language, a generally available way of speaking to God, which is now *not* available even for conscientious men such as the modern translators, who are therefore again in a world that is without form and void.

Moreover, though religious English has its own validity, and though the Bible and Prayer Book have to make any sense they can in themselves, in use, they couldn't do so if they were in a style disconnected from the other styles of the language. Religious

---

[14] Collingwood, *Principles of Art*, p. 282.

English is a distinct set of styles, but not insulated.[15] The religious styles matter to imaginative literature, too. This isn't simply the observation that a novel can use for its own purposes all the styles of a language. Religious English is a right of the great English novelist *in propria persona* as well as of his characters.

Shakespeare has a style of sober exposition or rebuke plainly related to the Bible by way of the Protestant sermon tradition and found, for instance, in the lay sermon Henry V preaches to Bates, Court and Williams the night before Agincourt:

Besides, there is no King, be his Cause never so spotlesse, if it come to the arbitrement of Swords, can trye it out with all unspotted Souldiers: some (peradventure) have on them the guilt of premeditated and contrived Murther; some, of beguiling Virgins with the broken Seales of Perjurie; some, making the Warres their Bulwarke, that have before gored the gentle Bosome of Peace with Pillage and Robberie.

But the connection with Shakespeare goes deeper by way of his rhythmic mode. There could have been no tragedy in English if it were not for the language of the Bible's great words and rhythms; the complete disappearance from contemporary literature of anything like tragedy (and the difficulty contemporary critics have – David Sims discusses it in *Human World* no. 12 (1973) – in recognizing the tragic in Shakespeare) is part of the same movement of language as the appearance of the N.E.B.[16]

The Bible had a lot to do with the survival of imaginative literature into the Age of Reason and our following age of technological arrangement. Johnson's *Life of Swift*, the nearest the English eighteenth century could come to tragedy (and *far*

---

[15] The 1611 translators showed their awareness of this in several ways – when, for instance, they give as one of their reasons for not always using the same English word to translate the same Greek or Hebrew word their wish to give the dignity of Bible language to some English words that might otherwise lack it. The fact that they put this rather funnily shouldn't make us think them unserious: they were witty people.

[16] As Mr David Holbrook wrote, in one of those letters which were a welcome gleam of critical life in the columns of the *Guardian* or the *Spectator* a few years ago: 'But the new version is noticeably deficient in the poetic rhythm and modes of the Authorized Version – and this is inevitable, since ours is a time when the poetic properties of language have been neglected, when, indeed, the capacities of English-speaking people to contemplate the mysterious and metaphysical through the word are weakened and unexercised ... The Bible is still at the root of such popular metaphorical inquiry by words as there remains to us.' (Letter to the *Spectator* (1961), p. 400.)

nearer than *Irene*) achieves its tragic seriousness by drawing on the rhythmic resources of religious English.

He now lost distinction. His madness was compounded of rage and fatuity. The last face he knew was that of Mrs Whiteway; and her he ceased to know in a little time. His meat was brought to him cut into mouthfuls; but he would never touch it while the servant staid, and at last, after it had stood perhaps an hour, would eat it walking; for he contined his old habit, and was on his feet ten hours a day.

This is obviously, in syntactic disposition, an eighteenth-century passage, and Johnson's individual style appears in the brevity of 'lost distinction' (i.e. lost the power to distinguish people from each other) and the weighty wit of 'rage and fatuity'; but the confidence of his rhythmic sense he owes to the Bible.

How was the novel possible – a work of the creative imagination, perhaps tragic, but written in the language of the science, reason and commonsense of the first industrial age? Part of the answer (which I would love to try to work out some day) is given by Professor Gifford when he quotes a passage of *The Rainbow*:

Anna's soul was put at peace between them. She looked from one to the other, and saw them established to her safety, and she was free. She played between the pillar of fire and the pillar of cloud in confidence, having the assurance on her right hand and the assurance on her left. She was no longer called upon to uphold with her childish might the broken end of the arch. Her father and her mother now met to the span of the heavens, and she, the child, was free to play in the space beneath, between.

It is often said that Lawrence brought English prose closer to the spoken language (which is not the same as 'ordinary speech'): it would be equally true to say that he brought English prose closer to poetry, by way of the language's religious tradition. How could he have written that passage except in the language of a people brought up on the Bible, i.e. brought up to take it seriously?

The Bible uses some special words and phrases but for the most part is a selection of the words and rhythms used elsewhere in the language. And some of the basic 'grammars' of the important words elsewhere depend on the religious styles. If you say 'I love God' with habitual insincerity, your wife would be well advised to look twice at your claim to love her. The N.E.B. is a diminution of our *whole* language.

The English Bible was made by those great generations around the time of Shakespeare, made through the effort of disciplined

and intelligent men who loved the Lord their God with heart
and mind and soul and who therefore did, amongst other things,
the necessary work on language. The proof of their love is *in* their
language. Those translators who have not done the work on
language by living with it, using it in a real religion, and under-
taking the intolerable wrestle with words and meanings, will be
betrayed by language; but any wrestling would be in vain without the language's co-operation. The 1611 translators summed up
in English the sense their sixteenth-century predecessors had
managed to make of the Bible. 'The memory of generations of
pious readers breathing down his neck must have had an un-
nerving effect upon a translator,' says Fr Baker. Why? The 1611
translators did not find it so: for them the earlier versions were a
guarantee, a sort of communion of saints, inspiring them, as ever,
to the salvation of souls:

So far off from condemning any of their labours that travelled before us
in this kind ... we acknowledge them to have been raised up of God for
the building and furnishing of his Church ... Therefore blessed be they,
and most honoured be their name, that break the ice, and give the onset
upon that which helpeth forward to the saving of souls.

They also defined their task as 'to make a good one better ... that
hath been our endeavour, that our mark'.

The collective sense made in 1611 was confirmed or modified
by later generations in reading. I am willing to believe that
some of the most important work on the 1611 English Bible went
on in the eighteenth and nineteenth centuries, after it had attained
its final form. That is only a rather striking instance of the work
that must be done on any book in every generation if it is to
survive, the re-creation which is the necessary new interaction
between the book and the different life. The familiarity of Bible
English, especially the familiarity of its rhythms, is an inestimably
precious possession of our language, though, like all such collective
achievements, open to abuse. The Bible could not have achieved
its English without the labours of many translators, but equally it
could not have been so right *for us* without the hundreds of years
of use in English life. There was no alternative to being married
and buried in terms of Prayer Book English, though of course
the sense made of the terms was a matter for each individual.
The outcome for us of the continuance of that language, the
interaction of countless individuals and the book, is the resonance
of the great words and rhythms (I don't mean booming sounds)

which we in turn are responsible for using, misusing or abandoning. This is a good example of the way that the state of a language depends on everybody who uses it and is indistinguishable from *their* state.

v

I am not discussing in this book the gross popular examples of breakdown or coarsening, and so refrain from quoting the results of the B.B.C.'s employment of the actors Sir Bernard Miles and Mr David Kossoff to travesty the Bible (the former in grotesque Zummerset) not as comic entertainment but as part of the religious broadcasting service. Nor shall I more than mention the increasing unseriousness of the denominational press which has on the whole kept time with the changes I discuss in chapter 4. I avoid these obvious subjects for the same reason that I avoid discussion in other chapters of the gutter press or 'hard core' pornography. They will not be seen to be 'obviously' what I name them, except by the standards of some centre, and it is the centre I am trying to consider. It therefore seems to me more alarming when the clergy cannot speak a religious language than when pop stars offer to fill the resulting vacuum.

There *is* a threat to the possibility of religion in life when an Archbishop of York generally supposed to belong more to the evangelical than the swinging persuasion – the same who signs the preface to the N.E.B. in the thoroughly traditional, not to say archaic form 'Donald Ebor', and who on 9 November 1961 moved a motion carried by the Church Assembly which 'welcomes, with deep gratitude, the publication of the New English Bible' – can say, 'Let us show ourselves adaptable. For long years complaints have been made that the work of the church is inhibited by old forms and antiquated methods of expression. I do not think we have gone far enough in meeting these complaints.'[17]

'Why,' he had asked earlier, 'should we make lusty young men and women refer to themselves as "frail and trembling sheep"?' Because in the sight of God, and in that sight of ourselves he may grant us the power to achieve, we *are* frail and trembling; and because in the language of the old forms without which there would have been no Church and no archbishops He is the Good Shepherd, who knows his sheep.

[17] *Times* report, 21 October 1967.

The question springs from the same failure of conviction, or of style, or of language, which left the N.E.B. translators also with only journalism to fall back on. The failure is quite general and central.

It is almost twenty-four years from the Church of Scotland's General Assembly in May 1946 to the publication of the complete Bible in March 1970. A whole generation has elapsed and the children of those who supported the original proposal in 1946 will have now grown up. Yet the time has not been wasted: progress, if slow, has been orderly and continuous; it is probably true that the resulting translation is the best that could be made in English at the present time.

Hunt, *About the New English Bible*, p. 75

Yes, that *is* probably true, and that is why I have a subject and may not unreasonably be concerned for the survival of English, at least as a language in which it is possible to speak of God. As one of the *Guardian* letters refuting me said of the N.E.B., 'It is hard to see how it could have been anything else.' Yes again; N.E.B. is no worse than the best-selling Penguin translation of the Gospels by E. V. Rieu, and is actually better than some of its more trendy rivals.

What ought the N.E.B. translators to have done? I don't know. I don't know why the root-and-branch replacement of the English Bible was thought necessary, except as part of the same loss of nerve that made its replacement the N.E.B. Continuity is often thought to be in more danger in the U.S.A. than over here, but as recently as 1952 a reasonably successful conservative reform of the 1611 Bible was accomplished in the American Revised Standard Version. If a modern idiomatic version was thought necessary in which the chattiness of the New Testament Greek was faithfully reproduced it was to hand in the version of J. B. Phillips. If one wanted a translation into good plain modern intelligible prose, there was Weymouth's version (which itself, published in the nineteenth century, gives the lie to the idea that English is fast changing).

And what is there to be done now by anyone who sees the need for a religious English? One thing we can't do is to set about manufacturing it – not, at any rate, as a matter of deliberate policy with definable ends.

But if we are to find ourselves at home again in a significant universe, we must somehow find, dialectically, a synthesis of what Cudworth asserted and Hobbes denied ... it is some analogue of the traditional deity we have to seek, and find, if the fundamental meaninglessness of the Hobbesian world, *our* Hobbesian world, is to be overcome.

Marjorie Grene, 'Hobbes and the Modern Mind',
The Anatomy of Knowledge (1970), p. 4

I intend no disrespect to the very interesting work done by Professor Grene and her group if I ask, 'Was ever a God found in this way?' He doesn't, apparently, exist; therefore it is necessary to invent him.

Rubin, in Solzhenitsyn's *First Circle*, tries to devise a religious language that will guarantee that the great events of life are taken with due seriousness:

In the preamble he spoke of the need to raise even higher the moral standards of the population (which, he emphasized, were already very high), to endow revolutionary and other anniversaries with greater significance, and to enhance with solemn ritual such occasions as weddings, the naming of new-born children, the reaching of adulthood and secular funeral services. (The author at this point intimated that these occasions tended to be observed in a perfunctory manner and that for this reason citizens were not always very aware of the family and social ties by which they were bound.)

The solution offered was the establishment all over the country of Civic Temples which should be architecturally imposing and dominate their surroundings . . .

The proposal laid particular emphasis on the need to ensure that all these ritual observances should be carried out in a proper setting, that the garments of the Temple ministrants should testify by their magnificence to the purity of mind of those who wore them; that the form of words employed in the various rituals should, by its rhythmic quality, achieve maximum emotional impact; that every possible means should be used to affect the sense organs of visitors to the Temple . . .   (ch. LXVII)

No, religious language cannot be called into existence in the interests of social health. One can just imagine what Rubin's services would be like – the boredom, the forcing, the ironies, the jokes, and the ceremonies as trivial as ever.

Any religious language is *ipso facto* ruined by the failure of the belief which makes it meaningful – and which it allows to be meaningful. The loss of faith which caused so much anguish to some Victorians, and which they so oddly ascribed to Darwin, was contemporary with the Church and Chapel voices which expressed the turning of religion to cant or hypocrisy. The people of our century have taken their revenge on a language which, from the lips of the faithless fathers, naturally set their teeth on edge, by abandoning it altogether. All re-creation of style involves criticism, asking oneself whether one is really saying what one means: for the N.E.B. translators and their age this led to the final criticism, complete rejection.

That doesn't mean that we can now start again from scratch. And it is tempting merely to accept the inevitable – a temptation to which we are at present much prone: there is something corruptly comforting, something of Shakespeare's Richard II, in the way we so often now recognize the inevitable, even with enjoyment.

The real English Bible, the possibility that we can still read it, is the sign of hope and that the new translators were altogether too defeatist. The N.E.B. laid claim to the great name of the English Bible; like the 1611 and 1885 versions it is published jointly by the presses of the ancient universities,[18] and in the Reading Room of the British Museum the library edition is shelved with those nicely-bound copies of the standard works of English literature amongst which the readers browse in the hours before their books arrive. Yet all hope need not be lost so long as we can see the situation more or less for what it is. The light by which to do so is given us by the language of the real English Bible and Prayer Book; they provide the standard in their record of a real religion which, such is their power, is always in danger of coming alive for any reader of goodwill who ventures unwarily into their pages.

'When all things began, the Word already was. The Word dwelt with God, and what God was, the Word was ... The real light which enlightens every man was even then coming into the world.' Who will ever be able to take those N.E.B. words as the Word of God or that light as the real light? If it does happen, those verses will be all too true for their readers thus enlightened. God will then be what that Word makes Him. But so long as our religious language allows us to see as much, it can still be true that God is not mocked.

[18] The Oxford University Press's entry in Cassell's *Directory of Publishing* (1966–7) says that 'profits are used to make possible the publication of works of scholarship and educational value which might not otherwise find a publisher'. The duller of the threatened 'works of scholarship' follow from N.E.B. as punishment from crime.

3
English and the Art of the Possible

Of dull and venal a new World to mold,
And bring Saturnian days of Lead and Gold.

I

Political events, one might suppose, just happen. Mr Edward Heath thinks so, at any rate, for in his ministerial broadcast commending us to 'Europe' he went further and said, 'Most history just happens.' (He was distinguishing Britain's accession to the E.E.C. as an exceptional case where 'we have an opportunity to make history happen'.[1]) But an event becomes a political or historic event only by being understood as such. Whatever 'just happens', it can't be history, for history is one thing we make of events, one way of understanding events, including the ones whose senselessness oddly leads to their being called acts of God. Politics may certainly be affected by things beyond the comprehension of politicians; but politics itself can only be what we do comprehend. Mr Heath's assumptions are commonplace enough to make it worth saying, then, that political events are simply the events we perceive politically, the ones that can enter the political consciousness of a community. A political event is therefore any event understood in its political significance. And *that* is understood in a language of politics; and the changes in a language of politics change events by changing our understanding of what things mean – which I have been arguing is not distinguishable from what they are. It is within a language of politics that all political judgments are made, all ideas of political justice understood, and all political consequences seen.

If a government is responsible to an electorate it has to communicate with the electorate, whether by deceiving it, debauching it, pandering to it, or striving to make political sense with it. Public opinion is essential to a society with representative government, for that is where communication can take place in the other direction, where criticism can enter the language of politics, and where a

[1] *The Times*, 9 July 1971.

66

change in political language may redirect political events by making different sense of them. (Of course, not all such changes are for the better.) So the way in which governments explain themselves and are criticized matters, absolutely, because that is the existence of the politics of any community.

The very existence of political events depends in this way on the power of politicians to address an electorate and of the electorate to be addressed and, in some cases, to answer back. Often, also, the success of a government in tackling what it regards as the most important political problems must depend not only on its own understanding of them, but also on convincing the people that its view is the right one; policy is not unaffected by the language of politics, and the latter *can* sometimes 'make history happen'.

The changes of style, over the last decade or so, in British politics (or in political English) can be exemplified in style narrowly considered – in diction, rhythm, and the nuances of intonation it is difficult to quote in this sort of book – and in the assumptions about the *effable*, in what everyone takes for granted about what is possible to the art of the possible.

I can give a couple of examples of what I mean by changed assumptions from the two political questions that happen to be dominating the headlines of British newspapers as I write. The Conservative government of Edward Heath, it is almost universally agreed, has taken a tough and stubborn line with inflationary wage-demands but in fact, because of one assumption, the government's position throughout the coalminers' strike of 1972 was one of obvious weakness. Given that the possibility of _breaking_ the strike was (as a colleague said) 'unthinkable', anyone could see that the miners could bring the government to its knees in a couple of months. If strikes are never under any circumstances to be broken, there are half a dozen unions which, granted some degree of organization and determination, can always get what they demand. This assumption, according to which all the parties spoke and acted throughout the strike is, in historic terms, quite new. (I remember enjoying rides in an army lorry when the Attlee government used the army to break a strike of provincial busmen, those harmless people.)

I think there is an even more basic changed assumption underlying this one. It is always intolerable for the law to be enforced if that involves danger to members of the public. It was after the

Second World War that Miss Anscombe wrote (in a pamphlet about the disgracefulness of awarding an honorary degree to Harry S. Truman) as something quite taken for granted and accepted by all speakers of the language, that

> the state actually has the authority to order deliberate killing in order to protect its people or to put frightful injustices right. (For example, the plight of the Jews under Hitler would have been a reasonable cause of war.) The reason for this is pretty simple: it stands out most clearly if we first consider the state's right to order such killing within its confines. I am not referring to the death penalty, but to what happens when there is rioting or when violent malefactors have to be caught. Rioters can sometimes only be restrained, or malefactors seized, by force. Law without force is ineffectual, and human beings without laws miserable (though we, who have too many and too changeable laws, may easily not feel this very distinctly). So much is indeed fairly obvious, though the more peaceful the society the less obvious it is that the force in the hands of the servants of the law has to be force up to the point of killing. It would become perfectly obvious any time there was rioting or gangsterism which had to be dealt with by the servants of the law fighting.[2]

On the contrary, because of our changed sense of the possible, this became *less* obvious to us all including the author of the passage, as rioting and terrorism in Northern Ireland increased.

Now I cannot pretend to be devoid of opinions about Northern Ireland or to be writing this chapter from some pseudo-monarchical position of untouched superiority. My opinion is, for instance, that though all killing is regrettable and the killing of thirteen people in Londonderry was grim, the killing was not in itself an outrage or a disgrace. I think that the only disgraceful thing was that successive governments had allowed public order in Northern Ireland to deteriorate to a point where the situation that led to the killings was not merely possible, but likely. I say this not because I want at present to enforce the opinion (curious readers can find the position I share worked out in an issue of *The Human World* I did not edit, no. 8 (1972)) but because it is my holding the opinion that gives edge to my remark about our changed language. I might not otherwise have noticed that the loud public outcry which followed the shooting of the thirteen on 'bloody Sunday' was over the fact, in itself, that there had been killing of civilians by the army. The centre of the orthodox

---

[2] G. E. M. Anscombe, 'Mr Truman's Degree', privately printed, n.d. [1956], pp. 8–9; reprinted in *The Human World*, no. 10 (1973).

sense of outrage was not the belief that the killings were unjust, nor that the paratroops were out of control (though those beliefs were present), and not that a policy of appeasing the terrorists would have inspired a peaceful response from them – though even that was extensively believed – but simply that the killing had happened. This was clear, for instance, in the *Times* leader of 20 April 1972 about 'that disastrous day': 'With the benefit of hindsight, over the graves of thirteen dead, one is driven to conclude that the operation was a mistake.' One must be driven to the conclusion only if *any* use of force against civilians to the point of killing is mistaken (and only, too, if expediency, the judgment of events by their consequences, is the *only* criterion of judgment in politics; a belief we shall see more of). A corollary is that anything which avoids killing is preferable. One of the Widgery Tribunal's conclusions was 'If the Army had persisted in its "low key" attitude and had not launched a large-scale operation to arrest hooligans the day might have passed off without serious incident.' It is therefore the opinion of the Lord Chief Justice that it would *not* have constituted a serious incident to permit an assembly of hooligans (his word) to shelter the gunmen who according to his report were active that day. These, too, were the grounds – and nobody challenged them – on which Mr William Whitelaw justified his abortive negotiations of July 1972 with the I.R.A. terrorists. 'I am not prepared to apologize to this House . . . for *any* [my italics] action which I took in the feeling that I might be able to save lives and damage to property. If I have to talk to anyone at all to honourably and properly follow that course, I would certainly do it.'[3]

The preservation of life and property is indeed an old and honourable political aim; the new thing is firstly that it becomes the *only* aim in riotous or warlike situations (to the exclusion, for instance, of defeating an enemy) and secondly that the time-span in which the aim operates is so short. Mr Whitelaw perhaps saved life for a day or two by agreeing to a truce with the terrorists, and that immediate gain is what exclusively counts. The total breakdown of Conservative policy in Northern Ireland, so that after 600 deaths Catholic and Protestant areas are 'policed' by inimical private armies, seems to me a most natural consequence of our new assumptions about the use of force. When there is a consensus that it is worse for the law to be enforced

[3] *Times* report, 11 July 1972.

than for people to be left to the 'law' of private armies, such results may be expected.

This is, I hope, the extreme point of a movement of language that began, perhaps, with the acceptance of the name 'Peterloo'. In the eighteenth century, in some ways a coarse age for all its enlightenment, it was ordinary for rioters to be shot with little fuss. Now, as a result of this very complex change and the exaltation of tolerance and compassion in senses that would not have been understood in the eighteenth century, we are (for better or worse) at an opposite extreme in which there are no final sanctions against rebellion, anarchy or even crime. These are changes in our political language, in the sense events make for us all and in the possibilities open to government. They are, in the broad sense, changes of political style, and examples of how a change in style matters as a change in political life. They may also begin to suggest how a concern for political style is not necessarily limited to the surface of life as contemporary politicians give the impression of supposing, and not separate from a concern for solving political problems, including the most material.

II

In one way, though styles of public speaking seem to be vanishing (Mr Harold Wilson's cult of informality is representative and leaves him sounding very odd on formal occasions) parties are now more interested in style than they have ever been. The Conservatives notoriously called in a public relations firm to titivate their 'image', the result being a poster of Mr Edward Heath looking even stiffer than usual and being called 'Edward Heath, Man of Principle'. Both parties talk a good deal about 'packages' and their conception of style is as a way of delivering the goods very contemporary with the packaging revolution in the grocery trade.

The Labour Party's 1964 manifesto – the one which for all anyone knows may have won them their tiny majority which did so much more for their morale and cohesion than their later thumping one – was, I thought, another indubitable sign of the times. And what one couldn't help noticing about it was the style.

The country needs fresh and virile leadership.

Labour is ready. Poised to swing its plans into instant operation. Impatient to apply the New Thinking that will end the chaos and sterility.

Here is Labour's Manifesto for the 1964 election, restless with positive remedies for the problems the Tories have criminally neglected ...

The ironies the next six years gave this document must not distract our present attention from its stylistic significance, as a noteworthy moment in the trivialization of our political language. It uses the style proper (if that is the word) to detergent advertising – a style, as Arnold said of Macaulay's, in which it is impossible to tell the truth. Many of the characteristic Omo–Daz nuances of style are prominent: the short sentences of thumping and portentous rhythmic structure (more or less dactyllic, with main stress early and few minor stresses), the calculated accumulation of emotional terms, the air of heady significance with a minimum of paraphrasable sense.

But poetry works in a comparable way; my remarks could have been a disgruntled account of the poetry of Gerard Manley Hopkins. What is it that makes that manifesto's style shabbily synthetic rather than poetic? and why are its effects conjuring-tricks rather than visions? Unlike poetry the manifesto is not as it is because nothing else would suffice; it is not stretching the language or forcing it into new meaning under stress of the urge to get something new precisely said; rather it is making a predatory attack upon the common language, manipulating its creative resources for a predetermined end. Nothing is being created; the common language is being drained and left lifeless.

> Come down, O Son of God! Incestuous gloom
> Curtains the land

wrote Oscar Wilde (in a sonnet called 'On the Massacre of the Christians in Bulgaria') in overwrought imitation of Milton. 'Incestuous' is a word glorified by an unholy halo. It gives off sparkles of wicked, or would-be wicked, fascination, and supplies guilty thrills to the innocent. But 'incest' and 'incestuous' are words with very firm dictionary definitions:

INCEST. Unnatural and criminal conjunction of persons within degrees prohibited.
INCESTUOUS. Guilty of unnatural cohabitation.

Johnson

'Incestuous' derives whatever thrill it may possess from the evil our culture and language ascribe to incest. The word is wicked because, in the way of looking at the world to which it belongs,

71

incest is evil. To use the thrill without any connection with its source in language and the life from which it receives strength and to which it gives shape is, as it were, to uproot the poison tree. In the Wilde sonnet language is cut off from life and commanded to thrill in the void. 'Incestuous gloom!' It fails because of the crudity of the attempt (one begins asking how gloom can be guilty of unnatural cohabitation) but, more generally, because no work has been done on language – because, that is to say, the interplay between language and 'life', which allows language to give us a grip on the real, is replaced by linguistic conjuring-tricks. The poet is mechanically drawing from the word-hoard of English in order to give us a *frisson,* with the result that we don't even get a *frisson,* because the coin is too tarnished.

But metaphor itself, *the* poetic device, is the use of the words in unexpected contexts. Metaphor makes us see something freshly, in a new meaning, because in language that is ordinarily used in a different situation and sense. Real metaphor, however, is not a decorative device for saying something the sense of which really exists elsewhere; it *is* the poet's new idea, his way of carrying a sense over into a new context, making a new connection, and so of extending language and consciousness. If in 'Nutting' Wordsworth could not have spoken of the visit to the copse in a sexual language he could not have recounted that experience at all, or written that poem.

The Shore manifesto (an attribution confirmed in Mr Wilson's Memoirs, *The Labour Government 1964–1970* (1971)) and the Wilde sonnet are alike in their anti-creative use of language. The manifesto uses 'virile' and 'sterility' just as Wilde uses 'incestuous', by trying to cream off the thrills. The effect is also, though crude, in both cases meant to be subliminal: the reader is supposed to be operated on, though coarsely, unawares. Mr Harold Wilson would perhaps be surprised, and with some reason, to be taken as having offered as head of government to outdo King Charles II in spreading his maker's image through the land, though that would indubitably be taking virile measures to end sterility. If the Labour Party did not intend 'virile' and 'sterility' to have their primary reproductive senses they might say that both words are in fact often used in milder, figurative ways. But if 'virile' is cut quite adrift from the primary use while retaining the emotional charge it derives therefrom, it becomes as disreputably magical a word as Wilde's 'incestuous' which – abracadabra! hey

presto! – changes one thing into another with no more effort
or understanding on the witch's part than it takes to pronounce
the spell. It is this lack of effort towards new understanding which
defines the sham and marks the difference between Mr Shore's
conjuring and the real magic of either poetry or politics, which
can change the world. To the best of my knowledge that manifesto was at the date of its publication unique in our modern
history in its descent to the senseless.

With 'criminal' its magical intent became more obvious and
more traditional, but not more intelligent. If Labour thought the
Conservatives had been guilty of crimes, their duty was to tell
the police or the D.P.P. Instead they smeared: smears, though as
old as language, are one of the more difficult linguistic conjuring-
tricks; they insinuate something forceful enough to be damaging
without being precise enough to be defined in a court of law. As
for the New Thinking (a phrase I first came across in the first
issue of the *Sun* newspaper, where it is exemplified by washing-
machines and trips to Spain) that too is thinking of a tricky kind.
It is thinking minus thought.

Dictators used to change the world by strokes of the pen, but
when Hitler drew a line on a map military action was likely to
follow to give it another reality. The Labour Party was more
economical and changed the world simply by conjurors' patter.
One of Mr Wilson's more prestidigious feats was to give a pledge
not to attack 'collective bargaining' in the same speech as a
warning that there can be 'no return to the wages free for all'.[4]
Now 'the wages free for all' (over the return to which, of course,
Mr Wilson presided) simply *is* 'collective bargaining' under another name. The only difference is a magical one. Under one of its
names the thing attacked is taboo, and the taboo is made to under-
mine the other, respectable name and attack the thing Mr Wilson
is promising to defend. It is as if he said, 'Of course, we are all in
favour of love affairs, but there must be no return to free fornication.'

Mr Wilson's own style is frequently, when he attempts flights
of oratory, like the manifesto's, and in one place at least the link
between that style and the idea of politics as manipulation comes
quite clear: 'This is what 1964 can mean. A chance for change.
More, a time for resurgence. A chance to sweep away the grouse-
moor conception of Tory leadership and refit Britain with a new

[4] To the T.U.C., 5 September 1966.

image, a new confidence. A chance to change the face and nature of Britain.'[5] The rhythmic alliterative phrases there allow Mr Wilson to make a cosmetic operation ('refitting with a new image ... changing the face') the same as changing the nature of Britain – which it is, though not as he intended the words.

A later Conservative manifesto was equally disreputable, though more feebly, as befitted the party doomed in 1966 to defeat. That spell spent thousands of words on promising 'action not words'. 'Action' is not an action but a word, and moreover a magically charged one. In modern English action is, generally speaking, all right ('stern, resolute action', 'immediate action') whereas inaction is a bad thing – that is the feeling of those words in our language although in political reality the contrary may well be true and we suffer a good deal from action for action's sake. (It is another unthinkable in modern English – so many unthinkables in our post-Victorian language – to say that the best thing for Northern Ireland would be to maintain the *status quo*. The language demands 'initiatives' and 'solutions'.) If you substitute 'a lot of actions' for 'action' the magic is lost: nobody would be expected to vote for a party offering 'a lot of actions and not many words'. Evidently 'action not words' didn't work, and it was dropped in 1970; but if anybody was influenced to vote Conservative by the slogan his behaviour is to be seen as response to a magical incantation. (And the best retort was that of the local poster-defacer who stuck the picture of a gag over the mouth of Mr Heath in the poster saying 'Action not words'.) It is too easily assumed that Mr Heath's style is radically different from Mr Wilson's. Certainly his reticence is a refreshing change from Mr Wilson's loquacity, but the difference seems to me all on the surface, covering a common language and a common belief that style in politics is a matter of manipulation and conjuring; as I will show by a final example of linguistic magic.

When Labour devalued the pound in 1967 there was a great hullabaloo, because devaluation was a sort of principal snake in Mr Wilson's conception of the game of politics. The Conservative devaluation of June 1972, on the contrary, caused hardly any commotion, because they employed a new linguistic trick. They got away more or less unchallenged simply by persuading every-one to call the operation 'the floating of the pound'. Now there

[5] *The New Britain: Labour's Plan, Outlined by Harold Wilson, Selected Speeches 1964* (1964), p. 10.

are uses of 'float' in which an object sinks: one may speak of thistledown floating gently to earth. But even that implies the buoyancy of what floats; and ordinarily things float on or up to a surface. (Another magical use of 'float' was the American soap advertisement 'It Floats', which *didn't* imply that one has to fish for the soap underwater in the wash-basin.) Would there have been that range of applause to acquiescence (the former led by the *Times* leader which called Mr Heath a great Prime Minister, 'It is right to float the pound', 24 June 1972) if the more accurate and less magical metaphor of sinking had been used? Could *The Times* have said 'It is right to sink the pound'? – which is what happened.

I am not objecting to emotive language in politics (all language is emotive) or even to magical language as such: there is a most important place in politics for truly magical language and, again, changing the world by a new way of talking is just what the poet does, as well as the great statesman. The proper magic of politics would have been, e.g., for Mr Wilson to have convinced us that there could and should be a viable prices and incomes policy, or for Mr Heath to have convinced us that 'Europe' is a good thing.

Magical activity is a kind of dynamo supplying the mechanism of practical life with the emotional current that drives it. Hence magic is a necessity for every sort and condition of man, and is actually found in every healthy society. A society which thinks, as our own thinks, that it has outlived the need of magic, is either mistaken in that opinion, or else it is a dying society, perishing for lack of interest in its own maintenance.

Collingwood, *Principles of Art*, pp. 68–9

But one must always do one's best to distinguish the real from the sham. Real political magic (Churchill in 1940, say), and even real political black magic, is a way of getting a grip on the reality of a political situation and of sharing that reality throughout the community. It is a form of language internally related to political understanding and the solution of problems; it doesn't come along (as Collingwood perhaps a little suggests) merely as a 'means to a preconceived end': it is closer to art and it may help to discover new ends. My objection is only that our new political magic is so shabby, so much more like conjuring-tricks. Style is detached from matter and made into a mode of manipulation not conviction.

The Labour government's failure with the area of politics it chose to make central, the management of the economy, can be explained as a failure of style. It may seem strange to say that Labour had no way of talking convincingly of money, for their whole endeavour was fixed on the development of the economy; but that is what I want to show.

Mr Wilson is still the only leading British politician who will habitually launch off a political speech without a word of introduction into the seas of balance of payments, cost of living, and gross national product. 'Prodoction' is his favourite word, occupying a place in his vocabulary something like 'life' in D. H. Lawrence's, and during his years in office one sometimes felt that Fielding was prophetically depicting Mr Wilson in a character who 'had, indeed, conversed so entirely with money, that it may be almost doubted whether he imagined there was any other thing really existing in the world'.[6]

Mr Wilson has not really been inconsistent about 'Europe'. He has always been aware that 'going into Europe' is a political question and that even its economic aspects are unquantifiable; but that has consistently meant for him that, since the question cannot be reduced to management of the economy, it can't be discussed at all. 'The decision', he said, 'will be made largely on subjective value-judgments, not capable of quantification.'[7] He seems to have thought that this exhausts rational treatment of the question, which is then settled by whim or guess. In 1967 his guess took the form of a pro-Europe *élan* that had abated by 1971, but the underlying position is the same. Mr Wilson's efforts to raise the essential non-economic questions always make them not merely unquantifiable but unspeakable and also curiously dead, to be brought to life only by a shot of economic euphoria.

In a speech to the Council of Europe, Mr Wilson, trying to speak of the general advantages of 'Europe', hid behind the vagueness of a few favourite mixed metaphors ('a unity the greater and more real because it builds on – and does not reject – the diversity of the nation-states whose national traits and characteristics will become stronger and more fruitful by being merged[8] in a wider, outward-looking unity',[9] but his speech came to life,

---

[6] *Tom Jones*, book xiv, chapter viii.   [7] *The Times*, 28 April 1967.

[8] Mr Wilson varied this sentence in his Commons speech of 8 May 1967 by substituting 'welded' for 'merged'. Sir Harry Legge-Bourke's word in October 1971 was 'coagulating'.

[9] *The Times*, 24 January 1967.

impelled by his characteristic energy, when he continued to this paraphrase of a Commons statement and lit upon a euphoric economic phrase:

'I want the House, the country, and our friends abroad to know that the Government are approaching the discussions I have foreshadowed with the clear intention and determination to enter the European Economic Community if, as we hope, our essential British and Commonwealth interests can be safeguarded. We mean business.'

That, Mr President, is our position. We mean business. And I am going to say why we mean business.

We mean business because we believe that British entry and involvement of the other EFTA countries, whether by entry or association, will of themselves contribute massively to the economic unity and strength of Europe.

(*Ibid.*)

Mr Wilson was so delightedly sure that in 'We mean business' he had found the right phrase because it is to business that his political language is restricted, as surely as that of Mr Heath's government of businessmen.[10]

When Mr Wilson does get off business, he fumbles like a beginner in a foreign language. In his Swansea speech of 10 January 1970 he did try, but seemed like the mythical child trying to learn to speak by way of ostensive definitions. He could only name things without having any idea of what to say about them; and names used in that way don't even refer to things. 'Add to these [economic problems] the issues of human relations, of individual freedom, of law and order and violence; the issues of race, equality before the law, human dignity.'[11] What sort of a sum will you get if you do add them? The names were, in Mr Wilson's speech, not those of 'issues' for there was no sign that he had thought about them or had any idea how to change them from the names which some other politicians were mysteriously bandying about into subjects of thought. So he returned without more ado to money, and the extensive report of the speech in the Memoirs[12] mentions nothing else.

But it doesn't follow that if politicians restrict themselves to

[10] Professor Walter Hallstein would not agree with him. He was quoted during the 'great debate' of October 1971 as having said of the E.E.C., 'We are not in business to promote tariff preferences, to establish a discriminatory club, to form a large market to make us richer or a trading bloc to further our commercial interest. We are not in business at all: we are in politics.'

[11] *The Times*, 12 January 1970.

[12] *The Labour Government 1964–70*, pp. 741–4.

management of the economy and give all their effort to it the economy will be well managed. The decade following those promises by Mr Macmillan's government of copious jam to-morrow which initiated the English economic monomania was not economically smooth. The Labour government failed in its economic management both because it was obsessed by the economy and because Mr Wilson did not sufficiently realize that managing the economy is managing not a machine but *us*. He failed to convince us, because he had no proper style for doing so.

In July 1966 Mr Wilson took (as he so frequently does) to the television, and there gave an impersonation of the late Sir Winston Churchill – not, to my mind, a successful one. The economy was said to be in such a bad way that Mr Wilson made a comparison with 1940 and appealed for the Dunkirk spirit. (According to his Memoirs he used the same imagery in a 'key-note speech' to the Labour Party Conference in December 1964, and now regrets it not because of its inherent ridiculousness but because 'A more accurate historical parallel, if one were needed, would have been the long period after Dunkirk and through to victory' (p. 53).) This was utterly inappropriate, the work of a man with no real sense of style. It could not possibly make sense. Nobody in 1966 had actually died in defence of the pound; there was nothing properly to be called poverty resulting from our economic situation. There weren't even any ministerial resignations, because Mr Wilson as usual returned Mr Brown's letter. Yet out of Mr Wilson's large information-bank of a mind there came, as the manipulator appropriate to the occasion and likely to make us take it with the right seriousness, the Dunkirk spirit. Perhaps Churchill *could* have appealed to seriousness as Mr Wilson was trying to – if so I suspect it would have been in one of his pugnacious or bantering styles, not the 'big bow wow'. In the event we had not Dunkirk but a very phoney war. There was no feeling of real crisis (a word ever on Mr Wilson's lips – he cries 'Wolf' too often) and without the feeling, without that way of taking the situation, which could only have been given by the government's command of style, there could not be the real thing, the turning point. Instead we were playing at the Dunkirk spirit.

Style affected the real nature of the event even more during the devaluation crisis of 1967. Here, understanding and dealing with the economic situation had largely to be convincing the electorate. But Mr Wilson appeared to be trying to disguise the very nature of devaluation. In a notorious phrase he appeared to deny that devaluation is a cut in the 'standard of living'. 'It does not mean, of course, that the pound here in Britain, in your pocket or purse or in your bank, has been devalued.'[13] He meant to say that we would not wake up next morning to find a tenth of our savings confiscated or that all prices had risen by that amount. That wasn't what he said, though: linguistic conjuring, altering reality by magical talking, is perilous close there to the lie direct. For if after the effects of devaluation imports cost five to ten per cent more, the pounds in our pockets have been devalued. That is what devaluation is, and Mr Wilson later contradicted himself by saying so. 'I have said that imports will cost more, and this means higher prices over a period for some of our imports, including some of our basic foods.' Yes, that's plain enough. But why had he to tuck it away after so thoroughly confusing the question? Why could we not be trusted with the truth?

It was impossible to know at the time whether Mr Wilson wasn't telling the truth because he wouldn't or because he couldn't, having lost the language and style for doing so. A passage of his Memoirs settles the question. The Treasury gave Mr Wilson a draft in what he calls 'far too technical and jargonesque' English, in which people were reassured that their savings were not to be confiscated; and Mr Wilson's comment makes it quite clear that that was indeed what he wanted to say himself, 'the fact that devaluation *had* not of itself reduced the cash value of savings and other bank deposits' (p. 464 – though even that isn't true in terms of gold or dollars). But the act of translating this into political English distorted it: in Mr Wilson's political dialect he simply could not utter that truth. The opposition were not, therefore, 'dishonestly and unscrupulously' misrepresenting him when they made hay of his phrase.

At the end of the devaluation speech Mr Wilson did try to speak to us, to ask for the co-operation of the people.

This devaluation has been a hard decision and some of its consequences will themselves be hard, for a time. But now the decision has been taken we – all of us together – must make a success of it. We must take with both hands the opportunity now presented to us.

Our exporters, industrial managers, our salesmen – and what a chance they've got now – our workers in every industry, our scientists and engineers, our designers, the professionals responsible for our invisible earnings, are

[13] *The Times*, 20 November 1967.

now on their mettle. Any who fail through laziness or self-seeking, any who frustrate the work of others by unofficial strikes will imperil the right of all our people to work, the right to work not only for themselves, but for the nation.

I have told you what led to this decision. I told you the alternative which we could have sought and why we rejected that alternative.

This is a proud nation. As I have said we have the chance now to break out of the straitjacket of these past years.

We're out on our own now.

It means putting Britain first.

The Times, 20 November 1967

But how am I to be on my mettle if I'm one of the majority who are neither managers, salesmen, workers in industry, scientists, engineers, designers or professionals responsible for invisible earnings? The answer is a very simple one, but Mr Wilson would not, could not or dared not give it.

What Mr Wilson could not say within the orthodoxy of our political language was that we ought to accept the reality of devaluation, i.e. that we were going to be at least for a time poorer not richer, and that the way to support the government was to understand and accept this. Mr Wilson could not make devaluation real: his effort, indeed, was in the other direction. He could not say something like 'there will be no increase in real incomes for some time and it is our duty to acept this not very terrible fact'.

In one sense Mr Wilson, forced into a devaluation it had been his basic endeavour for three years to avoid, could have only one thing to say. So he thought, anyway; and according to the Memoirs the question became how to titivate it up. There he regrets having followed Mr R. H. S. Crossman's advice to be aggressive and victorious[14] but because the ploy was not very successful, not because he now sees that any questions of truth or sincerity were involved.

At Friday night's meeting of ministers and my private office staff on the eve of devaluation I was pressed, above all by Dick Crossman, to alter the tone of the broadcast, and to drop the references to set-back and defeat,

---

[14] It is all of piece that Mr Crossman, an editor of the *New Statesman* and therefore a lover of truth, should have put forward (*The Journal of the Royal United Service Institution*, xcvii and xcviii (1952–3)) as a reason for preserving the B.B.C.'s reputation for veracity, that it could then, when the occasion arose, be used for deceiving an enemy.

and almost to exult in our decision. I believe I was wrong to accept this advice and a comparison today of my original draft with the text of my Sunday broadcast suggests that I should have stuck to my first thoughts.

Memoirs, p. 463

Can tone really be 'altered' like the tone of a radio-set?

The deliberately chosen style did create the particular event. The event would have been a different one, and our recent economic history a different story, if Mr Wilson could have spoken with conviction. But in that case style could not for him be a set of conjuring-tricks; nor would it be possible to apply to him the continuation of my Fielding passage: 'this, at least, may be certainly averred, that he firmly believed nothing else [than money] to have any real value'.

I am not saying that politicians should not manage the economy (though neither de Gaulle nor Churchill could raise much interest in it). I am certainly not saying, either, that politicians should be uninterested in questions of expediency. My criticism of the present state is that there is *nothing* in politics but economic management and expediency: and that means that even on its own level our politics is unsuccessful. A desire for prosperity is right and proper if it occupies a convincing place in a scheme of political value; and a readiness to do what is expedient is good in a statesman (heaven preserve us from the madmen who occasionally get into power and are not interested in expediency!) provided he sees it for what it is, and can also see that not all questions can be settled according to what is expedient. (For instance Mr George Brown's refusal to have Egyptian atrocities in the Yemen denounced at the U.N., 20 September 1967, on the grounds that to do so would be 'counter-productive' was an attempt to apply standards of expediency where they can't apply, as well as being wrong by its own standards; and another sign of the times is to hear the Archbishop of Canterbury, whose words can have only the sense of his office, intoning 'coun-ter-pro-duc-tive' about tactics in South Africa.) But when politics becomes wholly a question of what is expedient and of economic management, and particularly when that it disguised by moral tones and attitudes, there is something very wrong with the language of politics, one result of which must be economic mismanagement and inexpedient action. When a government's world is *wholly* confined to economic dodges for getting the economy moving one likely result is that the economy will get gummed up, for (like the rest of politics) economic management is management of human beings, which is just not restrictable to economics.

III

The reason Mr Wilson could not tell us that we were going to be poorer was that to have done so would have denied the central assumption of contemporary politics, that the first duty of government is to promote the growth of real incomes. Incomes must grow through the growth of the economy, but if the economy doesn't grow, incomes must go up in any case. Mr Wilson's devaluation failure is, in its representative way, the explanation of why we suffer from inflation.

It was Mr R. A. Butler, the best as well as the wiliest of recent Tory politicians, who offered to double our 'standard of living' within twenty years, and in the otherwise remarkably intelligent book *The Art of the Possible* (1971) he sees nothing to regret in the offer. Given our circumstances and language the advance towards that very material land of Beulah has had to be by way of the automatic annual wage-increase. The rule is that wages go up all the time a little faster than prices, and that anything else belongs to that large modern category, the unthinkable – quite suddenly in historic terms, for it is still less than forty years ago that if the nominal rate of wages altered it was more likely to be down than up. The automatic wage-increase is so much taken for granted as a necessary part of the world that it is perhaps more *Weltbild* than what is usually thought of as language. We act as if it were so, rather than talking of it; it belongs to that which cannot be contradicted without madness, like the belief that the world existed before we were born.

Yet this only applies to the political establishment – Westminster, the press, the B.B.C. At Westminster, for instance, when they discuss capital punishment it is unthinkable to bring in the considerations which dominate the parallel discussions in every pub in England: in Parliament the discussion is confined to questions of deterrence and therapy, whereas elsewhere justice may be mentioned. This political style which makes something here ineffable and there the subject of all the conversation, is something new in our present investigation. We are discussing all the time the multiplicity of ways in which language and life interinanimate one another, and the ways in which a change in standard English may implicate all or only some of its speakers. The changes in religious English are far more widespread than those in political English, but less clear-cut. To criticize the new religious styles I therefore naturally had to offer the older styles as a kind of perspective, and something similar can be done with politics. But here we can also use the perspective of commonsense, the rest of our contemporary language, for political English is in some aspects not so much a style or a language as an orthodoxy, capable of contradiction. To challenge it one has to go outside the orthodoxy but not outside current speech. And part of the trouble with what goes on in the Commons is that it is dislocated from the rest of English life.

Labour did at length turn the balance of payments deficit into substantial surplus and Mr Wilson is able to boast that 'No incoming Prime Minister, if Mr Heath takes over, in living memory has taken over a stronger economic situation.'[15] That is undoubtedly true of the balance of payments. Mr Heath also took over an unemployment situation which could not be improved without putting us back in the red, and a roaring wage-inflation such as this country has hardly known since the years following the Black Death. The latter was the direct result of the grammar of the unquestionables which I have described (that it is a general grammar of politics is surely suggested by the Conservatives' failure in their first two years to alter the situation): if devaluation was not to be passed on and understood, an enhanced rate of price- and wage-inflation was inevitable.

Within the language of post-war British politics, that is to say, the problem of inflation cannot be tackled. The very belated efforts of the Heath government, beginning with the 'freeze' of November 1972, were accompanied by assurances of continued 'growth' and money supply which make them look at least as unserious as Mr Wilson's. And that is a straightforward example of the failure of our words to grip reality, for inflation (though of course it has respectable economists to defend it as a good thing, as well as Mr Bernard Levin) can only work successfully as a kind of deception, by making people believe that the more paper money they are given the richer they have become; and devalua-

[15] Memoirs, p. 790.

tion accurately measures the extent to which we have deceived ourselves more than other nations. These are the fruits of our present style of politics.

How to generate a language fit for understanding and solving its problems is (in our terms of discussion) the prime question for any government. Forty years too late we have now a language capable of describing some of the problems of the thirties. But as regards wages, prices and economic advance, the present language is so restricted as to be quite predictable which, contravening Chomsky's necessary condition for a language, that it generate an infinite set of sentences, is one reason for thinking that we are here considering the sub-linguistic world of creed and orthodoxy.

Mr Wilson, the man of the age, is only a particularly striking example of what is generally true. You cannot hear five minutes of a British election speech or read five lines of a manifesto without coming on the essential belief (whether genuinely held or not is another matter) that 'growth' is the prime political value and motive. And the quest for the holy grail of growth is the mainspring of the effort to join 'Europe'.

To save space and take 'Europe' and 'growth' at once – and indeed they are often seen as the same thing – let us consider a few of the reasons for 'going into Europe' contained in official government publications of 1971. It should be realized that these all offer themselves as impartial and non-controversial, aimed only at giving essential information, and they are therefore particularly interesting as they speak the politicians' language of 'growth'-worship.

'The strength of Britain lies in the strength of British industry.'[16] Like Samson's in his hair? It is an equally unlikely place, or rather, what is meant by 'strength' is obscure. Yet the insistence on 'security and prosperity' together, that the former follows automatically from the latter, tolls through the surly sullen pages of the White Paper *The United Kingdom and the European Communities* ('praised for its style and expression of the ideals of the case for entry' as one *Times* headline said, 9 July 1971) both in phrases like 'the full range of modern technological and industrial advance, upon which both security and prosperity greatly depend' (para. 24) and in the idea of 'super powers whose strength is based on their great size and economic resources' (para. 27).

[16] Factsheets on Britain and Europe, issued by H. M. Government, no. 9.

Strength, that is, is a simple product of prosperity, on which all depends. (Cf. 'The economic base from which any influence and authority which we have overseas must spring . . .' – Sir Alec Douglas Home,[17] kicking off the 'great debate' with an idea which would have surprised many of his predecessors who *did* have influence overseas.) This is a doctrine Mr Edward Heath has made very much his own. Already in his Godkin Lectures quoted below Europe is seen as a mechanism to ensure 'prosperity, and consequently . . . stability' (p. 13).

'Differences of language and culture still make many reluctant to move from one country to another, unless there are compelling financial reasons for them to do so.'[18] But if there *are* 'compelling financial reasons', the innuendo is, we all troop obediently off. They are decisive. '. . . the economic progress which we all desire and which has eluded us for so long.'[19] '. . . [Britain's] inadequate rate of growth.'[20] The facing page of the Short White Paper shows that 'real' income per head in Britain increased by over a third in the eleven years 1958–69. This is 'inadequate' according to the orthodoxy. Inadequate for what? Not, evidently, inadequate to sustain a growing population in increasing affluence, but inadequate to provide the economic backing for the beliefs expressed in the words of all the politicians. 'The economic progress which we all desire . . .' We *don't* all desire our further economic overdevelopment; we don't all believe that this rate of getting richer is inadequate. It may well be damaging. But that cannot be said in the style of contemporary politics; any politician who did so would be suspected of believing also that the earth is flat.[21]

'The contrast between the experience of the Six in recent years and ours outside the Community shows that they chose the right road.'[22] Money is the measure of all things; that is the force

[17] *Hansard*, vol. 823, col. 918.
[18] Factsheet 10.
[19] Short Version of the White Paper *Britain and Europe*.
[20] White Paper, para. 40.
[21] Mr Jasper More did have the courage to speak the unspeakable in the Great Debate of 1971 when he said – though I cannot find that anybody paid any attention – 'We may have important things to do in this country and in this House before we get engulfed in the tidal wave of prosperity which the Common Market is to bring.'
Hansard (1971), col. 1296
[22] Short White Paper, p. 16.

of 'shows'. The right road is simply that which leads to most money. Mr Edward Heath put it more vulgarly in his ministerial broadcast of 8 July 1971, his trumpet call for entry into Europe made somewhat oddly in that adman's prose which comes so naturally to the contemporary leaders of the party of Peel, Disraeli and Churchill: 'Of course we all want increased prosperity as soon as we can have it.' And since Mr Heath does believe that a nation's 'performance' can be measured in comparative economic terms, he went on to ask 'Can you honestly say that there haven't been times in recent years when you've had the feeling that this country was losing out, in all sorts of ways?' In another speech he said 'The people of this country will not lightly forgive any group, whether it be a political party or among employers or inside the trade union movement, which is seen to obstruct the improvement in the standard of living which is now open to us.'[23] All manner of political sin and blasphemy shall be forgiven unto men: but the blasphemy against the holy growth shall not be forgiven unto men.

It follows that we must join the E.E.C., for that alone will make us richer quick enough. 'The differences between European neighbours are insignificant, compared with what we have in common.'[24] In our present language of politics this is a clear example of the basic assumption that the industrial system is the only reality. It is materialism run berserk. The assertion that differences between England, France and Germany are insignificant says again that only the means of production and exchange are significant. If England and Germany are both industrial countries, the differences between them do not matter: they are only 'differences of language and culture'. 'The member countries have far more interests in common than differences.'[25] It all depends how you measure and value the differences. This is a way of talking which in 'more' appeals to some numerical calculus which could only be economic. '. . . A Europe composed of states, which, in spite of their different national characteristics, are united in their *essential* interests.'[26] The different national characteristics are by this argument not essential to the European nations; it is no longer essential to a Frenchman to be French.

---

[23] *The Daily Telegraph*, 29 May 1972; not reported by *The Times*.
[24] White Paper, para. 32.   [25] *Ibid*., para. 24.
[26] White Paper, para. 15, my italics.

'There is no question of any erosion of essential national sovereignty; what is proposed is a sharing and an enlargement of individual national sovereignties in the general interest.'[27] (Rather, perhaps, as a husband proposing to add several wives to his marriage might assure the first that there is no question of eroding her essential interests, but of extending and sharing the marriage.) Here the language of politics has been simply taken over by that of mechanics. It is machines that can be designed, specified and controlled, machines which when they go wrong can be mended or the flaw in the design rectified. Mr Heath and the White Paper apply to 'Europe' the grammar of machines. He sees the United Kingdom of Great Britain and Northern Ireland as a regrettably little machine trying to switch itself into the vast machine of Europe. As Sir Christopher Soames put it, 'we must hitch our wagon to the European train' – which does at least vary the image more realistically in that it assumes someone else will supply the locomotive power.

Mr Wilson, the arch-mechanist of contemporary politics, naturally produced an even more telling phrase when he spoke of 'the industrial engine of our nation's greatness',[28] the trouble with which was in 1964 that it 'is underpowered, is not developing its full power, and is compelled for too long to idle on two or at best three cylinders'. The politician is in this image seen as a glorified professional machine-minder. Mr Wilson has in fact always been perfectly clear that Europe is a large technical arrangement. The vision he offered to stir the souls of the City men at the Guildhall, in 1966, was a proposal for

a drive to create a new technological community to pool within Europe the enormous technological inventiveness of Britain and other European countries, to enable Europe, on a competitive basis, to become more self-reliant and neither dependent on imports nor dominated from outside, but basing itself on the creation of competitive indigenous European industries. I can think of nothing that would make a greater reality of the whole European concept.

Memoirs, p. 300

Nor, it seems, could anyone else. The modern version of the belief in Saturn is naturally enough the belief in machines: the infinitely manipulable develops into the purely mechanical.

The whole position can be developed from 'Britain lives by

[27] *Ibid.*, para. 29.
[28] *The New Britain: Labour's Plan*, p. 43.

trade'.[29] By this simple sentence I hope I have made my point, for I guarantee that in itself it rouses no opposition. What could be more inoffensively true? We do live by trade, if working for organizations like I.C.I. or Unilever or B.L.M.C. is 'trade' – but only in the sense of 'earning a living'. Earning a living is important and honourable; more so than in the era of the automatic increase of wealth we like to believe. But it is not the whole of life. The debate about the entry into 'Europe' has throughout its ten boring years been conducted as an attempt to judge the whole of our political life by the standards that apply only to earning a living. 'Britain lives by trade' is therefore not a harmless fact, it is a declaration of orthodox faith which in turn is a sign of that contraction of our language of politics which renders it incapable of discussing anything but the economics of a modern industrial society – and therefore unable to do even *that* convincingly.

The unanimity of assent to a rudimentary materialism embraced 'marketeers' and 'anti-marketeers' alike, as well as Mr Harold Wilson. Sir Derek Walker-Smith, a principal Conservative 'anti-marketeer', took the chance of a controversy in *The Times* with the Duke of Edinburgh to assert the superiority of his own attachment to the economic orthodoxy. The Duke had pointed gently enough to the social disruption caused to Italian peasant farmers by the Community's policies of growth; Sir Derek's retort was that the whole thing should go much quicker (perhaps, I thought, at the pace of Stalin's collectivization?): 'The principal criticism of the Common Market in this regard is not that its technological zeal is having a disruptive effect on agricultural practice. It is rather that they are prolonging, and perhaps perpetuating, an out-of-date, inefficient, costly and socially divisive agricultural pattern.'[30] Cf. Mr Ernest Marples on the other side of the Great Debate: 'The Common Market countries are now trying to get people off the land. They are considering paying £600 for every job created for a farmer aged 55 or his children who will leave the land and go to another job. They are, therefore, making these changes in a very humane fashion.'[31]

The idea of 'Europe', the meaning of the word in contemporary politics (and my reason for putting the word in inverted commas)

[29] Factsheet 5.
[30] *The Times*, 24 June 1971.
[31] *Hansard*, vol. 823, col. 1131.

is thus remarkably restricted to a set of economic arrangements. 'Common Market' is a universally acceptable synonym, and the B.B.C. has even begun the process of composition by sometimes calling it 'the Commonmarket', with the accent on the first syllable.

Tacked on to the Mammonism there is, I hasten to concede, a political argument for 'Europe'. Only by uniting Europe can the wars between European states which have wrought havoc twice this century be in future avoided; further, such a united Europe could speak with one voice, a voice as loud as those of the Superpowers. This has been the argument from all the parties and in all the debates. Mr Wilson's version, during his pro-'Europe' period, was:

The drive to European unity received a great impetus from the suffering which conflicts within Europe imposed upon the people of Europe and, before the final reckoning came, upon the world. It was in the determination that this must never be allowed to happen again that men and women in Europe – and, of course, we are in Europe – talked and planned and began to work for a European decision so to unite Europe that differences between nations could never again be a cause of war here in Europe ...

Because we seek this friendly relationship with both the great powers we do not accept the notion that ... the great issues should be left for settlement direct between these powers because we in Europe are not sufficiently powerful economically – and, therefore, [*sic*] politically – to make our voices heard and our influence felt. *Hansard*, 8 May 1967

In 1972 Mr Heath was still using the same argument:

We're in a world of super powers, and what matters in Europe is that in fact it has very little voice or influence in what the super powers do, and this is where I think we've got a very high priority ... And we in Europe, I believe, can be a force on our own which stands for the things which Europe believes are important.

Times report of a B.B.C. interview, 25 January 1972

What these important things are we are never told (any more than we are told what are the grounds of the assumption – extraordinary if one thinks of European history – that if Europe speaks with one voice what it says will be composed in equal measure of sweetness and light) and I shall come back to the relevance of that lack to the vacuity of Mr Heath's concept of Europe as a new 'entity'.

The span of agreement about this idea of 'Europe' extends far out to the wings of both parties, and when 'Europe' is opposed, this is still the idea of it which is assumed. Mr Duncan Sandys expounds this noble post-imperial ambition almost every time the Commons debate the E.E.C. and he is so confident he has the right words that he always uses almost the same ones: 'In this age of super-states, Britain by herself is no longer in a position to exercise any really effective influence in international affairs . . . Neither can Europe without us claim a seat at the top table. But together we could be one of the giants.' And Sir Geoffrey de Freitas in the 1967 debate took the logic of the argument to its extreme by declaring, 'I see the last two wars as European civil wars, and they have convinced me of the stupidity of the European nation state' (*Hansard*, 10 May 1967).

That rather lets the cat out of the bag about part of the argument, for what 'rotten parchment bonds' can ever prevent civil war? But I waded most of the way through the *Hansard* report of the marathon Commons[32] debate of October 1971 without finding any substantially different argument.

There were two things, however, that emerged from that debate, to me rather surprisingly. One was undisguised military defeatism. Several members spoke of fathers or other near relatives who had been killed in one or other of the great wars, in order to draw the conclusion that the deaths had been an unnecessary waste. It was not, apparently, worth the sacrifice of any life to prevent Hitler's unification of Europe. 'We recognise that war is unacceptable today and at any time in the future', as Mr Christopher Brocklebank-Fowler put it.[33] That is itself a kind of death-

---

[32] Perhaps it was different in the Lords, for some clergy have been advocating 'Europe' on what they take to be spiritual grounds. 'He does not argue for entry on the ground that it would lead to greater prosperity, but concentrates on the advantages of belonging to one European family. "I have lived through two European wars and, like many of you, I have lost relatives and friends in both," he writes. "If we are to avoid a third conflict we must turn Europe into a family. In the past Europe has been a group of independent warring states at the cost of thousands of lives. Had there been a genuine fraternity of nations these terrible tragedies might have been avoided." ' – *Times* report, 3 September 1971, of an article by the Bishop of Southwark in his parish magazine. Dr Stockwood must live in a blissful world where families never quarrel (if he thinks it is the real world almost the first story in the Bible would have disabused him) and seems also to believe that this world can be produced by Act of Parliament.

[33] *Hansard*, vol. 823, col. 1283.

wish to opt out of a world where there can never be a guarantee against war, and where all states (even a hypothetical world state) must always have the right to order their citizens to risk life. 'Europe' could not prevent the loss of life where at present it is taking place, in Northern Ireland; and a federal Europe would need the right to make war.

My other surprise was that the speakers who imagined (like Shelley in *Prometheus Unbound*) that the world can begin again from scratch as we 'cast off the shackles of the past'[34] all spoke from the so-called Conservative benches. It was Sir Harry Legge-Bourke, for instance, who said 'We must try to wipe the slate as clean as we can and look forward to what we think Europe ought to be.'[35]

Was a great power ever so wished or machined into existence? Perhaps so, for history is infinitely various. This policy, if it can be so called, yet seems to me woefully unreal in its conception of Europe.

For despite our politicians Europe is a great and potent actuality; it is not in process of being created except as this kind of achievement must be created anew in each generation, and it is composed of nations. The nations do not compose Europe as parts compose a whole without which they are senseless; nor is Europe some definable core Europeans have in common. On the other hand Europe isn't something *added* to Europeans and European nations; it is their nature to be European. Our modern 'Europeans' sometimes seem to be looking for Europe outside all the European societies, in some special place, much like the mythical Victorian anatomist searching the human body for the precise location of the soul. 'Is he French or does he come from Paris?' 'No, I'm not English, I come from Yorkshire' – these are the kind of absurdity implied by Mr Heath's position in his Godkin lectures *Old Word, New Horizons*,[36] involving through the shallowness of the idea of Europe an even more disastrous unawareness of the nations which compose it. 'For [the new generation]' Mr Heath writes, 'national boundaries have little meaning. The teenager in Frankfurt has the same feelings and ambitions as the youngster in Manchester.'[37]

One retort would be to ask how he knows, since he speaks the language of neither. And the answer would have to be that they

---

[34] *Ibid.*
[35] *Ibid.*, col. 990   [36] 1970.   [37] p. 12.

must all feel the same because the language of economic advance is universal and omnipotent.

People in Europe today are feeling European. For the young in particular older nationalisms are rapidly disappearing. But with the removal of customs barriers the old frontiers have less and less meaning. With the almost universal use of television everyone can see what is going on in his own continent every day of his life. And the ubiquitous scooter means that not content with seeing the world on the screen the young can go and see for themselves what life has to hold for their generation.   (pp. 35–6)

Life holds then, for these pitiable youngsters, no more and no less than can be seen on the telly or from a scooter. The obvious fallacy here is that the statement has nothing to do with 'Europe'. Television cameras have penetrated the U.S.A., and scooters do not suddenly cease to scoot on reaching the Urals. The more important misunderstanding is the supposition that customs barriers are what divide nations, rather than barriers of the other sort of customs. It is part of the idea of Europe that European languages are related, but that nobody speaks European. Unless one sees that the people of Manchester and Frankfurt are very unlike because they are respectively English and German one will never understand why it matters that, all the same, both Manchester and Frankfurt are European cities.

Mr Heath's belief that national boundaries are no longer meaningful must be evidence of the amazing power of a language to make one believe almost anything. If national boundaries are no longer real, what does Mr Heath imagine he is Prime Minister of ?

But Mr Heath's reduction both of Europe and the European nations looks extraordinary only in this kind of commentary. You can find the same thing all over the national press which (with the exception of the Beaverbrook papers) supported 'Europe' with a unanimity which in itself suggests we are considering an orthodoxy rather than an argument. *The Times*, in particular, distinguished itself by the fervency of its despair of Britain, and supported Mr Heath in 1971 as loyally as ever Dawson supported Chamberlain.

All the recent lessons, good and bad alike, drive home the dominant argument: in the modern world of advanced and highly expensive technology – expensive both in money and highly educated men – a population of fifty million is not enough.   24 June 1971

The young can now look forward to leading a life with the whole of Western Europe as a home land ... Membership of Europe, and the exchanges with Europe this will produce, will encourage and revitalize the creative activity of Britain; they will end this atmosphere of staleness and pettiness of purpose.   8 July 1971

As well as showing the same belief that the world begins in economic gigantism this is the same determination that 'Europe' shall be a civilization distinct from those of its constituent nations. It looks to me, I admit, more like a prescription for a shot in the arm, less respectable even than the depression it is supposed to cure. As Mr Heath said in that broadcast, 'For 25 years we've been looking for something to get us going again. Now here it is.' *The Times* even went so far as to assert that 'There are very few purely national problems any more.' (23 February 1972: that was in a third leader on a day when the first two were called 'The Crime at Aldershot' and 'Judging Health Service Complaints'.)

The Commons debates on entry to the E.E.C. ought, if the subject is as important as everybody says, to have been the political events of the decade. They should have been like the French Assembly's debate on E.D.C. which not only made a decision (and the right one) but defined the sense of the decision, made it what it was. There is a certain appropriateness in the question of Europe's being the one our politicians are least competent to discuss; for it is the one that demands the keenest sense of the nature of our nation and of Europe. It is, indeed, in such discussion that Europe and Britain are defined. As far as the orthodox language of politics goes, the nation is what it is there made. The politicians were at work, in the way proper to them, on an idea of the political part of our nature: and a petty nature they have given us, too.

The bright idea that European wars are civil wars (provided, one supposes, that they are within the capitalist half of Europe – I have not met the idea applied to the likeliest next European war between 'Europe' and the rest of Europe, which *would* be a civil war as far as Germany is a nation) is in itself a good example of the way our language of politics is losing sense: firstly it is losing the sense of the kind of reality possessed by the community using it.

It is no longer commonplace to say that their nation matters in people's lives in Europe; some of the 'Europeans' have almost lost that sense. But the reality of nations makes the quest for a European entity (of, as far as one can guess, the same kind as the nations) look very wishful. The nation has been, after all, for 600 years in Europe, and is, the large community; in it individuals, families, towns, find a place as they cannot in either 'Europe' or Europe. The nation, not Europe, is simply our ordinary frame of reference. If you read in a newspaper 'Unemployment Tops the Million Mark' or 'Divorce Rate up Again' the paper doesn't mean the European unemployed or divorced and there is no reason why it should. We don't vote in European elections and are not subjects of the King of Europe. More important to this discussion, in Europe (as against India) nations, on the whole, are co-extensive with languages.[38] Nations are wholes because (with the obvious exceptions – Belgium is not the great characterizing instance of the European nation) composed of people of common culture, people, that is, who can argue with each other and who can therefore create politics in the way I began by discussing. That simply cannot happen in Europe as a whole; European unity could not be of that sort.

I used to think that the final destruction of the idea of Europe as a super-power was, 'But nobody could ever be asked to *die* for the Commonmarket?' 'Yes I would be willing to die for it,' replied a European. I refrained from using the retort said to have been made by a distinguished philosopher to a man who boldly asserted he liked having conversations with a computer: 'Then you must be a bigger bloody fool than I took you for.' 'A local state is not a God', said Arnold Toynbee to the Delos Symposium.[39] 'It has been treated as a god. People have sacrificed their lives for it. But a local state is really just a public utility, like the gasworks, the electricity grid or the telephone system.' He went on to recognize that he had just said something rather odd: 'In public school in England I was taught that for a man to give his life for his country is very noble. But if we were to say he gave his life for the electricity grid, that would sound comic.' Yes, it would and it would sound almost equally comic to say that a man gave his life for that larger utility, the European Economic Community. So long as in common speech one's country occupies a

---

[38] Nations which have a common language in the grammatical sense are closely related, but my argument doesn't commit me to saying we are really the same nation as the U.S.A. There is a close family relationship, but American English is very different from ours. We do *not* speak the same language; we have a different set of associations, assumptions, styles and references; and I would not dispute that in some ways our language is closer to French than to American (though to follow the analogy that would be friendship more than relationship).

[39] 10 July 1972.

different place from the electricity grid, Mr Heath's 'entity' of Europe will be comic.

'Europe needs a European press', said *The Times*, helping Mr Heath with his entity,[40] and set about providing one by the simultaneous publication together with *Le Monde* (which ought to have known better), *La Stampa* and *Die Welt* of one of their usual pull-out supplements, which bring in so much advertising revenue. (The one the week after was on new developments in the floor-covering industry.) The leader didn't even think it worth mentioning that the other papers publishing the supplement did so in various foreign languages.

There *are* people about who try to be European as against English, French, German or whatever. I met one who had, he said, all but lost his first language; as far as I could see he hadn't replaced it. His English was flat and with an unidentifiable accent we may, I suppose, come to know as European. We tried French and he spoke it grammatically and with a better accent than my English one – but, again, with a certain lifelessness. The experience was rather sinister, for it seemed to me that this man wasn't a human soul; he seemed somehow to have been displaced from humanity. There was a kind of breakdown and incoherence in his face. If you are at home everywhere (which of course Mr Heath isn't) how does that differ from being at home nowhere?

What is to be similarly fragmented and disoriented in the service of the new 'Europe' is, simply enough, our lives. This is what is to happen to the political part of being human. 'Europe' condemns us (even apart from the practical results which, I will not disguise, seem to me likely to be massive human dislocation, misery and dullness) to a life which in its political aspects cannot make sense. Mr Wilson's vision, shared by Mr Heath and the rest, of 'a Britain which had become part of a market of getting on for 300 million people'[41] defines the life appropriate to the formulation. (The national élite is then surprised that this prospect of industrial oligopoly – 'the European ideal' as the B.B.C. habitually calls it – arouses little enthusiasm in the young.)

Stupidity is usually thought to be innocent if not harmless, but there are degrees and kinds of stupidity (one meets some in the academic world) which are indistinguishable from malevolence, and that is one corollary of my discussions of the idea of 'sincerity'.

[40] 23 February 1972.
[41] *The Times*, 9 May 1967.

Our contemporary political English is a stupid orthodoxy which in its effects is not distinguishable from hatred of English life.

> To be prejudiced is always to be weak; yet there are prejudices so near to laudable, that they have been often praised, and are always pardoned. To love their country has been considered as virtue in men, whose love could not be otherwise than blind, because their preference was made without a comparison; but it has never been my fortune to find, either in ancient or modern writers, any honourable mention of those, who have with equal blindness hated their country.
>
> *Taxation no Tyranny*

The obsessions of the orthodox are of a kind that makes it hard for them to be really conscious of anything; it seems likely that they know not what they do. But, applying the doctrine of 'by their fruits ye shall know them' one can say that Johnson's numerous present exceptions would have to include those who receive foreign prizes and domestic congratulations for (in effect if not in conscious intent) hating their country.

IV

Mr Heath's and Mr Wilson's style, those two sides of the same doubly devalued coin, shows that they consider themselves to be the manipulators of 60,000,000 economic units which, in their grand way, they esteem a paltry number.[42] Churchill, on the contrary, talked – even when he was talking reactionary obscurantism – as if to human beings. 'Were it not for the leaping and twinkling of the soul, man would rot away in his greatest passion, idleness. A certain kind of reasonableness is its advocate, and a certain kind of morality adds its blessing. But to have soul is the whole venture of life.'[43] Jung might perhaps have agreed that in idleness of soul there is nothing necessarily inconsistent with either the manic activity of a Harold Wilson or the stubbornness of Edward Heath, Man of Principle.

Churchill's style, for all its surface grandeur and its occasional obfuscations, was a style for identifying and tackling problems –

---

[42] Cf. Mr Charles Pannell's much-respected contribution to the Great Debate: 'We can, if we wish, be a small red spot on the map – no longer red splashed over the globe – of 50 million people; a derisory number against the market that is open to us in Europe.' – *Hansard*, vol. 823, col. 1292.

[43] C. G. Jung, *Collected Works* vol. IX (1959), p. 27; he is following a La Rochefoucauld *pensée*.

it was what, if he were a poet, one might call a 'technique for sincerity'. And to miss this, to see only oratory or rhetoric in Churchill, though there is certainly an element of that, is very like seeing only beauty or orotundity in the English Bible – both are signs that one is reading a dead language.

The striking thing about both Churchill's war speeches and his *Second World War* is how constantly he had to keep coming back to work on his sense of the nature of English life, of what it was that we were defending. He does this not through discussions or arguments but through the convinced use in his story and speeches of the general political terms of the English language, such as 'parliamentary government' as well as ones like 'courage'. What Churchill was defending, and defining, was (though he wouldn't ever have put it this way) the life of political English. It is this life that in the age of the Common Market and the growth-orthodoxy has somehow evaporated.

Perhaps we have no serious political problems (at least we are unable to make Ireland a serious problem) now we have got rid of the Empire and super-power status and retain the British tradition of not treating things like social change, sexual revolution and the developments of the machine age as political. At all events, the sinking into dullness of mind of our political language does seem a particularly English disease. (The English disease of which the weeklies are full seems to me to be diagnosable as sheer feeble-mindedness.)

I am not suggesting that this English disease is curable by an act of will (or that the image should mislead us into thinking there can be a diagnosis followed by cure). We can no more have a political style than a religious one just by wishing, though wanting one is certainly one of the necessary conditions. The present situation obviously comes from deep in the history of our century and before, and the new political élite of 'Europeans' cannot suddenly be expected to develop what at present they lack, a language for understanding their inheritance from the old governing élite of landed aristocracy and middle class. Yet they might be made to feel that they are kicking against the pricks (though not by the people who *should* be criticizing them in an ordinary day-to-day fashion, as I demonstrate next chapter). Our new élite[44] is drag-

---

[44] One flattering unction laid by *The Times* to the Europeans' soul is that though a solid majority of the electorate appears to be opposed to 'Europe' a majority of the thinking and educated classes is in favour.

ging us (kicking and screaming, as Mr Wilson said elsewhere) into 'Europe)' as proof that we *are* reducible to the language of
economic management and 'growth'. The dragging is against the
other pull of whatever it is that gives us nationality – in political
terms, against our nature. Our sullenness may be evidence of our
bloody-mindedness (which in itself might be something to be
glad of) but can also be seen as a more hopeful sign that we
might still find in national life a criterion to judge present politics
by.

For there is another England and another English as well as
those of the politicians. In England we all believe in technology,
growth, prosperity and therefore stability, security and progress;
we drive our cars along the motorways and pocket our automatic
annual wage-increases. But occupying exactly the same territory
and created by the same people there is also a great England, the
England of Shakespeare. To it some of its statesmen (Cromwell,
Gladstone, Churchill) have belonged. Mr Wilson's devaluation
speech was an insult to this 'proud nation' because he does not
know what is great in it. And it isn't the great England that is
'going into Europe' any more than it is the great Europe she is
going into, for to the great Europe the great England naturally
and necessarily belongs. The great England provides the standards
of political judgment. The commonsense by which we judge the
politicians and their ways of thought is effective because unlike
their style it can still connect with that greatness of English which
is the possibility of the real and the sincere in our political life.

There must come a day when our statesmen once again see
that their responsibilities begin at home and are not to be shrugged
off by going 'into Europe' or anywhere else. It is to what is great
in this Island (as Churchill liked to call it) that politicians are
responsible; to the possibility of a serious human life whose
language is English; and it is by that standard that they will, like
the rest of us, be judged, should judgment survive.

(Cf. Patrick Wall M.P., *Hansard* (1971), col. 1177.) The first and best
retort to that is a rude noise; the second that, alas, when you transfer the
discussion from votes to thinking, issues are not settled by majorities at
all, unless in the reformed jury system. It doesn't follow either, because
150 economists signed a letter *pro* to *The Times* and another 150 *con*,
that the economic arguments are evenly balanced, or that they would
have been less evenly balanced if one side had drummed up a couple
of hundred.

4

The Vulgarization of 'The Times'

tam saeva et infesta virtutibus tempora
                                                    Tacitus

It is as far from the truth with regard to journalism as politics that events just happen. There are, of course, the events that are caused by journalism, as when television camera crews inspire people by their presence to behave in an extraordinary way. They are not primarily what I mean, though they are connected with the examples I am after by such intermediate cases as the following. On 20 June 1971 the B.B.C. Radio 4 programme *The World This Weekend* led off across countless Sunday dinner tables with the story of a twelve-year-old girl who had been refused a National Health Service abortion and had later been aborted at a private clinic. The child's mother and the officers of the clinic were interviewed at length and in detail in order to make an adverse criticism against the general practitioner who had decided against the abortion. Of all the people concerned, except the child, only the G.P. kept his mouth shut – which was in turn used by the B.B.C. programme as an adverse criticism. On page 1 of the next day's *Times* (21 June 1971) these events were reported under the following headline: 'MP Defends Doctor who Refused Abortion to Girl of 12.'[1] Now in ordinary life, it seems pretty clear, what happened was that a girl of twelve, not well looked after, became pregnant and suffered the consequent traumas, which were complicated by her experiences in public and private medical hands. Afterwards, said her mother on the radio, everything was forgotten. For the journalists, however, the event in question was that a doctor had made a particular decision, and another doctor another decision, and that a well-known Roman Catholic M.P. and others had taken to the air. What happened was turned into what was of interest to journalists.

Anybody who has ever read a newspaper account of an event

[1] Throughout this essay *The Times* is quoted from an early edition, usually no. 3 or 4 of the possible eight.

at which he has been present will understand the truth we have to keep coming back to that the style of expressing a thing affects the thing expressed. 'Were we really there?' we may wonder, or 'Is he writing about the same thing?' To the latter of these questions the answer is *no*, newspapers aren't quite writing about the things we see and experience, because they are following the rules of a language which isn't quite the ordinary language, and which changes the events depicted.

The gross example is newspaper cliché. Newspapers must tell a story about an event in such a way as to make it immediately comprehensible. 'Girl, Three, Escapes from Embrace of Boa-constrictor.' In one sense – the sense proper to newspapers – this tells us immediately what happened. But what happened is very different for little Alice, for her mother, and for the reader of the sentence (not to consider the boa-constrictor). For the newspaper-reader the actuality is analysed simply into the most ordinary categories, so that the story of the event is imagined in terms of girls, ages, very simple action.

In that way newspapers are a primitive example of how a style of language creates a world. The style even of the *Sun* is the form of a life. 'Most news is made by man, though some can be made by bacteria,' said *The Times* in its manifesto of 21 September 1970. No, *all* news is made by men. Bacteria may be the occasion of news, but it is only within a particular way of speech and thought that bacteria 'make' news – in this case the particular way that is a newspaper's style. But there is no need for a newspaper's style to be cliché or its world to be unrecognizable.

The developments in *The Times* in the 1960s were one of our most obvious signs of change in the decade. I want to inquire into the kind and degree of significance they had, and what the change in the world of *The Times* means for our common world. Commenting on the history of a newspaper is particularly difficult, for the memory of something even as dependable as the old *Times* fades rapidly and is not easily revivified by quotation which, in the nature of the case, has to be highly selective. I will not pretend, either, to have read the paper all the way through every day, especially since 1968, when my judgment of the changes increasingly took the form of unwillingness to waste much time on the paper. (And unlike Northcliffe, who used to amaze his *Times* men by delivering a detailed criticism of the whole paper every morning, I haven't either inside information

or a secretary to read *The Times* for me.) All the same, I think
what has happened is quite plain enough.

I

The Times has been twice revolutionized since 1965, not counting
the minor changes and the effort at counter-revolution in September 1970. The immediately surprising thing is that the revolution
under the *ancien régime* was much more thoroughgoing than that
which followed Lord Thomson's takeover. What happened?

The important part of the first revolution, according to *The
Times* as well as other newspapers and the B.B.C., was a change
in what I shall call surface style: the placing of news on the
front page, where the small advertisements used to be. This is
what caught the public fancy, as it was intended to, and one of
The Times's later recollections ran, 'So, a year last May, news
was put on the front page, other features were introduced . . .'
(1 January 1968). Behind this, the real transformation of May
1966 escaped apparently unobserved – partly because *The Times*
itself published no letters on the subject until, weeks later, one
attained to the dignity of the new women's page. Some of the
main changes in 1966 were the re-styling of the leader page, the
introduction of a women's page, a gossip column and cartoons,
the remodelling of the main news pages to include advertising,
and the reversion to the typographical style of the inter-war years,
with Stanley Morison's Times New Roman face set leaded as it
was intended to be.[2] This last made *The Times* the most hand-
somely printed and legible European newspaper (until the reduction of type-sizes in September 1970 and the earlier narrowing
of columns and use of inferior paper) on the leader page, at least,
where the print was still found unmolested by the competition
of big pictures, bold headlines and so forth which went with the
revolution. That this transformation was more than a face-lift
is difficult but necessary to establish.

The second, or Thomsonian revolution occurred in two stages
early in 1967, with gentler later repercussions, and provided, as

---

[2] In 1972, the year of the publication of Morison's biography, *The
Times* went over (Morison's politics proving more durable than the typo-
graphy that was his real achievement) in apparent imitation of the
Guardian to a kind of degenerate Baskerville which would hardly have
been countenanced, I think, by either John Baskerville or Stanley
Morison.

well as another rearrangement of the order of pages, a Business News separable from the rest of the paper (Lord Thomson's own inspiration, the rumour goes, which explains why it survived for three years), the naming of correspondents, the suppression of the fourth leader (in which last asylum the English Essay had daily appeared in its disgusting and whimsical senility) and a very substantial relaxation of the house-rules about such matters as size of pictures and headlines. Prose style was, as we shall see, pepped up. Both changes greatly increased *The Times*'s bulk. Other changes before September 1970 included the provision of a Saturday Review which gathers and somewhat expands the book reviews, the bridge, chess and cooking features and so on.

These formal changes, so innocent-looking as here described, expressed the deep disintegration of the paper's idea of what it is and does. They embody a changed idea of news.

What counts as news is the first difference between the new *Times* and the old. Two pieces of legal news achieved the front page on 5 October 1967; the one, in three column-inches, that for the first time in English history a jury had been 'sent out to reach a majority verdict', the other, in twelve column-inches, that a barrister had appeared in the Inner London Sessional Court wearing a turban instead of a wig. For the new *Times*, true to its belief in the importance of surface style, the latter was much the more important departure from tradition. On 4 September 1967 the B.B.C. broadcast news of mysterious flying saucers, apparently made of plastic and emitting bleeps, which had been collected at sundry places. I waited with interest to see what *The Times* would make of this 'mystery' if it wasn't solved before the paper went to press. In fact it *was* solved in plenty of time but still filled a column on the next day's front page. What is the point of a gossip column if hoaxes can't go into it? Would *The Times* ever, before May 1966, even in the silly season of August, have run as its second story on the home-news page the information, illustrated by two photographs, that the then Mrs John Lennon had missed a train and wept? But the new *Times* explained un-blushingly in its obituary of Brian Epstein (28 August 1967) that The Beatles[3] are the best-known people in the world – and therefore, it followed for the new paper, the best worth reporting on all occasions. Pop stars' pictures at about the same time began

---

[3] 'Quartette vocal britannique de musique légère' – *Grand Larousse*, supplément.

alternating with royalty on the court page. *The Times*'s rather clumsy *penchant* for pop stars, it is fair to say, did not endure (it was later in part replaced by one for sports stars so that, for instance, on 8 January 1972 the dropping of George Best from the Manchester United team occupied a more prominent part of page 1 than the suicide of a leading American poet) but while it lasted it looked as if *The Times* were engaged in self-punishment. The real pop papers wouldn't have fallen for a story-line as threadbare as the *how I wish I could be a straight actor and not a filmstar/club entertainer/cabaret-singer/pop star* one: 'I hope by Christmas to have killed the "pop star" title. I want to be "actor Jess Conrad"' (9 September 1967).

The new *Times* is very much longer than the old, but (as I shall illustrate) the solid day-by-day recording of facts which was the backbone of the old paper has not expanded, and the editorial problem seems to be to find enough matter of the requisite un-seriousness to fill the pages. The effect of making a little go a long way can fairly be called sensationalism, if sensations can be boring. One of the opportunities given by more space is to treat some subject relevant to the news in some depth. But so often (and especially after the changes of September 1970) depth turns out to be length, too like an extension of the gossip column on whose page the investigations by the 'News Team' are found. Exception-ally informative and interesting articles have appeared, sometimes, like the ones on the workings of the Greek Colonels' régime, of a kind the old *Times* might have been too stuffy to print. But there is far too much like 'Why Wilson Lost against all Odds', a News Team narrative which had the air of having been hastily assem-bled to replace a 'Why Wilson Won' story (20 June 1970). Despite the 'why' of its title this article consisted simply of a detailed, gossipy and inaccurate narrative of some of the trivia of the 1970 election. ('In the shadow beyond the glare of the television lights the normally imperturbable Mr Reginald Pye, a rubber planter, a Canadian Army captain and a dealer in foreign stamps before he became the Conservative agent in Bexley in 1949, was almost overcome . . .' and so on.) The 'why', confined to the last two paragraphs, was on this level of intellection:

What went wrong? A Labour Party worker said sadly: 'Like Jack Dempsey, we failed to duck.'

Across the square, at Central Office, a party worker captured it all in a phrase: 'It's the greatest comeback since Lazarus.'

Don't agree with him here!!

That is the kind of phrase that does capture the fancy of the new *Times*. It would be unreasonable to expect an explanation of a surprising result the day after an election: the offer should therefore not have been made.

It is good that news is no longer confined within the Victorian categories, and Mr Harry Eddom's remarkable survival on a raft in the Arctic after his trawler went down was certainly worth reporting. But need *The Times* have done it like this, with the telephone conversations *verbatim*? – 'I spoke to him on the telephone. He said: "How are you, mum?" and when I said: "How are you, Harry," he said "All right, mum" ' (7 February 1968). Important speeches are not so reported. One wonders, therefore, whether the paper reprinted *The Irish Times*'s long interview with Miss Bernadette Devlin M.P. about her pregnancy for its political interest or its value as gossip (3 July 1971).

The 1967 devaluation of the pound was an important event, but important enough to need the whole of *The Times*'s front page and six other separate reports and leaders as well as the whole Business News (20 November 1967)? The real information could have gone comfortably into a short paragraph. In fact it was altogether omitted, at least in the early edition, and the omission was disguised by all the column-furlongs of print. For after the initial announcement, the important devaluation news was the reaction of other countries. Would there be other devaluations which would undo the effect of ours? *The Times* not only failed to report other changes on 20 November 1967; it also failed to comment on the possibility. The lengthiness is properly a form of gossip, but the collective bulk of the pages floating past the reader's eyes gives him a vague sense of importance that may or may not be properly attachable to the events. That can be called a kind of sensationalism. If the legendary Victorian editor, Delane, as Kitchin observes, expected his readers to spend 'their entire waking day quarrying in the columns of *The Times* for the news which had therein been buried overnight'[4] Mr Rees-Mogg apparently expects *his* readers to spend all day wandering idly amidst broken columns of 'comment', 'background' and other solemn or not solemn chit-chat.

A more obvious kind of sensationalism goes with the introduction of banner headlines. Once they are possible to a newspaper

[4] F. Harcourt Kitchin, *Moberly Bell and his Times* (1925), p. 39.

there is a kind of pressure to use them and be sensational. Devaluation of the pound perhaps deserved a banner headline, but by the following year so did the results of the *borough* elections ('Triumphant Tories Sweep the Country', 10 May 1968). It seems to me that that inflation of importance is only another aspect of *Times* headline English which now also makes G. H. Lewes in a Saturday Review article 'the Bloke George Eliot Lived With' (30 March 1968), says of a runner 'Cool, Real Cool, this Young Man in a Hell of a Hurry to Win Gold' (16 July 1971), and summarized words of de Gaulle correctly translated 'If your answer should be "No", it goes without saying that I should no longer continue my duties' with the phrase 'Back Me or I Quit' (25 May 1968). By a not very strange coincidence *The Times* shared that last headline with the *Daily Mirror*.

In 1971 *The Times* launched one of those poster campaigns which must do so much for its losses, aimed at persuading the public that it is still an utterly dependable newspaper of record. (One poster showed an unwinding microfilm reel of a copy of the paper which had an unfortunate momentary resemblance to the paper's disappearing into a waste-bin.) But *The Times* is a less reliable and complete document of record than it was in 1960 and *much* less than it was in 1900. Even allowing for the fact that *The Times* now thinks that Western Europe is not overseas, the amount of space given to overseas news, the pride and joy of the Victorian *Times*, has not increased, and what there is is far flimsier. (Saturday is not a good day for foreign news, but it was still remarkable on 29 May 1972 that in the newly European paper foreign news was down to one page out of fourteen, including the newly-separated 'West Europe' news, and that half the page was the text of the Strategic Arms Limitation Treaty. There was still room to tell us that the clock had been put on in Italy for the seventh successive year and for stories about the Anglo-German Everest expedition and a football match played in Spain by Glasgow Rangers.) The paper is as far as ever from its nineteenth-century policy of reporting important speeches *verbatim* (the only exceptions I noticed in seven years were some Common Market speeches in 1967 and again in 1971; they did also print Mr Barber's 1972 budget speech complete – a sign of an odd scale of values). Parliament gets truncated reports from which, even if they were well done, one could get only a hazy idea of what had been said. Even the Business News, even in its most distended days,

1967–70, didn't reprint the *Stock Exchange Daily Official List* of bargains marked, as *The Times* used to do until the early sixties. To the paper's credit, however, they did print the White Paper on Common Market entry complete.

Another aspect of the new *Times*'s failure as the paper of record is its determination to be up-to-the-minute. (This trouble afflicts the B.B.C. more severely – when it deigns to broadcast the important news at all. Both the *Daily Telegraph* and *The Times* were worried on 14 June 1972 in case a vital Common Market vote might be lost in the Commons: at 8.00 a.m. the following morning Radio 4 didn't mention the result. When the news is broadcast in the morning, you must get it while you can, for by 1.00 p.m. it is either history or the subject of lengthy comment from which you try to infer the news.) Anybody looking at *The Times* on 7 June 1968 to discover whether Senator Robert Kennedy's wounds had proved mortal would have had to search for the information or infer it from the presence of an obituary (not in itself conclusive evidence since all newspapers from time to time make the mistake of publishing an obituary of a living person): the news story on page 1 was too up-to-the-minute to mention Kennedy's death. 'Woman Sought in Kennedy Inquiry' ran the headline, introducing one of the non-stories of which there must have been more in *The Times* since 1966 than in its whole previous history. The *Daily Telegraph* handled this better (one of the ironies of our recent past is that Matthew Arnold's *bête noir*, much truer to its traditions than our other newspapers, is now the nearest we come to something dependable): its head-lines went, 'Robert Kennedy Dead/Johnson orders Day of Mourning/[and only then] Police hunt Woman seen with Sus-pect'. Even the death of a former King of England was not some-thing the new *Times* could simply record in a headline. Instead (unlike the *Telegraph*, which got it right with 'Duke of Windsor Dies at 77') they went on to the funeral arrangements: 'The Duke of Windsor to be Buried on Monday after Lying in State in St George's Chapel' (29 May 1972). One could infer that the duke was dead; but should reading newspapers outside the Soviet Union be so much a matter of inference?

On Monday 18 March 1968 *The Times* appeared with a main headline 'Bankers Agree on Plan to Avoid Monetary Collapse' and the story began, with a self-contradiction that whetted one's appetite for the news. 'The main lines of the international bankers' strategy to stave off a collapse of the monetary system were settled yesterday. The emergency meeting of the gold pool ended in Washington, as it had begun, in absolute secrecy.' 'All yesterday,' said the Business News, 'the world held its breath, waiting for the news from Washington.' The news itself became available after the early edition of *The Times* had gone to press. It so happened that on that Monday I saw no other papers and was not able to hear any B.B.C. news, so I looked at the next day's *Times* with some interest to find out whether the world monetary system had collapsed. But by then the news was so old that *The Times* didn't print it at all. Instead we had the usual pages and pages of 'reactions' from which the news could after a fashion be guessed. I turned to the parliamentary report; but the news had been cut there too. The Business News had a collection of stories headed 'Day 1 of the New Monetary Deal' without saying what this 'new monetary deal' was.

It is often easier to discover from the new *Times* what it thinks will happen next week or next century than what happened yesterday. Some of the predictions are quite unnecessarily risky. *The Times* was in good company when it took for granted de Gaulle's devaluation of the franc, for *Le Monde* was even more categorical in its 'reports'. ('Le conseil des ministres fixera samedi le taux de la dévaluation . . . Dix ans après la grande réforme monétaire de 1958, accompagnée d'une dévaluation qui devait être définitive, le gouvernement du général de Gaulle se trouve contraint à nouveau d'amputer la valeur du franc' (23 November 1968). 'Le gouvernement définit les grandes orientations du programme économique qui accompagnera la dévaluation' (25 November 1968).) 'Among all forms of mistake,' as George Eliot says, 'prophecy is the most gratuitous.' The category of prophecy offered as report didn't, apparently, occur to her: 'Mr Heath has not won the support of the voters . . . One cannot say that Mr Powell's incursion cost the Conservatives the election; it has certainly made a recovery much more difficult' (17 June 1970). I am not merely objecting that *The Times* was misled by the opinion polls about what it insisted on calling 'Election 70', but that its lack of caution in the week before the election was so extreme as to bring in question its power to distinguish fact from guesswork. It is the nature of an election that the result cannot be discussed before the votes are cast. A newspaper which knew this elementary fact wouldn't have needed as *The Times* did after beginning 'A general election in

West Germany is now provisionally planned for December 3' to continue 'Nobody knows who will win' (11 July 1972).

But *The Times* is now very fond of crystal-gazing as news. 'Consultants Upset by Pay Offer' began 'Consultants in regional hospitals *are likely to* lead senior doctors in a campaign against acceptance of *an expected* 5 per cent government offer...' (4 August 1970, my italics). Habits of sobriety would have ruled these out, and would have postponed reporting and discussion of the James Report until publication.

They would also have prevented this sensational scare-story which *The Times* printed on its front page: 'A small army of militant extremists plans to seize control of certain highly sensitive installations and buildings in central London next month...' (5 September 1968) – a tale which contains a great deal about that very publicity-minded revolutionary Mr Tariq Ali, by whom the old paper would surely have been less impressed and whose affinity with the new *Times* used to be shown in his appearance with comparable frequency in the news columns and the gossip column.

The changes in lay-out and the general debilitation of the sense of news chime harmoniously with the new prose. The news is processed into a new kind of newsiness.

Other figures in the report which indicate the human cost of apartheid include ... a swinging 25,933 strokes of corporal punishment, and a total of 340 deaths in prison. But the grimmest figure of all discloses that 84 people were hanged during the twelve months, which enables South Africa comfortably to maintain her traditional place at the top of the world execution table.

Dan van der Vat, 6 August 1970

This wit is rather ghastly, though not in the way intended. The old *Times* would simply have reported these figures, and that would have revealed their grimness more effectively than Mr van der Vat's amusing us with what they 'disclose'.

This kind of brightness seems to me all of a piece with the more obvious kinds of coarsening of prose style – the split infinitives, the solecisms (even 'disinterested' is now misused), the clichés, marking the abandonment of the old *Times*'s style-book which must have been as near as England ever came to the definiteness of the Académie Française. 'AUTHORITY AND INTEGRITY; the key words for TIMES SPECIAL REPORTS' *The Times* itself told us in a corner of one of them which it hadn't managed to sell (12 August 1971); presumably that is its explanation of the style for describing drivers in a special report on motor-racing (16 July 1971):

Quicker, most agree, than any alive today. Showman and money-minded. You see him small but striding, always smiling [The photograph of a very fashionably grim face accompanies the words.] . . . Baby faced, but the whiskers are on his helmet . . . Always the bridesmaid, never the bride . . . His career has been studded with luck. Took over the number one seat for the Colin Chapman team after Jochen Rindt's death at Monza . . . Sensitive and small, you see him crouching in a corner of his car. Pale and balding, 'There's so much that's stark and functional in the world, so much sickness and evil.'

So many clichés, too. One could sum it up by using one: there is nothing new under the sun. The mixed metaphors in which the new paper – taking a leaf out of the *Guardian*'s phrase-book – disports itself, occasionally give a glimmer of pleasure as the blank day breaks on the bald street. Poor Mr John Lindsay 'lacks the grass-roots' backing in the Democrat machine' (12 August 1971). The following came all at once in the same article:

However, in his sweeping purge of the Egyptian administration, which was surgical in its precision and painlessness, President Anwar Sadat has spirited himself on to the exalted throne long regarded as the place of Nasser alone . . . The one thing that is common of [*sic*] all those whose heads have fallen in the past week is that they formed the pillars of the Nasser régime . . .[5] What is so impressive about the way in which Mr Sadat dismantled the old administration and established one modelled on his own image is that he has left not a stone unturned. The so-called 'centres of power', generators in the Egyptian powerhouse under Nasser and dangerous pockets of opposition to his successor, have disappeared. But the purge has not stopped there . . . The momentum gathered in his original stroke . . . after his own administration begins to get off the ground . . .   (19 May 1971)

All this is worse than a relaxation of Victorian standards. The intention shining through so much of the new *Times*'s prose is to vie with its Fleet Street competitors – to take its standards from them.

Aid to poor nations has a past to live down. Present efforts to boost assistance to developing countries are therefore that much more difficult. Experience however has taught many lessons. These are being applied increasingly. The management of aid has become a highly sophisticated business. Great strides have been made in the last few years.

                                                                        (30 October 1967)

[5] The falling heads are a figure of speech: there were no executions.

That has the air of an ordinary complex sentence translated into the style of the *Express*'s 'Opinion' column. 'From his first day [Sir William Haley] set about improving the paper . . . getting stories and leaders written "in words of one syllable"' (1 January 1968). His efforts bore that fruit.

It is not always easy to know whether a new *Times* sentence is just very badly written or, for some reason, self-parodying. The nicely-mixed metaphors I quoted are perhaps simply the slackness which is brightness's other face; but may not these, about talks in the car industry, have been done on purpose? – though *what* purpose is hard to say:

There were many then who thought that a working part at the level proposed by B.M.H. was a non-starter and anything lower down the ladder would operate with one hand tied behind its back.

Such, however, is the standing of the new body that the very fact that it is in being now offers both sides probably the best form of safety valve in times of stress the oft beleaguered car industry has ever seen.

(21 August 1967)

This is the style to be expected of a newspaper ready to admit in its own columns that 'the *Daily Mirror* has continued to be the most powerful newspaper in the country' (24 January 1970). The old *Times* would not so unironically have condemned itself to powerlessness by confusing circulation with influence. 'How is it possible not to be influenced by the belief that power is a matter of size?' asked a columnist (21 February 1970). How indeed? But if *The Times* cannot answer the question there is no hope of a respectable British newspaper.

Some *Times* leaders are very good; ten years ago it was our only newspaper capable of proper criticism of the Robbins Report, and in recent years it has risen to some occasions in ways I think it could not have managed under Sir William Haley. No other newspaper seriously raises the questions of pornography and censorship (see next chapter), and *The Times* was the only daily or weekly journal to make any sustained criticism of the 1970 election. But some kinds of feebleness of argument came into *The Times* with the revolutions and would have been impossible before. One of the best of the 1970 leaders on the triviality of the campaigns, 6 June 1970, made as good a shot as I have seen anywhere at discussing how and why 'Inside a few years, British elections have passed from being debates to being spectacles,' and why that matters. This was far better than the last election leaders under the old dispensation, which gave us (prophetically for the paper as well as the country) such nonsense as 'This weekend's new Government has to get Britain going at once' (14 October 1964). But *The Times* itself is affected by the disintegration and coarsening of political language, and marred the series by making hysterical and irrational attacks on Mr Enoch Powell. 'Now he talks nonsense, dangerous nonsense, but nonsense nevertheless' (15 June 1970). There was no effort to sustain the rhetoric by argument.

Of course fear is a real power . . . Hatred has a power too. Yet it is ludicrous to suppose that any British party could ever now be led by Mr Powell . . .

His hysteria, because it is hysteria, is to be pitied; as it is directed against innocent people, people poorer, less secure, less well housed, less well educated, less fortunate in almost every way than himself or most of his followers, it is to be hated as well as pitied.   (*Ibid.*)

But not, apparently, to be refuted. Perhaps, now the dust is settled, the hatred and fear may be seen to belong more to that passage than to the donnish Mr Powell – as well as the rashness of prophecy, for during the next couple of years many people grew to think it far from ludicrous to imagine Mr Powell as the successor of Mr Heath. At any rate *The Times*'s own weapons were rhetoric and emotion of a kind that the old paper might have thought, without supporting argument, rather disreputable.

The Times too is perpetually mystified by Ireland and always dismisses the Rev. Dr Ian Paisley without the slightest attempt at refutation or explanation. To *The Times* what he says isn't strictly language at all; it doesn't fall within what the paper can recognize as politics or religion. The effect, which some will think extraordinary, is that *The Times* seems more prejudiced, more out of touch with the world, and less able to conduct an argument than the right wing of the Tory party and the Protestants of Ulster. Sometimes the new paper slips into a kind of infantilism one would not have expected from the old. It made, for instance, the extraordinary though truly British suggestion that the Rhodesia question should be harmlessly settled by inflation of the Rhodesian currency.

In fact, if prices remain stable, on these qualifications, and even assuming considerable prosperity in Rhodesia as the result of British aid at £5m a year, it might take 30 years, and perhaps 50 [for Africans to get as many parliamentary seats as Europeans]. But inflation benignly erodes income and property qualification barriers, so that if the actual figures are entrenched and cannot be altered, the period of time would be shortened, perhaps to a short and acceptable transition.   (26 November 1971)

Of course, inflation might benignly erode British aid too. Also, a Rhodesian government could hardly be blamed if it won the game by inducing deflation. My point, however, is that the idea that the future of a polity, the sense its political institutions make, can rightly be determined by transparent financial deception, is a kind of childish cleverness one associates with the new paper not the old.

At a more comic level one notices how afraid the new *Times* can be of its own logic.

It would be more convincing to argue – although outside the Commission's brief – that the advertising [of detergents] achieves no purpose in increasing total sales; it is merely an additional cost, borne in the end by the housewife.

But this is true of all advertising. It would be very hard to pinpoint the social usefulness of any particular piece of advertising. Is it therefore a wasteful use of resources? The mind reels at the possibilities inherent in allowing a government power to nominate practices it did not like for the axe. The rest of us could, with equal justice, nominate, say, all spending by the parties.   (27 April 1967)

'Is it therefore a wasteful use of resources?' The answer to the question in that context, and without prejudice to detergent-advertising, is simply YES. But some minds reel easily, and the 'possibilities' here are those envisaged by a reeling mind, not those entailed by the argument.

When the new paper attempts comment on moral or philosophical issues it is apt to come out with such speculations as these about 'Life in a Test Tube': 'The cheapest and surest way for any small, impoverished country to improve its wealth and influence would be to concentrate on breeding a race of intellectual giants. So much depends these days on the intelligence of a nation's manpower' (15 April 1969). The idea that persons of supreme intelligence could ever, whatever the advances in biology, be bred in test tubes, is a misconception of the nature of intelligence. Much happens, after all, between the conception of a human being and the contribution of his intelligence to the national economy. A *Times* which had any understanding of the importance of, for instance, its own history for 'the intelligence of our nation's manpower' would not have got into the muddle. And that is the kind of connection between the changes of style and the failure of critical comment which I must try to draw.

During the revolutions correspondents began to be named, some correspondents were promoted to be columnists and new ones were brought in (the culmination of the development was the appointment of Mr Bernard Levin, on whom a little more in section IV, below). I will not spend long on the contributions of Mr Philip Howard, whose appointed task was to be frivolous about such matters as demonstrations by people in wheelchairs or members of the Greenland Liberation Front in a style which is a kind of pepped-up version of the old fourth-leader whimsy. ('In his timbered local in the depths of Suffolk, the oldest regular clutches convulsively at his pint of mild to ward off the tidal wave of children. In the snug they look up from their shove-ha'penny in a wild surmise . . .' (26 July 1967) etc., etc. – Mr Howard has all the fourth leader's weakness for hackneyed quotation. He later extended his scope and on 19 February 1969 was loosed upon the Oxford Professor of Poetry.) I must however make a few remarks about some representative correspondents.

The Times appeared to signal its conversion to enlightened views on education by appointing Mr Brian MacArthur education correspondent (though the case was not quite so simple since correspondence and leaders often disagreed and there was in the latter some survival of *The Times*'s admirable and lonely opposition to the post-Robbins university explosion). Mr MacArthur, so, I am afraid, it seems to me, has no understanding of education. He never felt any need to argue his case for the continued expansion of the universities; educational progress for him was always and consistently numbers going up, class sizes coming down, and lots more money spent. Asking 'what significant shifts seem to have occurred in education' in recent years, Mr MacArthur came out with the remarkably self-confident answer, 'Undoubtedly, the crucial issue has been money, a problem which will continue to dominate all discussions about education for several years to come (11 January 1969: the years referred to were those of 'student power', of the continuing debate about comprehensive schools, and of the impact of the Robbins, Crowther and Newsom Reports). He happily prophesied for universities 'an increase in productivity and a more intensive use of university plant' in the course of recommending universities as a moral duty to worsen their staff–student ratio (28 December 1967; by 'plant' he meant equipment – computers and the like, not books – not that delicate weed, the only true result of 'productivity' in a university, namely, thinking). He would like 'each university, each department [to] be allowed to excel at something, whether it is solid-state physics or medieval English, but the situation can no longer prevail in which all of them attempt to do so' (*ibid.*). A mind that supposes academic excellence – thought – to be so easy to arrange (presumably as another question of money) or that excellence or mediocrity in one department has no effect on the others, or that any university is likely to have *any* distinction if its senior members are not trying to master their subjects, has failed to understand the nature of thought and the idea of a university, and is unfitted to comment on educational problems. 'Such are the ideas in the air as Britain's booming system of higher education moves into the 1970s' ('Education Revolution just Beginning', 7 December 1968). Yes indeed, and the new *Times* could be relied on not to miss the bandwagon.

I thought with the appointment of Mr Stephen Jessel *The Times* had come to its senses about its education correspondence and he is certainly a great improvement. What really happened, however, is that the paper gained accidentally by promoting Mr MacArthur to run the illegible new *T.H.E.S.* where he continues to give satisfaction to Times Newspapers Ltd even to this very day without, so far as I can see, having learned anything about education.

For some years before the first revolution *The Times*'s newspage report of Parliament had been getting chattier, but the revolutions have made more than possible a full imitation of *Guardian* brightness. The parliamentary correspondent has the *Guardian* weakness for an extended metaphor which runs the wind of the poor cracked phrase to death – for instance:

Mr Heath hit back vigorously today in the Commons at Mr Wilson and other Labour MPs who have been needling him over his yachting activities ... Mr Heath replied with a Nelsonian flourish that he had been asked to captain the Admiral's Cup team and he intended doing so ...

When ... Mr Wilson ventured off on the same tack, [he] sailed into a force 9 prime ministerial gale ... At this point the Speaker joined in. It was time to get back to the fairway, Mr Selwyn Lloyd said. Conservative MPs leapt for joy at the reminder of Mr Wilson's prowess in and out of the rough.

(16 July 1971)

[margin handwriting: typically Thomson]

114

I am not against amusement, though I was not very much amused by that style, week in week out, and in bulk. My point is that it belongs to a range of ways of talking the total effect of which is to make it very difficult to guess whether there had been anything worth reporting. The correspondent's way of going for titbits, jokes and sensations makes one never quite sure whether he is on to anything or not. The natural consequence of this style of reporting is such a story as 'MP Fails to Make Longest Speech' (19 February 1969) in which Mr Hugh Noyes held up Mr Robert Sheldon to extensive ridicule because he had spoken for two hours and ten minutes. Was it not rather inappropriate to do so in the longest story on the front page? It may be that any just description of parliamentary proceedings would bring out their ridiculousness; but the parliamentary correspondent's style is not one that can be trusted to make just descriptions. It was not possible to infer from what he wrote whether Mr Sheldon was speaking for or against a bill, whether he was trying to talk it out or demonstrating against Parliamentary rules. (It was, in fact, the last case.) This is the opposite of reporting, for one couldn't find out what had happened. The important thing, the thing that got expressed, was the correspondent's own style – so personal and so stereotyped – a directionless irony that gives nothing but the writer's sense of superiority to what he describes.

Once again Brother George [Mr George Brown] is the darling of the Labour Party. His critics are routed, at least until the next time he decides to go frugging, and more important for the nation, conference has given the Government a clear and overwhelming mandate to go ahead with their Common Market negotiations. (6 October 1967)

The corespondent's interest is so obviously not in what is important for the nation. 'Starting slowly and gradually warming to his task, the Foreign Secretary left the Opposition – Douglas Jay, Manny Shinwell, Alf Morris, Uncle Frank Cousins and all – in the undignified posture of men who have suddenly had their chairs withdrawn just as they are about to sit down.' The style is a poor substitute for any effort at understanding the subject.

One great thing in the old *Times*, especially before the Northcliffe takeover, was its foreign correspondence, uniquely reliable and informative if only because the *Times* man often had unique access to information because he *was* the *Times* man. The style of the modern correspondents, as of the parliamentary correspondence – their restriction within the barest Western clichés – makes it often impossible to get beyond the surface of events to any understanding of them. (I discuss the main recent example in section IV of this essay.) What was the 1970 revolution in Oman all about? To the *Times* man that was a very simple question: the people were simply emerging from the 'sleep of centuries' into 'hopes, shared by most, that the doors of the twentieth century are at last open to them' (31 July 1970) – the twentieth century consisting of roads, hospitals, electricity, schooling and so on, the alternative being simply 'medieval', whatever that means. Seeing this situation through such modern spectacles has the effect of making it literally unimaginable. For 'a job in itself will be to create the proper infrastructure for development. At present, in an age when the rest of the Persian Gulf is bristling with luxury hotels, ports and airports, Omanis are just seeing the foundations laid for the first hotel in the sultanate.' In that case the Omanis cannot be craving for Western materialism; they cannot be said to know what they are wanting. I will also confess that I'm not as sure as *The Times* that they will be better off when they get it, and I don't find the destruction of ancient civilizations by the wholesale construction of infrastructures and hotels necessarily an inspiration to trust in progress. ('Undoubtedly it was the fact that the Sultan turned his back on progress that precipitated his downfall.') How could what I quoted account for the correspondent's description of the new Sultan's receiving from his people 'a welcome reserved for those who come as saviours'? If he *did* come as a saviour there was something deeper and more passionate in the outburst than the wish to scream oneself into the modern world; and if the new Sultan is simply the modern liberal technocrat he will be in trouble before long. But those are observations gathered not by reading *The Times* so much as demolishing it. Mr Peter Hazelhurst, of whom more later, is comparable. His solution to the problems of India can fairly be summarized as contraception and slaughter of the sacred cows. He writes of the latter, 'Ancient Hindu priests gave the cow her religious sanctity to preserve her for her milk yield' (9 May 1970). As if anything could be 'given' sanctity like that! That statement is a prime example of a failure to *see* brought on by the modern Western prejudice that only economic management is real and that everything else follows from it.[6]

---

[6] Cf. 'What narrowness of spiritual life we find in Frazer! And as a result:

Whatever the shape of the new régime, the tasks facing it will be the same – to end the country's isolation, particularly from the West, and to embark on a development programme which will move **** towards the twentieth century. (15 January 1970)

That is Nicholas Ashford on the Yemen, but it could be any new *Times* correspondent on any 'underdeveloped' country. So the 'Prime Minister, Mohsin al-Aini . . . represents the forces of moderate pragmatism' (*ibid.*). My objection is not merely that I'm not much impressed by moderate pragmatism after our own recent experiences of it: I don't know what in the context of the Yemen it could mean; and *The Times* nowadays can't make any shot at telling me.

I haven't read the new women's page very often. When I do, it seems more thoughtlessly enthusiastic about the new 'pop' world than the rest of the paper, and equally unable to raise the real questions.

First she thinks she has to overcome the public's image of her. 'People think that everything I do is evil and wicked. Well I know I'm not what people think of me. So I got married when I was very young, so I got divorced, so I'm in love with Mick Jagger . . . Well, I can love everybody. It doesn't matter what they think of me' . . .
The publicity has left its scars . . .
But there is a note of hope in her voice. To be beautiful and a good actress is almost too much to wish for. But [she] looks like making it. (14 February 1969)

Is it only publicity that leaves scars? May such a life as is here suggested *not* be one to be envied? *The Times* in the old days would have thought this article a simple condoning of immorality and perhaps I am making a related point if I say it made me feel compassion for its subject. The article is evidence of something

how impossible for him to understand a different way of life from the English one of his time!
'Frazer cannot imagine a priest who is not basically an English parson of our times with all his stupidity and feebleness . . .
'Frazer is much more savage than most of his savages, for these savages will not be so far from any understanding of spiritual matters as an Englishman of the twentieth century. His explanations of the primitive observances are much cruder than the sense of the observances themselves.' – L. Wittgenstein, 'Remarks on Frazer's *Golden Bough*', transl. A. C. Miles and Rush Rhees, *The Human World*, no. 3 (1971) pp. 31–2, 34.

more alarming, of a lack of all values, a return to chaos in which 'morality' and 'pity' would be equally meaningless.

'Classless, indifferent to established religion, politics and authority, this new young breed [of "drops-outs . . . and students"] is seeking a fresh approach to living. They certainly look like a force of change. But they are all growing older. Can they keep that questioning energy into the thirties, the forties?' (18 December 1968). Any 'seeking' is here taking place in a void, where nothing could be recognized if found. This is describing not a 'force' but a chaos, with which the writer feels empathy. It is desperate to try to see groups as hopelessly disinherited as these as 'a force for change'. But the new *Times*'s fellow-feeling for them is not confined to the women's page: another sign is the gossip column's weakness for the *Red Mole* and those other very well publicized 'underground' creatures.

The same style is to be found in the arts page. The new *Times* has in the first place a very unreliable sense of what is art and what isn't. Arthur Askey is part of the general knowledge of our age, but an article on 'The *Art* of Arthur Askey' (20 March 1971, my italics) is the confusion of kinds. 'The refashioning process is made easier by a creative continuity from one play to the next.' Scofield in Shakespeare? No, an article called 'Coming of Age for the "Whitehall farce"' (3 April 1971) which went on, 'No less than the National Theatre or the Royal Shakespeare Company, Mr Rix believes in the ensemble principle.' Why ever was the Berliner Ensemble and Brecht left out of the comparison? Mr Rix smiled out of the accompanying photograph with an appropriately ironical expression lost on the reporter. An article on 'the novelist, John Fowles' called 'The Writer as a Recluse' (12 May 1971), after describing the subject as 'probably the most successful and least known serious English novelist published in the last quarter of a century' and defining his seriousness as 'indicating the rejuvenation of the romantic novel, and the decline of the gasp and grope sex novel' also defines his style of being a recluse:

Now he travels occasionally to the United States, where *The French Lieutenant's Woman* has just appeared in paperback, to submerge in the promotional circus of television chat shows. 'I stay drunk most of the time', he says smiling. 'With seven or eight shows a day you can't help it.'

It is all of a piece that Mr John Russell Taylor, the regular film reviewer, should have no idea of what counts as seriousness in films. (See also below, 'Pornography'.) One day he defined true liberty, apropos of *Mysteries of the Organism.*

Benevolent and serene as it stares out at us from photographs, his face therefore haunts the film with a sense of paradise lost in a world where true liberty, as expressed by a naked couple who are briefly seen climbing all over the room in one long, ecstatic orgasm of animal joy, is inevitably stifled by creeds, dogmas and political necessities.

(19 November 1971)

If that is true liberty one would have thought it more likely to be stifled by physiological than political necessities.

The superior solemnity of this next quotation benefits its appearance as a leader:

There need be no affectation in admiring [the brief great age of Hollywood, a moment of glory] a generation later – or, for that matter, in thinking that a time when Cole Porter and Noël Coward were at the top of their form, and when vintage Wodehouse appeared with any luck twice a year, was an age of almost Augustan riches.   (11 December 1971)

No affectation, in the new *Times*, certainly – but evidence, perhaps, of the collapse of any serious standards of taste? 'Old heroes are best', as Richard Williams said (2 November 1971). The old heroes, on a page entitled 'The Arts', are a 'pop' group called the Beach Boys, and the article recounts something of their history. They go back as far as 1967, when '"Surf's Up" had been acclaimed by the few who had heard it as one of the greatest pop songs of all time. It was said to be Wilson's masterpiece.' How long is all time in the history of pop? 'Old heroes are the best heroes, particularly when they can make 1971 feel like both itself *and* 1967. Four years wasn't such a long time to wait, after all.' This makes *The Times* itself (an eighteenth-century foundation) as well as Shakespeare, Mozart and so forth, merely prehistoric.

In commenting on these changes in the style of a vast flood of printed matter I have necessarily had to simplify, perhaps in suggesting that the old *Times* disappeared overnight. Of course, some bits survive, though *as* bits rather than parts deriving from the new paper. The obvious case is the obituaries. All 'quality' papers carefully accumulate a stock of obituaries ready for use, and it cannot easily be replaced. In its early months the new *Times* was still publishing obituaries of colonial administrators, scientists, musicians and literary figures which it must have filed years before. I saw no internal reason to date the *Times* obituary of Mark

Rutherford's second wife (28 July 1967) later than 1930. In such cases the paper is still its old self: very full and careful as to facts, tending to stuffiness, but sometimes even rising to a thought-provoking judgment. (The obituarist of Margaret Kennedy used the occasion to suggest rather persuasively that there might after all be something to be said for her novels.) One odd side-effect is that earlier *Times* styles and attitudes can momentarily reappear, as when the Nizam of Hyderabad received a very full obituary, of the thundering kind, which was found so insulting by his family that they were allowed to publish in the paper a kind of counter-obituary. But with obituaries that must have been prepared recently, *The Times* is all at sea: it becomes particularly clear that *The Times* has not developed any coherent alternative to the old establishment values. It used to be obvious who deserved an obituary, and at what length. But what is the present standard of importance? Charming bits of olde-worlde *Times* survive, as when the obituary of Sir Thomas Innes, 'Former Lord Lyon King of Arms' ran to about 24 column-inches and told us things like: 'He had that childlike quality that characterizes the truly great . . . and . . . an eldritch sense of humour that made him coveted as an after-dinner speaker . . . He removed the fear of snobbery from heraldry and showed instead that it was fun' (18 October 1971). The obituary of Krushchev (whose career ended before the *Times* revolutions) showed the strength of the old style: full, informative, sober, but not shirking judgments (13 September 1971).

But was the death of Brian Epstein (manager of the 'pop' group, The Beatles) really a national event? Perhaps it was, but *The Times* was incapable of knowing what sort of event, or of coming up with a style suitable for the occasion. Epstein was treated in much the same tone as Bertrand Russell, as if he were a comparable Grand Old Man, in an obituary packed with words like 'stature' which must have seemed very odd to Epstein's admirers. One wished long life to all teenage idols.

For some months the worst thing of all in the new *Times* was Mr Clive Irving's Saturday column on 'media' – worst because it seemed so representative, the characterizing expression of the paper's coherent and achieved new identity or, as it would say, 'image'. Mr Irving's work, reminiscent of Marshall McLuhan's in its mixture of hectic belief in progress with pseudo-technical jargon, used to appear under headlines like 'The Reincarnation

of Radio Reporting' and always assumed that the most desirable
thing in our society is change in and for itself.

With B.B.C. radio undergoing one of its most sweeping reconstructions
this autumn, the pirate radio operators can look on with justifiable chagrin
as their kind of music programmes are taken over by the corporation.
Without the pirates it is doubtful that the B.B.C. would have moved so far
so fast.

But not all the new ideas are coming from outside. There's still some
steam left in steam radio . . .

(29 July 1967)

So long as things move far and fast the direction is unimportant
and *what for?* A question not to be asked. Mr Irving's articles
brought *The Times* fully contemporary with a Prime Minister
who was reported to have said, 'The Labour Party is like a
vehicle. If you drive at great speed, all the people in it are either
so exhilarated or so sick that you have no problems. But when
you stop, they all get out and argue about which way to go.'[7]
The submission to the spell of technology that is another aspect of
Mr Irving's meaningless élan came out here:

In the end, in a nightmare world where everything can be quantified in
the research departments, we may be able not only to predict psychological
attitudes to particular publications, but also, by measuring them, be able
to control them. For the moment, though, this is an argument to be heard
only in the publishers' propaganda . . .

The television companies, who are, by the nature of Independent Television, automatically united through one outlet, do a better collective job
of selling the medium. They fight solely with the figures, and do not seem
to need to talk about atmosphere or states of mind.

(27 July 1967, supplement)

This 'nightmare world' *is* a nightmare, though Mr Irving seems
to relish it: it is a vision of a horrible but mercifully impossible
state. 'The end' would be after the end of humanity; so long
as we are human it can never be possible for 'everything' to be
quantified and predictable. But this nightmare was, in the years
1967–70, the unrealizable state to which *The Times* seemed to be
looking as an ideal and towards which it was trying to progress.

II

In the leaders that announced the various changes, *The Times*
made some show of justifying them; as with the translators of the

[7] Ian Trethowan's column, 30 January 1968.

N.E.B. one can ask what they *thought* they were doing, as well as what they did. The first manifesto, 'Modern Times' – the use of the name of Chaplin's great attack on our age was presumably accidental – devoted most of its effort to justifying news on the front page: 'Now *The Times* also puts first things first. The prime purpose of a newspaper is to give the news. It should do so in the quickest and most convenient manner' (3 May 1966). Not, one notes, 'the steadiest and most reliable manner'. Even about this change in its surface grammar, the most striking break with *Times* tradition was the feeling that because it was unique it was wrong. (After all, *The Times* got on very well in its first century without anything you could call a main news page.) Where the main news page comes isn't very important, but it does matter that *The Times*'s horizons should not be bounded by contemporary Fleet Street. (Cf. its curiously insular tribute to *Le Monde*, 23 December 1969, in which *The Times* was surprised by aspects of that newspaper's style which it shares with almost every journal in the world outside the Anglo-Saxon nations.) After dealing with news on the front page and such essentials as the changed position of the weather forecast, 'Modern Times' went on to the real changes in this way:

The page opposite the court page has been assigned to matters principally concerning woman and the home. A Diary has been introduced on the leader page. Some readers have been alarmed by reports that it is to be a gossip column. There were far more vehement fears when The Times started a crossword puzzle. (That angry and vituperative correspondence from the eminent and unknown was one of the social curiosities of the age.) We hope The Times Diary will come to be as eagerly awaited and as highly regarded as The Times crossword now is.

But what if I ask (not being in the habit of eagerly awaiting the *Times* crossword) whether those who thought neither the crossword nor the gossip column a change for the better may not have had some reason on their side? The leader gave no more of an argument than appears in the quotation. It is, instead, a rhetorical device discounting all opposition, in advance, and with that compound of indulgent contempt and failure to argue which is our modern enlightenment's habitual response to criticism. It was the same with the manifesto of the second revolution: 'There are a few of our readers, particularly those who have read The Times for a very long while, for whom all changes seem equally unwelcome; to them we can only offer our understanding' (11

April 1967). That contrives to suggest, without exposing the suggestion to argument, that everyone who doesn't like the changes is (a) unreasonably averse to any change whatsoever, (b) an insignificant minority and (c) since they are in their dotage in need of (d) being humoured. Nowhere in 'Modern Times' was there a closer approach to reasoning than this:

The question has been asked why there should be change at all. Change is the law of life. If things do not evolve they die... Newspapers serve society; if they are to do so successfully they cannot divorce themselves from its habits. Placing news on the front page of The Times is one more step along a road this paper has been treading for 181 years. Uniqueness is not a virtue if it becomes mere eccentricity. There is no future for any newspaper as a museum piece.[8]

Change may be 'the law of life' but dying is also a very good example of change. Continuity is also a law of life. And if change is so much more important than continuity how is the road trodden by Sir William Haley and colleagues the same road as that of the paper's first 181 years?

The leader evokes the general reflection that if this country had any coherent conservative tradition its reformers would be forced to be less woolly: in particular one asks, why these changes in *The Times*? The answer is, to conform – a verb expressing more succinctly what the leader called *not divorcing itself from contemporary habits*. But *The Times* became a great (and very profitable) newspaper precisely by not conforming to the journalistic practices and mental clichés of the early nineteenth century. How can a newspaper serve society unless it is able, sometimes, not to conform? – unless, for instance, it divorces itself from habits that work against the formation and expression of public opinion. 'The [Saturday] Review is a further stage in the editorial redevelopment of The Times that began earlier this year with the launching of the Business News. The principle behind each is the same: to offer the reader what he wants to read on the day he is best able to read it' (14 October 1967). Who is 'the reader' and what does he want? 'The books pages ... will aim to represent the interests of a very wide range of readers' the first class of whom was 'the amiable middle-brow'. This makes an

---

[8] On this last point Northcliffe for one moment thought differently: he conceived the idea of bequeathing *The Times* to a body which was to include the Archbishop of Canterbury and the Trustees of the British Museum.

instructive contrast with the insistence (discussed below) of
Moberly Bell during the Northcliffe takeover that 'the paper
shall ... appeal to the better-educated portion of the public'.[9]
This leader also promised that the 'Review' will contain 'information on art and gramophone records, pop and classical'. 'There
may be some,' said Mr Grobe very gently, 'though perhaps
amongst them you would find no dean or bishop who would have
preferred that you put God's name before Grunter's'.[10]

III

What happened to *The Times* in 1966–7 makes an instructive
contrast with its history from the turn of the century to 1908,
when it was ordered to be sold, and was snapped up by Northcliffe. The contrast is between two different senses of style.

I am not trying to produce a commentary on *The History of
'The Times'* and can only sketch the salient features of the earlier
situation. Moberly Bell, the assistant manager at the time (a post
which because of *The Times*'s extraordinary and very complicated
constitution, lucidly explained by Kitchin, gave him general control of the paper) was determined to keep *The Times* going in its
established character despite a falling circulation and the apparent
impossibility of making it meet its expenses. He did so by involving
the paper with various unjournalistic enterprises (the most
famous being an arrangement to associate *The Times* with a reprint of the ninth edition of *Encyclopaedia Britannica*) which were
advertised in *The Times* in displays that breached its usual standards of decorum in their stridency. This was, I think, a change
in surface style, which did not much affect the deep character of
the newspaper; but Bell seems to have had no conception of the
risks he was running.

Bell was a stickler for good English and a fanatic for the paper's
integrity, but he made no connection between those concerns
and the way the print was disposed on the pages, or the appearance of the advertisements. Sensationalism of typography, banner
headlines and the like, would have been instinctively rejected if
the possibility could have arisen – the first time *The Times*
extended a headline over more than one column had not been
auspicious: it was to announce the publication of the (forged)

<hr>

[9] *The History of 'The Times'*, vol. III, p. 548.
[10] T. F. Powys, *Mr. Weston's Good Wine*, chapter 27.

Parnell letter – but neither Bell nor Buckle, the editor, had any sense that the character of the paper might be expressed in some way by the appearance of the pages.

Before Northcliffe's day *The Times* was designed (if that is the word) by the foreman printer – not any member of the Walter family, principal proprietors and printers, who were country gentlemen by the end of the nineteenth century, but the man supervising the presses. News went in where there was room, and if there was no room the news was held over indefinitely for the 'outer sheet', which provoked Northcliffe's very understand-able outbursts against *The Times*'s belief that news, like wine, im-proves with keeping. So before Northcliffe the make-up of *The Times* was a matter indifferent to manager, editor and proprietor. 'In the days of Delane there was no such thing as a technique of display and make-up of news.'[11]

Yet in its Victorian heyday there is a certain obvious congruence between what *The Times* was and what it looked like. One could make a pretty good guess that *The Times* of the Delane period was conducted with 'responsibility' and expressed 'massive stability' merely by turning over its pages without reading them. They look solid, stable and dependable, as well, to the modern eye, as more or less unreadable. In those circumstances the sur-face appearance naturally took the form appropriate to what the paper really was.

Fifty years later, in Moberly Bell's day, cross-heads had been introduced; but the heavily-crowded pages of small print still look daunting and solemn. These Bell peppered more or less indis-criminately (though the foreign news page and leader page were sacrosanct) with advertisements which offended some readers. Some were sleazy, for Bell was anxious for what income could be had (though he would certainly have drawn the line at one togged up to look like a scientific report, 21 June 1972, 'Contraception: the official statistics' according to which 120% [*sic*] of married couples use one or more of five methods, without any percentage reserved for the procreators and the don't knows, but all too few the ones manufactured by this scientific benefactor: 'Which is sad, when you consider that simple, effective contraceptives are so easy to obtain'); but more striking were the strident announcements of *Encyclopaedia Britannica, The Historians' History of the World*,

---

[11] Kitchin, *Moberly Bell and his Times*, p. 39.

the (later) Times Book Club, and so forth – 'strident', that is, in context: they would look quite restrained in today's *Times*. These

made a horrid mess of the once decent pages of *The Times* news-paper. That unhappy journal broke out into a rash of ugly block type, even upon its orderly front page, and classes of illustrated advertisements were accepted which to look upon must have curdled the hereditary Walter blood.

Kitchen, *ibid.*, p. 161

There were many protests to Bell about the Hooper and Jackson advertisements but, with what Kitchin calls a 'sheer lust for battle', he went on with his policy. At the paper's moment of supreme crisis Bell's contempt for questions of mere surface style led him almost to fail in his heroic effort to preserve *The Times*.

The circumstances of the Northcliffe takeover, though a fasci-nating tale, can concern us here only as to the bargain Bell made with Northcliffe. Bell agreed to get Northcliffe in, despite the plans of Walter, the chief proprietor, on certain conditions:[12]

(a) That the main changes will be in matters relating to the mechanical production of the paper.
(b) That changes will be made in the arrangement and get-up of the paper, but that in other respects the tendency will be to fuller and more complete reports ...
(f) That the paper shall avoid sensationalism, and appeal to the better educated portion of the public.

The History of 'The Times', vol. III, p. 548

It seems to me that Bell here is, as usual, making his manful effort on very dangerous ground. For is there not some natural con-nection between the 'arrangement and get-up' of a newspaper – its outward and visible form – and less tangible expressions of its character like English style and editorial policy? Almost Bell was inviting interference with the body, expecting the soul to be unscathed. Yet, because he was very clear about what I will call the deeper aspects of style, he almost got away with it.

The critique I have attempted of the new *Times* has been of its deep style which determines its sense; sometimes I remarked on the appearance and surface features as symptomatic of the bent of the paper, sometimes on other matters. But once again in the

---

[12] At the very last moment Bell had to admit Northcliffe on the single condition of the maintenance in office of the key editorial staff, but in subsequent years, Northcliffe, Bell, Buckle and Chirol all seem to have behaved as if the original agreement was in force.

new paper, my argument runs, there is no disconnection between the real character and the immediate appearance of *The Times*, and Bell's attempt to disconnect the two was, in the long run, against nature, as Northcliffe well knew. The surface style follows from the deep style, the sense of what is news. A serious paper will *naturally* not go in for sensationalism, banner headlines and so on. Bell's mistake was to suppose that the surface style is therefore a kind of face that can be indefinitely manipulated without altering the character. If Bell's resistance to Northcliffe's predictable pushes of *The Times* towards the *Daily Mail* was not fully successful, it was because Northcliffe, with his instinct for popular journalism, knew that the line between form and content cannot finally be drawn and that changes in the former will affect the latter.

In our day the *Times* men had an easier passage:

I thought it might take a year for the two sides to size each other up and really get together, and at least another year for the new company to get into full swing.

As things turned out, I was hopelessly over-cautious. The two sides came together from the start, and the staffs of the two papers found they had a healthy respect for each other. It was clear from the start that the only desire of Lord Thomson, his son, and Mr Denis Hamilton was to enhance the prestige of *The Times* and the service it could give to its readers.

Sir William Haley, quoted 26 September 1967

The case the men of 1966 would wish to make is that they did nothing worse than manipulate the surface style, while maintaining the general character and nature of the newspaper. The difference from Bell is essential. He *did* want, passionately, to preserve *The Times* – at the expense of some lapses of taste. In 1966 the change of expression followed a change of sensibility. The loss of faith in the paper preceded the changes, and was expressed in a great upheaval in the deep style which, naturally enough, was then also expressed on the surface.

'Readers will rapidly become as accustomed to the new look as they were to the old. It is what a newspaper is that matters' (3 May 1966). I can't say that I have ever become as used to the new paper as the old, but the main objection is that a mistake which looks like Bell's is actually an unintentional camouflage for really basic change for the worse. 'There is no intention of altering the essential character of The Times. The same people have produced today's issue as did yesterday's. They will continue to have the same sense of responsibility and the same standards' (*ibid.*). Whether a person is the same when his language changes is a good question: it is at least clear that changes of language are changes of standards, and that what happened to *The Times* in 1966 was a disintegration, for which Sir William Haley was responsible, of its total language, and the substitution of a worse. Sir William Haley's confidence that his own continuity was the same as *The Times*'s was thus, unlike Bell's, a comic example of the blankness about the nature of *The Times* which led to the changes.

The takeovers of *The Times* by Northcliffe in 1908 and Thomson in 1967 both have a historical rightness which will no doubt be dispassionately pleasing to future historians of the sect which is fond of the word 'inevitable'. In both cases the paper succumbed to the spirit of the age. When Newnes, the Harmsworths and Pearson founded the English version of popular journalism they can have had little thought of influencing the London morning dailies. At the turn of the century *The Times* was flanked by half a dozen contemporaries all with circulations less than our *Morning Star*'s, all more solid and dependable than our *Telegraph*, not to mention our new *Times*, and all losing money in a modest way. But, though leaves are many, the root is one: Northcliffe's takeover of *The Times* was a fine illustration of the unity of English culture. Ultimately *Answers* competed with *The Times*. A few years ago radio pirates affected the Third Programme and today the *Daily Mirror* has had its effect on the *New Statesman*. The new thing is that today the influence is all one way. (It couldn't have occurred to the *Guardian* in 1966 that really it was about time they stopped the personality cult of naming correspondents and the vulgarity of news on the front page.) In Bell's day *The Times* influenced Northcliffe and his *Mail*, as well as *vice versa*. But in our day the capture of *The Times* was made easy by the internal rot. Haley *wanted* Thomson and did not know that there were any passes to be sold. (I have no knowledge of the events leading to the Thomson takeover and look forward to the next volume of *The History of 'The Times'* – assuming the paper is still thought to be having a history. My remark is a stylistic observation.)

Under Bell and Buckle it was the 'total language' of *The Times* which was great, almost, in some cases, despite the things the paper in fact said. Bell was reactionary and romantic. He was enthusiastically pro-Rhodes, disinclined to believe any ill of Jameson even after the Raid, and took delight in this prophecy, now close to a fulfilment he could surely not have imagined:

Personally my own view is perhaps an extreme one, for I look forward to the time when, not in the Colonies only, but here in England, it shall be regarded as disgraceful to employ a white man on mere manual unskilled labour, and when the lower races shall be the universal hewers of wood and drawers of water.

The Life and Letters of C. F. Moberly Bell (1927), p. 219

But when *The Times* organized a history of the Boer War, Bell's insistence, despite his passionate commitment to the wrong side, was the one dictated by the language of *The Times*; and he could write with convincing sincerity to a correspondent collecting information from captured Boers, 'Try to impress upon them the fact that it is *History* without any political object, and all we wish to do is justice to both sides' (*ibid.*, p. 216). Even when the paper was wrong it was wrong in a way that could be discussed and refuted. The maintenance of these standards was the form taken by the devotion to the paper of Bell and his colleagues; and that is the difference they made to the civilization of their age. Northcliffe could not destroy their tradition. Kitchin is convincing when he says 'I fancy, in their hearts love of *The Times* and love of country were the same sentiment. *The Times* was England' (p. 36. Morals could be drawn about the relation of the new *Times* men and *their* country). With the new paper one's objection is so often of the form 'You can't talk about it *in that way* at all.' There is something incorrigible about the new *Times*: that is what I mean by damage to its total language.

So (despite the assurance of a very senior English literary critic that '*The Times* has shown us recently that it is possible to be contemporary without any loss of dignity whatever'[13]) *The Times* now finds it hard to speak, even when it has something to say. A minor example is the damage the new self-advertisements do to the things advertised. Mr Winston S. Churchill's reports from Biafra were amongst the best things in *The Times* of recent years, in the real old *Times* tradition of telling the plain truth (easier said than done, as I argue below); but those despatches made their way, perhaps a harder way than Delane's solid unannounced column-feet on the Crimea, against the grain of their prior announcement (1 March 1969) which irritated the reader by

[13] F. W. Bateson, *Essays in Criticism* (April 1971).

giving what looked like the main page 1 news story, with huge picture and seven column-inches of text, to an *advertisement* for a 'hard-hitting series starting in The Times on Monday'. Can you imagine anything less likely to strike one than what the new *Times* calls a hard-hitting series? A lot of page 1 on 17 February 1968 was devoted not to news from Vietnam but chatty bio-graphies ('he has at times been helped by his Australian wife, Judy, whom he married last December') of the *Times* men in Vietnam. This is bound to make one pay less attention to what they say. Similarly a paper which is so proud to announce on page 1 (5 January 1967) that it has received the accolade of Granada Television in the title 'Paper of the Year' is asking to be taken with the seriousness appropriate to the award. 'He said that under the new editorship of Mr William Rees-Mogg changes had been rapid.' Yes.

More seriously one observes that even the best of *Times* leaders nowadays fails to carry the old weight simply because the con-text is more trivial.

Even assuming the worthwhileness of the enterprise, there is still room for anxiety about the academic aspects of the Open University. The informa-tion that the Humanities course is designed 'for all students who are in-terested in man, his history and his cultural achievements' – which university student is not? – is an ominous preface to a course which seems to try hard to find the most appealing combination of triviality and frag-mentation – a nibble at Vasari, a chunk of Descartes, a bite at St Mark's Gospel.

(14 August 1970)

That was well said. Ten years ago, in the old *Times*, it would have been magisterial. But in those days it could not have appeared in an issue whose first page 1 story was ' "Queen" in magazine merger' and which said:

As Queen Harper's the magazine will try to retain the best aspects of both original publications: the famous column of social chat, 'Jennifer's Diary', will continue from Queen, as will the horoscope and the restaurant feature. But the publishers hope to strengthen the long-standing authority of the originally American Harper's Bazaar in fashion.   (*Ibid.*)

Turning this cutting over I see that the back is filled by a long nudist-colony story, by a woman reporter. Putting these together one feels that one or more of them must surely be written with tongue in cheek and, if so, in the new *Times*, most likely the first. All were no doubt perfectly sincere, the full expression of a writer's intention: but anything serious in the paper now is disconnected from the bulk of the contents. I have already paid tribute to *The Times*'s effort to raise questions about the general health of our civilization; and its attack on 'commercial radio, which, as is well known in advance, will be a mindless repetition of faded popular songs, "musical chewing gum"'' (3 September 1970) was first-rate. The same leader made a central and true criticism of recent artistic fashions: 'Only a society in deep despair about itself would accept the hostility to meaning of some of the artists of the 1960's.' But it was the same newspaper (10 September 1970) gossiping about a new musical, which commended it in these terms, 'It has been described as a "dark and lovely rock-folk musical" and has obvious *Hair* undertones.'

Rebuking the B.B.C. convincingly for the television series on the British Empire ('A respectable historical case can be made against as well as for the Empire. What matters about this series is that it presented no respectable historical case at all') *The Times* reached this conclusion:

> The trouble goes back some years. When Sir Hugh Greene was director-general there was a considerable liberalization. This was a necessary process if the B.B.C. was to keep sufficiently in touch with public opinion, but it went too far. Old taboos were swept away but there was a progressive loss of nerve in preserving and enforcing those standards which were still necessary. In removing unnecessary constraints the B.B.C. lost its sense of direction.
>
> (29 April 1972)

Fine, at first – until one remembers that, reading 'Sir William Haley' for 'Sir Hugh Greene' the judgment applies more strongly to *The Times* itself. One might then be provoked into asking whether the taboos should have been swept away – whether, in fact, in these cases that wasn't the same as the loss of a direction which might have shown people why the old constraints of formality, anonymity and dignified prose were valuable. The 'but' should be an 'and'.

IV

By 1970 it was plain that the revolutions had diminished *The Times* as well as spelling financial disaster, and in September there came a quite determined attempt to reconvert *The Times* into a respectable newspaper. (The gossip was that *The Times* was to be the British *Monde*; another pleasing irony if one recalls that *Le Monde* was founded largely in imitation of *The Times*.) I don't think the attempt succeeded, though it is certainly a relief to be spared the banner headlines.

After one week of the new dispensation I wrote a quite hopeful and encouraging account which may be found by any curious researcher in the first issue of *The Human World*. Since September 1970 there have indeed been more attempts at serious articles than there were in the previous three years; the mixture is not as before. But it is still true that *The Times* is a great mixture, and that its consistent character, to the extent that it has one, is more the lowest common denominator of the mixture than anything like its old standards.

All the things I have objected to the new paper go on being true: it still has the undigested conglomeration of the serious, the po-faced and the frivolous, the small-type solemnity with the with-it and flighty; the best leaders are still printed on the backs of the stupidest features. The new seriousness is perhaps best characterized by the appointment of Mr Bernard Levin as columnist. Mr Levin was once an excellent critic of television in the *Guardian*, and has graduated, by way of *That Was The Week That Was* and being the first man to use 'four-letter words' in the *Spectator* (4 November 1960) to become an attempted Walter Lippman of Printing House Square. Some of his satire still has a little of the old bite, but whenever he attempts straight statement he displays on his sleeve a heart of pure hogwash:

What the *School Kids' Issue* [of the once notorious *Oz*] is about is not sex, but pain. It is mainly written by adolescents, and what runs through almost everything in it is the agony of youth facing the incomprehension of their elders; a reader can almost hear the bars rattle as the children beat their fists against the imprisoning cage of No.

'New Martyrs for the World of No', 10 August 1971

Mr Levin's soft-hearted belief is that there could be adolescence without pain – if we turned the world into a World of Yes, presumably. The following counted for Mr Levin as part of an argument:

That one of the drawings in the *School Kids' Oz* depicted a middle-aged teacher manipulating his own penis with one hand and a schoolboy's buttocks with the other is not coincidence: and it is not obscene, either. It is a defiant statement that if it is all right for the children's fathers to tell jokes like the one about the barmaid and the commercial traveller it should be all right for the children to feel sexual desire, and even express it, without their fathers calling the police. *(Ibid.)*

The derivation of the defiant statement from the picture must be according to the principles of medieval allegorization, of which Luther justly remarked that it could make the words in Genesis 'God created Heaven and Earth' come out as 'the cuckoo ate the hedgesparrow'.

In choosing the Columnist of the Year the panel had, unusually, found itself in complete unanimity before discussion even began. Mr Inglis said: usually it takes time for a columnist to play himself in . . . But Levin started off airing his idiosyncratic views, in the idiosyncratic style, without fear or favour, as though his niche at The Times had been just what he was born for.

(20 January 1972)

The other aspect of this undoubted truth is that Levin fits his niche just as if the new paper had been designed for his peculiar talent. He is so much at home there, indeed, that he even occasionally runs to authority and pomp: 'I have made clear my views of the Home–Smith pact, and do not need to repeat them now . . .' (10 February 1972). He is equally authoritative on productions of Shakespeare and performances of Beethoven. It seems a rather unnecessary extravagance for *The Times* to employ anybody else.

A style once destroyed is not easily supplied; especially is it not easily supplied as a by-product of the search for financial viability. The thing missing in the reformed *Times* is the old standards, the old steady convictions, renewed day by day, about what matters, what has to be said and how.

One difficulty is to give enough evidence without labouring the obvious, *ad nauseam*. I will try to complete my case by considering *The Times*'s treatment in 1971 of one important news story, the developments during that year in the Indian sub-continent. I choose this subject as a test of the paper because it is from an area where *The Times* is traditionally strong, and because the way events fell out did give the paper a whole series of chances to be informative and to develop a picture of what had really happened. I also choose it because I think it led our opinion-formers as a whole into certain relevant traps.

The British consensus that the situation in East Pakistan after the *coup de main* by President Yahya Khan was a simple and easily understood one stretched from *Red Mole*, *Private Eye* and the

Morning Star to the *Spectator* and *The Times*. This was the occasion of Mr Tariq Ali's celebrated rupture with Chairman Mao; and the *Morning Star*, whose range of thought is limited, later called Chinese intervention 'unthinkable'. The *Guardian*, naturally, bawled its compassion louder than anyone else, but there was absolute unanimity from left to right that the situation was to be described in very simple terms. The Awami League, having won a majority, should have formed a government, but instead was brutally repressed by a military dictatorship.

This allowed the most sweeping and simple moral judgments and political prescriptions – the latter including the suspension of aid to Pakistan, presumably to ensure that the Bengalis should be starved if they survived the massacres. (Cf. 'Aid Officials Fear that East Pakistan Faces Year of Famine', 24 June 1971; 'The British Government should not resume consortia aid or economic aid to West Pakistan in the view of Mr Peter Shore', 3 September 1971.) Yahya the butcher must get out and make way for Sheikh Mujib. All this with considerable self-congratulation: 'Britain has hardly spoken out during the Bangla Desh tragedy: but we have not fawned or looked away. We have not entirely pawned our moral integrity' (the *Guardian*, 6 July 1971).

Now I, too, believe in representative institutions and have the usual British distaste for military dictatorship, nor am I going to suggest that executions without trial, or massacres, are ever justifiable. But when the *Guardian* begins talking about our moral integrity in relation to events so safely far from home I begin to smell a rat. And when Senator Edward Kennedy celebrates the triumph of right by linking himself with 'General' Abdul Qadir Siddiqi, 'leader of the Mukti Bahini in Dacca, who took part in the bayoneting of four youths here on Saturday' (21 December 1971), as 'brothers in liberty, and no man, no policy, no government can change that fact' (15 February 1972 – Mr Siddiqi had just called the Senator 'suffering humanity's best friend') my disillusion with the consensus is complete and I can't even manage to see the conversation as inappropriate.

What happened? And what sort of judgment could be offered of these events? 'Mass Slaughter of Punjabis begins in East Pakistan', 'Political and Intellectual Leaders being Wiped out in a War of Genocide', screamed *Times* headlines (2 April 1971) and one of the reports began, 'The Pakistan Army is alleged to have waged a war of genocide in East Pakistan. The objective is said to be the elimination of the political and intellectual leadership, and it might well have been achieved.'

'Genocide', freely used by *The Times* in the first weeks, was a word certain to mislead in one way or another as applied to the Pakistani imbroglio. One trouble is, 'genocide' looks transparent: it must mean, we suppose, 'intentional extermination of a race'[14] or 'extermination of an ethnic group'[15] because of its derivation from roots meaning 'tribe' and 'killing'. There have been instances of genocide in this obvious sense in this century. In Germany and places occupied by Germany during the Second World War, a deliberate and organized effort was made by the state to murder all those of Jewish race. The attempt was made with the planning and persistence necessary to such a project, and so successfully that there are now hardly any Jews left in Germany. That was genocide. A less deliberate example of the same thing accompanied the replacement of Red Indians by Americans: 'The only good Injun is a dead Injun' is a genocidal sentiment. It was at least plausible to accuse the Nigerian government of the attempted genocide of the Biafrans (and Mr Wilson's government of complicity in attempted genocide) because the federals at some stages of that war seemed to be trying to starve whole races to death. To accuse Pakistan of genocide in this obvious sense was never remotely plausible, yet to read *The Times* or listen to the B.B.C. in those early weeks one would think Yahya Khan's policy was to exterminate all the races of his enemies.

The rebuke to the paper cannot, however, be quite so straightforward. For though 'genocide' is all too familiar in our language and world, the word itself is, as words go, very new. It was coined by Raphael Lemkin in his book *Axis Rule in Occupied Europe*[16] and he used it to mean two things which ought, perhaps, to have been kept separate. As well as the sense we have discussed (and the word *was* invented to describe Nazi atrocities) Lemkin uses 'genocide' to mean the destruction of a nation, and he gives as examples the forceful imposition on one nation of the institutions of another, or the persecution of people *for* their nationality. Now the inventor of a word has no responsibility for its subsequent career, and my own sense of how the word is used is that this second sense is extraordinary. It would be odd to say that in 1968

[14] *Oxford Dictionary of Etymology* (1966).
[15] Ernest Klein, *Etymological Dictionary* (1967).
[16] 1944.

the Russians committed *genocide* in Czechoslovakia, and I have
not heard the word applied to the English even by those Welshmen
who do in fact believe that the English persecute the Welsh by
forcing the institutions of one nation upon another. However, I
believe that the word is sometimes used in Lemkin's second sense.
Grant this was the sense intended, *The Times* was still irresponsible and tendentious, for 'genocide' in this second sense confuses
precisely the point at issue between the combatants, whether or
not Bengal is a nation – and in just the same way that Mr Harold
Wilson begged the essential question about the war between
federal Nigeria and Colonel Ojukwu's Biafrans, by calling it a
'civil' war. In no sense could the Pakistan army be accused of
genocide with any approach to illumination, truth or even
decency.

This fixing of simple and inapplicable labels badly obscured the
next development, the movement of the millions of refugees into
India. For *The Times* the explanation of this movement was
simple enough: the refugees were fleeing the wrath of the Pakistani
army, which intended to kill them all. On the contrary, as far
as one can judge from the mass of unauthenticated accusations,
the attempts at genocide and the massacres that did occur
followed the ancient pattern of the sub-continent: communal
rioting and slaughter.

In areas of Hindu ascendancy Moslems were butchered and the survivors
fled, and throughout the province, whether the army condoned it or was
powerless to prevent it, the Moslems turned on the 10 million Bengali
Hindus. Many were killed. Nearly half of them are refugees in India, never
to return.

Peter Gill in the *Daily Telegraph*, 22 July 1971

It took *The Times* some weeks to realize that the refugees were
overwhelmingly Hindu, not a cross-section of the Bengali population or the intellectual and political élite; but at length Michael
Hornsby did report (9 July 1971) 'At least 80 per cent., perhaps
90 per cent. of the refugees now in India are Hindus. Fear has
been the spur – fear not only of the army but also of the ven-
geance of Bihari (non-Bengali) Muslims, who were victimized
and in some places butchered during the two or three weeks it
took the Army to secure control of the province.' The recognition
that the army *was* in control was itself belated, *The Times* having
assumed before (and after) that guerillas were rapidly overrunning

the country and that the army was at best besieged in the important towns.

The mythology of the new *Times* demanded a large and successful guerilla movement offering democratic resistance to oppression; and that, rather than the evidence, too often determined the news. Things *must* be in increasing and spontaneous crisis in Bengal rather than either settling down or stirred up from without. By September 'Force of 5,000 Trained Guerillas Joins Bangla Desh Resistance as Reprisals by Army Continue' said a headline (13 September 1971). The story underneath offered no evidence for any of its assertions except Indian estimates, according to which 'an average of 40 to 50 Pakistan soldiers are killed every day'. One conclusion, therefore, after the admission that 'the Liberation Army occupies some territory, but only because the Pakistan Army allows it to do so', read like wishful thinking: 'However, the guerillas are destroying the credibility of the Pakistan Army . . .' The wave of sabotage in East Bengal was still rising on 11 November, according to another headline. On 9 November 'Bengal Guerillas Step up Number of Assassinations and Bombings.'

The zenith of enthusiasm for guerilla activity was probably the article Kuldip Nayar sent from Delhi (3 November 1971), which was also the summit of vagueness and assertion. 'For example, a foreign journalist who recently returned from Dacca said in Delhi that there was very little activity in the town after 6 p.m. He also testified that the population, particularly in the countryside, was helping the guerillas.' How vague can you get? Perhaps the question occurred to the writer, for he descended to statistics. 'The guerillas' claim is that they have killed nearly 20,000 Pakistan soldiers since March. The figure is probably exaggerated, but there is ample evidence to prove that Islamabad's forces have lost at least 6,000 men.' He didn't say where the ample evidence could be found or what it could be. So again the end was wish-fulfilment: 'Indeed, the increasing effectiveness of the *Mukti Bahini*, with their impatience to go all out, has created a warlike situation in the sub-continent.'

By the end of the year that was true, though not in the sense intended. As far as mere fact goes, all these reports of guerilla success were untrue, and one says so on the best authority. For the Indian government, which wanted nothing more than guerilla success, and was surely the best practical judge of guerilla progress, finally decided that, even with considerable help from their army, it was negligible. If the history of the conquest of East Pakistan by India shows anything it must show that before the war the Pakistani authorities were securely in control of their territory in the East. An army small enough to be defeated in a fortnight was yet big enough to control a province more populous than the British Isles.

The Times's determination that the West Pakistani policy must fail thus became indistinguishable from belief in Indian propaganda. In *The Times* India did have an amazingly good press throughout that summer, and Mrs Gandhi remained the heroine of the piece even after she had been abandoned by *Red Mole*.

Who was responsible for this drift of bloody events? *The Times* gave their correspondent Peter Hazelhurst his head – in fact Louis Heren, who after being a distinguished American correspondent has yet to find his feet as foreign editor, patted it several times – and Mr Hazelhurst, whose strong pro-Indian feeling went fittingly enough with his rather superficial knowledge of India, unhesitatingly named Mr Bhutto, the present President of Pakistan. His reasons were not convincing, because he was insulated from history and from reality by his language, the set of English clichés he took over with him. Mr Heren said, in a puff which took precedence over Hazelhurst's report,

Those who are so eager to impugn the integrity of men such as Hazelhurst never seem to realize that they work alone, far from family and head office, often in an alien environment, and not infrequently in considerable danger. Their job is to provide an honest version of what happens, no more and no less . . .   (7 June 1971)

Yes, but the worth of the honest version depends on the correspondent's power to describe what is real. I am impugning not Mr Hazelhurst's integrity but his intelligence – his sincerity in the poetic sense – and not his personally but that of the whole new paper, for which 'an honest version of what happens, no more and no less' is so much more difficult than it was for Moberly Bell. Mr Heren's plug was headed 'For weeks officialdom turned a blind eye to dispatches from The Times' man-on-the-spot/World wakes up at last but it may be too late' and began 'The unfolding tragedy of East Pakistan has been unfailingly reported from the beginning by Peter Hazelhurst . . . For weeks he has been patrolling the Indo-Pakistan frontier without respite and writing with controlled fury of what he witnessed.' The controlled fury expressed itself in the usual journalistic exaggerations (the cholera non-story, for example) and the simplistic judgments we shall end by considering.

Was the responsibility for the disaster Mr Bhutto's? He had his share (and it is imaginable that he may have helped on partition) – but was it *this* share?

Taking events to their logical conclusion there is no doubt that the present holocaust was precipitated by President Yahya Khan when he postponed the Assembly without consulting the Bengalis, but even more so by Mr Bhutto's deliberate decision to boycott the Assembly on March 3.

(4 June 1971)

According to the same article, Mr Bhutto's reasons for boycott were that 'he had heard disconcerting reports that the Shaikh was planning to declare that the Constituent Assembly was a sovereign body the moment it met'. In other words, the domination of the West over East would be straightforwardly replaced by the domination of East over West. Sheikh Mujibur Rahman seemed to give some colour to this prediction when he, again according to Hazelhurst, declined to agree to any share in his government for the Western party. I do not see how Mr Hazelhurst's argument, even in his own terms, supports his conclusion.

One can have sympathy, especially at the safe distance of a few thousand miles, with all the people caught up by history into that muddled, painful, perhaps tragic Indian life – caught up by a history in which 1971 was a mere episode and not out of the character of the sub-continent. Who was responsible? (Who is responsible for the existence of India?) History, and the historic question of an independent Muslim state there. One can make sense of the actions of Sheikh Mujib: carried on a wave of genuine popularity and indignation against Western dominance, he must have been overwhelmingly tempted to go for independence (which could only be the independence he has got, as a satellite of India). It ought also to be obvious enough that the president – any president – of Pakistan had to think hard before permitting the break-up of the country. If, as Hazelhurst also said, 'mass movement on the streets of Bengal had slipped out of Mujib's control', it was Yahya's urgent duty to avoid as much of the inevitable subsequent communal slaughter as possible; and one can see his point of view too. Called to power in an intolerable situation he had at last the certainty that in any case he would have a lot of blood on his hands. One can also sympathize with India. It was understandable that India should extract the maximum political advantage from the situation, and perhaps there *was* a certain inevitability in the war and its result. What I'm afraid I find it very difficult to feel any sympathy for is Mrs Gandhi's rhetoric. Whether she believes it herself I have no means of knowing, but as the year went on its political usefulness became increasingly clear, as a mask for the very astute Bismarckism of Indian actions.

The Times in those months never tired of reporting and applauding India's restraint, wish for peace, determination to get the refugees back ('on her own political terms' was not added) and general democratic sweetness. 'As you know, everybody admires our restraint . . .' – as Mrs Gandhi told us herself (20 October 1971). The admirers certainly included Mr Hazelhurst:

There are now obvious signs in Delhi that after exercising restraint for eight months Mrs Gandhi, the Prime Minister, is convinced that the efforts of the international community to achieve a political solution to the East Bengal crisis have failed and she has no other recourse but to embark upon a military action.

(29 November 1971)

'India had done its best to preserve peace on the sub-continent, but had been forced into war by the acts of the Pakistan military junta,' said Mrs Gandhi (11 December 1971). The delight of the Oxford undergraduates during her visit ('Several carried placards saying: "Thank you, India, for doing the world's job"' (3 November 1971)) was only one index of Mrs Gandhi's propaganda triumph which paved the way for the military one. Poor, poor righteous India! Forced against her will to achieve ambitions any Indian government must nurse! So with peace and patience ever upon her lips the Indian premier compassionately ordered in her army, dismembered Pakistan, installed a client government in Bengal and attained hegemony in the sub-continent.

The Times did not forbear to cheer. Mrs Gandhi's style is, at least, a prime example of the kind of insincerity I keep having to discuss, and *The Times*'s swallowing it was the mark of its failure either to describe or to judge what was happening.

The Times, the paper which recorded for so many years the acquisition and liquidation of the British Empire and the consequent historic changes in the power-structure of the world, was quite blind to the importance of the complex history lying behind the Indian trauma of 1971. It had no notion that British assumptions about democracy might be an insufficient frame of reference to explain what was happening.

I am not demanding instant history from a newspaper, but news that will not rule out the possibility of history. This is not an unreasonable demand: it took no more than a few months for the kind of perspective on Bangla Desh I am urging to begin making its appearance, even in newspapers (there was a very good *Observer* article by Mr Cyril Dunn). One of the best early accounts was by a journalist, appropriately enough from the *Daily Telegraph* not *The Times*, Mr David Loshak (cf. *The New York Review of Books*, 23 March 1972).

The old *Times* would have reported what could be reliably known, would have qualified its conjectures *as* conjectures, would have refrained from making premature judgments – and so would have allowed history to emerge, so to speak, in its own categories. And that is how the old paper used to create a different world from the new one of instant convictions and general cliché.

V

I chose to discuss *The Times* because I think its recent history is the most central case of the collapse that is my present subject, and because, as a steady *Times* reader for a number of years, I know more about it than the other possible examples. But I could equally well have concentrated on the 'quality' Sundays, the *New Statesman*, *The T.L.S.* or the B.B.C.

'Finally,' said the Archbishop of Cardiff in a letter to *The Times* (7 November 1969) 'do not let us be too hard on the B.B.C. They are simply following the trend.' On the contrary, that is the reason for being hard. As Mr Frank Gillard said to *The Times* in another letter (21 February 1970), 'You know from your own experience that a mass medium must change and develop because the society which it serves and the circumstances in which it operates are never static.' The question is whether the 'mass medium' has to follow the trend (and where does the trend appear if not in the mass medium?) or whether institutions like *The Times* and the B.B.C. ought to be centres of value not simply dictated to by trends. In both cases the thing wrong has been the following of such trends as are imaginable to the editorial mind; and in both cases I believe the difference between following and leading is not as simple as the Archbishop assumed. If in the circumstances of the B.B.C. you follow enthusiastically enough, you also propagate.

We have been considering, that is to claim, an instance of something quite general in serious British journalism, something which I think has to do with the language of journalism and its relation to our whole language.

Following the near compulsion of the writers of his age to refer to *The Times*, Shaw made Lady Britomart say, 'You will find that there is a certain amount of tosh about *The Times*; but at least its language is reputable.' She spoke more truly than Shaw knew.

A newspaper may be a very important example of the collaborative creation of a style of life which one means by civilization. One does not look to a newspaper for distinguished poetry, philosophy or mathematics or theology; it is obvious that a newspaper has to find its place in a world that includes higher and deeper things. There is yet a whole range of public affairs, made available to a public and created as a unity by a newspaper, without which, in the modern world, the higher and deeper things are likely to find life even more precarious. If public affairs – politics, economics, the arts as they become news – are to exist, if they are to be attended to, connected and understood by any coherent public (by *us*, that is to say, in finding what matters to us in the public world) newspapers are indispensable. There is a lot of serious reading of *The Times*, the *Daily Telegraph* and even the *Guardian*, in which civilization is created over perhaps half a million breakfast tables. This participation in life has to be through the written language, by taking in and mulling over information and comment in a way impossible to the television viewer. 'Once it becames possible to pre-select the kinds of information – whether editorial or advertising – that you actually want new every morning, the market for a "mosaic" product of wide general appeal will surely shrink.'[17] But a newspaper can no more be a 'collocation of specialisms' than a university. None of its subjects has its full meaning except by its bearings on the others within the whole; each needs the others even when there are no obvious links. No reader will take a comparable interest in all the pages, but the idea of a newspaper as the connections within a world, creating a category of specifically public events, and developing the language for them, is a necessary one and well expressed

[17] Christopher Driver, 'Why Newspapers have Readers', *Encounter* (November 1967), p. 91.

whatever goes on under them, in such titles as *The Times*, *The Observer*, the *News of the World*, the *News Chronicle*, the *Daily News*, and so on right back to the mercuries of the seventeenth century. Mr Driver's own image is against him: the parts of a mosaic considered separately are senseless bits of marble; it is only in their connections that they make a picture.

But have I not been objecting to precisely those features of modern newspapers that make a wider picture of the world than was possible to the old *Times*? When *The Observer* can celebrate the sixth anniversary of a pop group and when its colour supplement finds room for *all* the trend-setters of the affluent society, whether they be pornographers or philosophers, isn't that the achievement of a more genuine mosaic than when *The Observer* appealed to the better-educated portion? No, because the new pieces, if they belong together at all, do so thanks to the levelling process. The result may be a wide range, but to call it a picture is to debase the word, which does, after all, have implications of coherence and significance. If the new *Times* or *The Observer* do now offer pictures of the world it is only in the sense that the *Sun* might, too. When the all-composing hour falls it makes a kind of sludge rather than a mosaic.

Newspapers give one of the pictures of the world and speak in one of the languages we cannot do without. Without the kind of picture of the world the old *Times* used to give, without its language, the world it pictured has ceased to exist. (I do find that I know a lot less about what is ordinarily going on in the world than I did in 1965 – except when I happen to be keeping the resolution to read *Le Monde* daily.) And without this common public world the whole of life, our whole language, including the things we may think higher or deeper, is impoverished and disordered. Sanity in the ordinary public world is one of the aids to knowing what is high or deep.

The Times lost its 'sense of responsibility' and its picture of the world at the same moment of 1966 in what I have been calling the disintegration of its 'total language'. It is perhaps surprising that the old *Times* survived so long into the anti-élite age; and certainly it needed to change. By the mid-sixties the form of the paper was sustaining it against the intentions of the editor; sensibility had altered and was only prevented from breaking out by the old habits of expression. By then, too, Bell's determination that the paper appeal to 'the better educated portion of the

public' had descended into the nauseous slogan TOP PEOPLE TAKE
THE TIMES. The continued attempt there expressed to equate 'top
people' with an educated public had become an anachronism, for
is it not notorious that our rulers are now less interested in thought
even than they were when Arnold called them barbarians and
philistines?

If *The Times* was to survive with some continuity, if it was to
continue to be *The Times* in our different age, which the preservation of its old form gave it the chance to do, it needed to abandon the ruling classes in favour of the educated. How to do that
was a problem greater than any faced by Bell, Buckle or Dawson
before or after the Northcliffe tempest.

What in fact happened was that in 1966 *The Times* became
panicky about its Victorian tradition and in 1970 found that a
modern alternative was not easy to come by. Instead of bringing
The Times's real identity into a changed world *The Times* was
changed to suit the trends, and the result was the kind of newspaper I have discussed, a style, it would seem, for a nation with
little that could be called public opinion, with no capacity for
generating a language in which the political world can be discussed and where all political decisions (if they are now properly
so called) must therefore be left to people who cannot be responsible to a public. It was understandable that *The Times* should
become afraid that it was no longer living in its own age,
especially as it was losing money. But as it happened the attempt
to serve the present age became suiting the present age; dragging
The Times all too willingly into what Mr Wilson calls the twentieth century meant commitment to a very cheap idea of the
twentieth century. The paper's language had to change, but the
difference between change and decay was not understood.

The pattern of lower casting out higher in *The Times* is not
merely similar to what we saw in politics, it is the same; and the
spring and summer of 1972, when *The Times* found a consistent
new political character in rapturous and unconditional support
for those elements of Mr Heath's policy that make for pragmatical
management, is therefore a fitting time to end this commentary.

How *The Times* managed to persuade itself that Mr Heath and
his 'very rational government' (5 May 1972) are better managers
than Mr Wilson *because* of the policies that led predictably to devaluation (24 June 1972) I cannot conjecture. This was, however,
the moment when they chose to call Mr Heath a 'great' Prime

Minister. To *The Times* he is 'great', and *The Times* is indeed a paper now where he may be expected so to be.

We are all at work all the time, with whatever seriousness we can bring or find, on values. The development of values worth having – of a language for gripping reality – is the concern of the saint, poet or prophet as well as the rest of us following critically after. 'To seize the right to new values – that is the most terrible proceeding for a weight-bearing and reverential spirit.'[18] Values worth having are not created by opportunism, failure of nerve (however self-confident) and the pursuit of profits. But those who cannot create values can sometimes destroy them.

[18] Nietzsche, 'Of the Three Metamorphoses', *Thus spoke Zarathustra.*

5

Notes on the Language of Love:
I, the Definition of Pornography

The beating down of the wise
And great Art beaten down

I

So far, it may be thought, in considering uses of language as public as church services, political speeches and newspapers we have been on safe ground, at least in the sense that there is nothing secret about the objects of discussion. On the contrary, the parsons, politicians and journalists are all competing and clamouring to be heard. It seems not unreasonable to look for the religion of an age in its Bible and Prayer Book, or the politics in public speeches; and I argued that these are not comprehensible apart from the styles of the language: to understand one is to understand the other. But the *love* of an age...? How can we see that? (Even sexology has not progressed so far, for it has to confine itself to the observation of sexual activity.) It is certainly easy to assume that here, at least, we can be ourselves and make our world unhampered by what is said elsewhere. Yet I still want to work out why, most of the time anyway, I find myself in agreement with Rush Rhees.

Consider the language of religion and the language of love – I mean of the love of man and woman. I would say that there could not be religion without the language of religion, and that *just as little* could there be love without the language of love.

Without Answers (1969), p. 121

Let me confess that I do find this discussion difficult. I hope I am not going to try to minimize the new world of love, the obvious experiental fact that two lovers *are* on their own, quite free to make a new heaven or hell. It is equally obvious that individuality is intense here. We must discuss how, nevertheless, Rhees may still be right.

If he is, we are confronting the domestic part of our subject which cannot but strike home to every man and woman. It is

146

possible more or less to scramble through the world without anything recognizable as a religious sense or at least without ever reading the Bible; it is certainly possible to ignore politics, and I incline increasingly to C. R. Attlee's view that sensible men only look at newspapers to discover the racing results. But from love – or from sex, anyway, and I shall not distinguish the two yet – there is no escape this side senility. And if I can show that our sexual experiences make any sense they might only within a language of sex, and that that (as much as our other 'languages') is inevitably an aspect or style of the common language of our place and time, I shall have brought the subject within the scope of this book and be able to point to certain conclusions which can be taken equally to be about language or about life.

It is a mark of the insufficiency of our common notions of the individual and the community (discussed in chapter 1) that that may well look paradoxical. Of course I am not suggesting that anybody is likely, because he speaks a common language of sex, to take to his psychiatrist the fear that his sex-life is happening to somebody else; and if he thinks he is being mysteriously controlled by others the psychiatrist will rightly diagnose paranoia. But it is always as true of our sexual experiences as the others that they exist as meaning. If sex matters to us – and God help us if it doesn't – it means something. But it is the nature of one meaning to exist in its connection with others (which connection is, at widest, what one means by language). The meaning of sex lies in such connections even, or especially, when the experience is at its most individual, unrepeatable or timeless, and when the significance is expressed in the experience itself rather than in any later remembrance or thought of it.

It remains true (to put the other way round the remark that meanings connect) that sex, like everything else, has its significance within a context which is at widest the context of a whole life. And the possibilities of our whole lives vary, notoriously, with the 'circumstances' in which we live; the possibilities of what sense we can find in sex will therefore vary too. Pederasty could not have been the same in classical Athens as in a modern English public school, except by the rules of biology: to see the difference is to understand the languages of sex of two very different cultures. Or how could sex be the same – except, again, by the rules of biology – in a polygamous as in a Christian marriage? The different contexts must make different senses. Experience – necessarily one's own experience – is essential, obviously, for any language of sex. And we all develop our language of sex willingly, in the interaction between ourselves and others. There is no compulsion and nobody is forced to conform to anybody else's sense. But these things do not distinguish the language of sex from other parts of language, yet we do all find ourselves in possession of a common language.

The voice of commonsense will here, I know from experience, still be heard asking 'But isn't sex natural?' – and I cannot afford to ignore the questions of commonsense. Yes, of course sex is natural: I am only pointing out, as usual, that the nature in our case is inevitably human nature, the nature of the creatures who talk. 'Natural', though a necessary and important word, is too easily misleading in our post-Hobbes, post-Calvin world in which it so easily sketches a picture of an untouched biological foundation on which is built our artificial humanity.[1] (Cf. above, p. 9). Love, hate, and the gamut between them are final and infallible and as natural as can be. We cannot choose to love (though we can sometimes take evasive action or modify the sense of love in other ways) any more than we can choose to live without bodies. Love is always a revelation or inspiration – but always in *our* life, which in its inalienable physicality is also necessarily human.

Take the cases of 'being a man' or 'being a woman' and of 'father' or 'mother'. Without *la petite différence* these categories would not arise; and (despite the famous cases of transvestism and so on) it is not possible to *choose* whether to be a man or a woman. It depends on one's organic constitution. Yet it depends on language too, on the idea, the grammar of the words, the style of being a man or woman in the place where one lives.

There could not be fathers without begetting; but begetting does not exhaust the sense of 'father'. Professor Phillips, after saying '"Because he *is* your father": what does this mean? Surely it refers to the fact that this is the man who begat you; this is the man to whom you owe your existence. There is only *one* such man', says also

We appreciate the force of a reminder of our obligations when someone says, 'Remember, he is your father.' He does not have to add, 'And you ought to give special consideration to your father', since to understand

---

[1] The cover of the paperback *Female Eunuch* even extends the idea of the unnatural superstructure erected on some basic foundation of human nature to include the feminine anatomy, which it depicts, rather horribly, as a dress the woman (?) puts on.

what is meant by calling someone your father is to understand that one has certain obligations towards him.

It seems, then, that the status of being a father entails certain rights which the children of the father have obligations to satisfy. It is possible to argue from 'He is my father' to 'I ought not to leave him destitute', for example, since the understanding of the latter statement is involved in the understanding of the former.

Faith and Philosophical Enquiry (1970), pp. 225, 226–7

Yes – within our language. It is natural within our language for 'father' to have this sense, but the only guarantee in nature that it must is that we naturally so use our language. Moreover our language can make fathers out of men who have done no begetting. One of the most convincing touches in George Eliot's *Silas Marner* is the naturalness of Eppie's calling Silas 'father' while her 'real' father remains only 'Mr Cass'. Yet this wouldn't work unless it were usual and natural in our language for fathers to be begetters. We always see the biological function as it makes sense in our whole life – unless, of course, we're mistakenly trying to apply biology to the whole of life.

So with 'man' and 'woman'. They are natural categories, but within our language and varying styles of life. 'Being a man' or 'being a woman' has a sense not exhausted by our genetic composition; if someone exhorts you to 'Be a man!' he doesn't mean 'Get yourself the male hormones' but 'act the role of a man as we understand it'. 'Being a man' or 'being a woman' is the form our biological constitution assumes in the life of our whole language.

It is this, as far as I can see, that the extremer exponents of 'Women's Lib.' are raging against. It therefore doesn't demand the use of any inverted commas to say that what Miss Millett, Miss Firestone and Miss Greer are trying to liberate women from is being women. It is possible reasonably to argue that there is something wrong with our language, that our 'being a woman' is restrictive, the role stultifying. But if you envisage a new womanhood free from child-bearing, you have gone far beyond the possibilities of the natural in our language – or, I'd guess, in any other, for it is not part of my case to argue that the freedom of circumstances to shape life is unlimited. Women without childbirth seems not within the limits of what a language can make us see as natural.

I doubt whether sex without the possibility of procreation can in general ever be natural, either. There are instances of heterosexual intercourse where conception is naturally impossible – if one of the people is barren, too young, too old, or if the woman is pregnant. But could there be a society in which the connection of sexual intercourse with reproduction drops out of the picture? (A writer in *Marriage Guidance*, May 1972, almost suggests it when he thinks 'childlessness or adopting children' should be 'of equal status [for any couple] if not superior to having their own' – p. 7.)

I am going to show that one great endeavour of our modern establishment is to disconnect sex from reproduction; and that does seem to me right at the nether limit of the power of language to shape life or to recognize what is real. D. H. Lawrence almost denies the connection in a passage which shows well the peculiar limit of his understanding.[2] But he didn't quite mean to advocate what *Cosmopolitan*'s first issue called 'the most beautiful thing a man can do for a woman', quoting a man who had done it. This most beautiful thing is the surgical operation of vasectomy, the modern refinement of castration which leaves a man with sexual appetites and performance but secured against begetting children, and this gentleman did it for his wife. 'I first got the idea when I read a funny article in the *Guardian*. The man made it sound so easy and civilized.' 'And there be eunuchs, which have made themselves eunuchs for the kingdom of heaven's sake.' In India some men undergo vasectomy because they are so wretchedly poor they feel unable to support more children. But I had never before heard of anyone improving on Origen in quite this way and doing it for the sake of his sex life. Before the disconnection of sex from reproduction which the surgery perfectly expresses that would have seemed self-contradictory. It does still seem to me unnatural. Greater love hath no man than *this*?

It is symptomatic of the state of our language of sex that the Pope's views on contraception in the encyclical *Humanae Vitae* should have been not merely disagreed with in the West but

---

[2] 'Now what is the act of coition? We know its functional purpose of procreation. But, after all our experience and all our poetry and novels we know that the procreative purpose of sex is, to the individual man and woman, just a side-show' – *Fantasia of the Unconscious*, chapter IX. It certainly is a side-show in *Lady Chatterley's Lover*, and one of the crude unrealities of the book is that Connie shouldn't ever worry about conception. How odd that Lawrence, who was so good at seeing that men and women cannot be unisex, should not be able to realize that women are *naturally* interested in babies. (Contrast *Anna Karenina*, part VII, chapters XIV–XV.)

greeted with the blank rage we reserve for the hopelessly unen-lightened. Yet he had, at least, a good hold of the central truth which we are tending to lose, that if procreation is not amongst the circumstances of sex, sex is necessarily unserious. One need not go all the way with the Pope to say so: contraception can be a way of recognizing the link of sex with conception and of taking it seriously. That, however, is not the view of it given by the British Medical Association (below) or some of the writers in *Marriage Guidance*. And if contraception is a device for appeasing what Mr John Eppstein calls 'the Western World's obsession with sexual intercourse and copulation with impunity', for turning sex from that which has naturally to do with procreation into a controllable pleasure, then it is an attack on any natural language of sex.

The natural fact that this is how children are procreated is one great hint, for those who need it, of the seriousness of sex. (That is why there cannot be homosexual marriage and why in homo-sexual relationships, however seriously they are taken and however important in the lives concerned, there must always be a certain natural frivolity. Shakespeare's homosexual love in the Sonnets attains a different kind of seriousness when he tells the beautiful youth to go and breed.) But, to come at this from the other direc-tion, the hint is only to be spoken in a language of sex. Procrea-tion may be casual, accidental or the result of rape: there has to be a certain language-dependent grace for its importance to be seen. Yet it could still not be natural for procreation not to matter.

Conversely abortion (even if it is seen as a necessary evil) could not in any fully human language lose its aura of the horrible and the unnatural, and if it is doing so that is not because of any Act of Parliament or statistics or the activities of any clinic, but be-cause at that point our language is going against nature; and an editress's announcement that her woman's magazine shall mention babies only in connection with abortion is a determination to speak against nature. 'At forty-three', said one actress in a squalid *Cosmopolitan* page called 'These Women have had Abortions', 'it would be ludicrous to start a family again. I'd have it out like a tooth.' No, a woman *can't* have a baby out like a tooth because abortion can't be thought of in the same way as a visit to a dentist as long as our words retain their power of distinguishing things, as long as our language gives us the power of knowing what is natural. (The natural is not the same as the normal and particularly not the same as the ordinary. I am assured by a friend, though I somewhat doubt it nevertheless, that abortion is so frequently and traditionally practised by working-class married women as to be ordinary. That would certainly not make the practice natural.)

What is natural in sex is then a question to be decided not by biology but by what our language gives us the chance to see the facts of life *as*. Without the biological facts they couldn't be seen as anything; but the high level controls the lower here as elsewhere, and our natural sex is sex in our nature.

I spoke of 'circumstances' as a way of allowing the obvious truth that the sense we make of sex is not restricted within words. (As Dafydd ap Gwilym somewhere says, 'There is a certain magic in two words, though contentment is not to be had merely by adding a third.') There is yet an intimate connection between 'circumstances' and verbal language which I think not different in kind from, say, the connection between the verbal language and circumstances of religion. The links between all one's way of making sense of experience, the existence of experience in one's whole life, and the spoken language, are pretty much the same with sex as they are anywhere else.

To understand marriage is, *inter alia*, to speak that bit of English. We all, married or not, use the word in making sense of our unique circumstances and our individuality, but, as ever, we can do that because everybody else is also using the word in *their* unique individuality and circumstances. The common sense, 'marriage', is our common way of tackling all our uniquenesses, and the common language can vary, here as elsewhere, as well as the individualities.

For instance English reserves 'love' for use on important occasions. Do you really love him? The alternative is *like*; and the love/like distinction, unusual in the European languages (*aimer*, suitably qualified, serves for both in French) is the way we really see the world. 'Liking' goes with ease, control, criticism: in our language it is often much further from love than hate is. Here one is talking simultaneously about what happens in our life and how we use English. One complication is that sometimes (for example Merton Densher in *The Wings of the Dove*) people say 'like' when they mean 'love'. But the force of that depends on the same 'grammar'. So when the *Vanity Fair* 'Guide to the New Sexual Etiquette' (discussed below) argues that loving and liking are really the same, it is preaching a new style of love and sex by changing the verbal language.

Even to say 'ways of looking at or thinking about loving and liking vary with language' would be misleading, for that would make the object, love, separate from the beholders, us. The point, and the difficulty, is my perpetual one that we cannot have the thing without the way of seeing it, and that for us it's quite natural to like someone without loving him, whereas in French it's equally natural *not* to be able to say 'je l'aime mais je ne l'aime pas,' except as paradox or unsureness.

Change in verbal language here as elsewhere can change a thing by changing its meaning. This is most easily shown from very general examples involving large vistas of life. The obvious recent case is 'divorce'. People who begin to accept the ordinariness of divorce have changed the 'grammar' of marriage, for better or worse. The change is not *merely* verbal and not *simply* in the experience of disconnected individuals, it is the kind of change in sensibility and value which again helps to show that in talking about the one we are necessarily also talking about the other, from whichever aspect we begin.

If we can manage to observe even the verbal language of sex we shall therefore be observing behaviour far more effectively than Masters and Johnson can possibly do, for we shall be seeing what sex means.

But even if it is agreed that the sense of sex depends on the varying 'circumstances' of sex and that that is reliably seen in the verbal language, is it not still true that the kinds of verbal language that are most important to making love are often not quotable? Isn't the spoken language here notorious for its ability to do without mere words? And may not even 'spoken' be misleading when so much depends on the different styles of silence?

Love is famous for getting itself expressed in eye-beams, 'eyeblinks' and so on. These are part of the common language, not merely private-and-personal. There is no difference in kind between the way a blush or tears work, and a sentence. The full meaning of all depends upon a context in language and life; all can be uncontrollable, but all are also interceptible. Anyone of the same civilization as the gesturer can understand a gesture as well as a sentence; that is why the makers of films and novels can use the fact that a glance can be caught, understood or misunderstood by people not intended to see it. (There are French gestures and also, I suspect, Indian gestures though there is no Indian language.) But how to quote such things? We may follow Collingwood in seeing language as originally 'total gesture'[3] but how to record and discuss that?

Copulation is only the extreme example of gesture as language: a series of movements whose significance is in itself but depends on its total context in the life of the individuals in the life of their society. Copulation shares with verbal language the power of modifying the sense of the preceding life ('After we said/did that, things were never the same again . . .') and it also shares the possibility of being simple nonsense. But, thank God, copulation can't be quoted or subjected to practical criticism; and even if it could be quoted it would make no more sense than an isolated scene of a play.

I have to bring this discussion not only to the level of verbal language, but to what is publicly producible. But even when we come to words do they not depend on precisely the intonations and nuances which cannot be quoted, and which could only be written down at all by a phonetician or a novelist? Almost any imaginable human utterance can belong to the language of sex or love, including shouts, grunts, threats, scientific abstractions, and the Prayer Book; but to produce the meaning in print, to show that they are indeed examples of a language of love, would one not have to tell a story, to supply a full context?

Verbal language might work here by being as it were overloaded. You fall in love, touch her hand and feel – 'as if an electric current flowed between us'. This is a cliché, but if the cliché is overloaded with the experience may it not be redeemed and made meaningful? This is a place where even the deadest-looking phrases may be suddenly resurrected into new life. But simply quoted they would have their usual written status as dead phrases or cliché.

Even so, though spoken language need not be very important to love or, if important, quotable, it is worth remembering that it *can* be both. It is certainly possible for the communication of love to take place in words, even written ones; they may in some cases be a very full and reliable expression. Total gesture here as elsewhere *can* be on the page. For instance love letters are some people's way of discovering, creating and exploring their love; and it is possible to achieve in a letter, and send through the post, a

[3] *Principles of Art*, pp. 234ff.

sudden true statement that alters a situation as completely as a sudden grab; sometimes, also, the meaning of such communications will be open to third parties. And if all words are ambiguous, especially the words of love, it's also true that a poet or novelist can show us, in words, exactly the shade of love the words express.

> Oh thou weed:
> Who art so lovely faire, and smell'st so sweete,
> That the Sense akes at thee,
> Would thou hadst never bin borne

– Othello's words are a 'total gesture' which bodily movement could not replace. For Othello to achieve his tragic and evil love he has to find these words.

I conclude that sex does vary with language, but that the kind of evidence I can adduce will not be representative of anyone's whole language of sex. What can be quoted are the styles that make up the levels of the language I distinguished in chapter 3 as 'the age' – the language of women's magazines, newspapers, films, poems, and the manuals of sex education, marriage guidance and sexology. The effect of 'the age' on our total language, i.e. on sex in people's lives, is immense. I concede, however, that the immensity is both incalculable and undemonstrable. I issue this caveat as a hopeful remark: there are many grammars of sex in English as well as that of *She* or the *New Statesman* (and they are not all quotable). For instance one system of value, a very old one, makes it right for men to marry virgins; another, of moderate antiquity, encourages men to go to bed with women but not women to go to bed with men, whereas in the language of the publications I am going to quote all sexual experience is good if it makes us happy. Different styles are here pulls different ways, we have to fight it out with what help there is and what sense we can make. The plight of the adolescent girl, told by her language to do so many contradictory things, is particularly confusing – but after all, it might be worse if the place of sex in life were rigidly fixed. The present situation can be seen as a kind of challenge, even if one that daunts or destroys some people.

It is the determined effort of 'the age', perhaps as against some of the people who live in it, and certainly as against some of the levels of our language and psyches, to make sex unserious. If I say that the age has a language in which sex is frivolous I am not necessarily saying that *people* are frivolous, except to the extent that they willingly live in their age – and except the leaders of opinion, poets, trend-setters and critics who define the age. I am not asserting the opposite, either, that people *are* serious about sex. Whether that's true as a general proposition, or of a majority, only God knows. We are discussing possibilities not statistics.

I am no believer in the golden age, but I do believe *The Times* was demonstrably a better newspaper in 1965 than 1967. In the case of the language of sex I can't offer any such picture of a simple superiority of past over present and I shall not be arguing that our plight is generally worse than that of the Victorians. The drive of some eminent Victorians to abolish sex and destroy any language of sex – a culmination of the Christian tradition which would on the whole much have preferred there to be no sex – meant that in some respects (names for the organs, for instance) we are without a common language of sex at all. The Victorian situation ensured agonies, senselessness and profound disconnections within the human psyche. All of which is no excuse for the failures of our own age. Whatever the Victorians did they at least didn't fall into treating marriage as a game or a social service, and I shall even suggest that in some ways passion came easier to them.

II

It is an obvious fact that there is much more pornographic material on general offer now than there was ten years ago, at least by the standards of ten years ago. I shall not be discussing the bumper crop of 'hard core' pornography raised in the hothouse of Soho, nor the increasing boldness of the men's magazines which were always inclined to the scandalous. (Cf. two informative articles in *The Times*, 23–4 August 1971, by Chris Dunkley.) I am not, either, much concerned here with publications which are *offered* as didactic; though I don't concede that the works of Mr Richard Neville (the Tariq Ali of the world of sex) or the drawings of Mr John Lennon are not pornographic because they do it righteously and deliberately. I am more interested in what our language counts as ordinary, and in the difference of style ten years has made.

To get to the scantier store of books in the local W. H. Smith's you now have to pick your way past an array of paperbacks which, unless their covers are designed to deceive, exist only to titillate. Almost all the new films in the West End depend for their appeal – again, unless the photographs outside are lies – on sexual rather than histrionic performances and, often enough, on the depiction of some hitherto undreamed-of perversion; while on the B.B.C. things are done before the cameras which used to happen, if at all, only in bedrooms. The newspaper founded as a successor to that bastion of Labour respectability the *Daily Herald* is saved from financial collapse by the introduction of an unprecedented quantity of what according to *Private Eye* its proprietor calls 'tit'. The latter rather serious magazine is banned from W. H. Smith's, no doubt because it would take up space more profitably occupied by the new generation of women's magazines which are replacing with pornography the cosy and deadly moral offerings of the fifties. *She*, for instance, ran an illustrated feature on the Cerne Abbas Giant (January 1972) with the subtitles 'Vivian Bird exposes a long-standing member of the English countryside' and 'Carved out of the hillside hundreds of years ago, the giant's penis is a sixth of his height. By that reckoning 6' blokes would have 12" choppers. Ho-hum, anyone for tennis?' At a loss for an ending after her tales of 'actual sexual intercourse' over the 'figure', the writer tried for direct stimulation: 'And if one visits the giant alone, or with the right kind of female company, then one will be stirred by the intensity of the feelings aroused.' The history of contraception on the next page is alleviated by a fashion-flash, which happens to be the re-introduction by two tall Japanese of codpieces.[4]

4 I chose to single out *She* from the rich field largely because I happened to see that the managing director of its publishers is announced as Marcus Morris. The history of Mr Morris is in itself an abstract and brief chronicle of the time. He first appeared, as the Rev. Marcus Morris, editing *Eagle*, the post-war boys' comic which was meant to combat the unwholesome influences of the excellent productions of the D. C. Thompson company of Dundee. *Eagle* was already perhaps a sign of a self-righteousness rather like the kind one associates with much pornography, for it offered a nauseous mixture of would-be Christianity (a comic strip about St Paul on the back page) with undisguised capitalist advertising (a character called Tommy Walls, who performed more whopping miracles than St Paul's after eating the relevant ice-cream and making a magic W sign) and moral homilies from the editor; and its effort was to divert readers from the very solid (no comic strips), decent and imaginative *Wizard, Hotspur, Rover* and *Adventure*, with the general approval of the establishment. The interesting thing is that Mr Morris is still to some extent on the same tack even with the obviously porno-

Not to be outsold *Vanity Fair* published a supplement called 'Nice Girls Do/Vanity Fair's Guide to the New Sexual Etiquette', a complete do-it-yourself seduction kit. The staff later deserted and started their own *Over 21*. Problems in the heart-to-heart column of the first issue (May 1972) included transvestism in its sexual-performance aspects: 'He used to be a good lover before all this started but he can't *perform sexually* [my italics] when he's dressed up.' (Who could, in 'frilly knickers, padded bras and fish-net tights?' – obviously this character prefers other performances, if he isn't, as one strongly suspects, a mere figment of the editorial imagination.) A couple of months earlier, back at W. H. Smith's, my eye had lighted – after drifting over a magazine whose cover asked the piquant question 'Do you still wear pyjamas?' and showed a couple outside their bed who didn't, but whose carefully shaved pudenda were mostly hidden by the brass bedstead – upon the March 1972 issue of *She* which was featuring one 'Have you a Third Nipple?' story and another, 'There's Always a First Time' of tales by former virgins giving what in evangelical circles

graphical *She*. There is a column by a parson, and the leading feature on witchcraft in this same January 1972 issue concludes with the sage and reverend advice 'To non-witches who may be tempted to try out the procedures I describe, I say: seek out a coven, or a responsible occult teacher, and work under guidance. Otherwise you may get dangerously out of your depth.'

Almost the last thing I noticed before closing my file on pornography on the grounds that I couldn't walk the streets or read newspapers with-out superadding to it was the next step in Mr Morris's career, as managing editor of *Cosmopolitan*, which has already been cited. Its style is, consistently, a certain kind of insinuating immorality: the constant suggestion that unless you fornicate a good deal you are not with it. (In the May 1972 issue the editress gently twitted a contributor for asserting that 'other men and women actually expect [every adult female who is single, widowed or divorced] to pack up her sexual equipment and store it until she gets married' with 'Surely Dr Reuben there can't be many people who really believe that these days?' What one expects may be different from what should be the case, but at this level the retort to one who launched off her first issue with 'Certainly with a divorce behind me and who-knows-what in front, I've got my share of emotional hang-ups . . . And that's why we are producing *Cosmopolitan* – to give help and advice' is, '*You* will never get another husband!' Other educative things in the issue included 'The Art of Lying' – i.e. lie when it is politic – 'How to Marry a Married Man' and a poem 'Abortion' which ended 'Never mind love. Well, here we go again.')

The Rev. Marcus Morris still figures in the current *Crockford's* as, *inter alia*, hon. chaplain of St Bride's, Fleet Street.

they call their 'testimony'. Even *Golf World* that month had a nude on the cover – leading, it appeared, to a story about the effect of sex on one's game rather than *vice versa*. (All this while I was looking for the *Family Doctor* booklet on marriage, of which somewhat below.)

As for the supposedly respectable press, *The Times* now publishes Saturday by Saturday advertisements for King Key-Wear (*read* 'Kinky Wear') in 20-denier see-thro' nylon, and included amongst *Times* Stocking Fillers ('Large presents are only part of the Christmas problem as well as these are the small, inexpensive, and yet personal gifts' 4 December 1971) 'Brief Gifts/Apollo briefs for Xmas/Fun brief in stretch cotton-knit . . . Backless pose pouch in misc. colours.' Earlier in the year the same paper had published a glorious full-page nude as an advertisement for a fertilizer firm. By 29 April 1972 they had descended to a much sleazier nude advertising a 'vibro massage belt' with a legend which made it look at first glance as though *she* were on offer at a 'special introductory price only £6 plus 30p P & P'. (In the *Telegraph* version she was clothed, getting her vibrations, with a different oddity, through a swimsuit.)

Respectable publishers mix filth into their advertisements as if it were the most natural subject in their world. One Cassell advertisement listed, in this order, 'Published for/H.R.H. PRINCE PHILIP/on his fiftieth birthday/THE TWELFTH MAN/*Foreword by H.R.H. The Prince of Wales* . . . SIR EDWARD GREY/ A biography of Lord Grey of Fallodon . . . IRVING WALLACE/THE NYMPHO AND OTHER MANIACS/*stories of some scandalous women* . . . JACQUES-YVES COUSTEAU/ LIFE AND DEATH/IN A CORAL SEA . . .' before descending to what must be the primal mud:

COPROPHILIA
or *A Peck of Dirt*
TERENCE McLAUGHLIN

With a delectable, dry sense of humour Terence McLaughlin delves deep into the dunghill of history to reveal the elegance and finery of previous eras in their true light – as the trappings of periods of uninhibited filth and squalor. £2·10.

(*T.L.S.* 2 July 1971)

The zest of that prose might say something about our own period. In the same month W. H. Allen ('over 170 years of successful publishing in Britain') followed *The Duchess of Kent* ('A tasteful, informative biography of this charming member of the Royal Family'), Beverley Nichols's *The Gift of a Garden* and a book on Stefan Zweig with:

THE FUNDAMENTALS OF SEX
PHILIP CAUTHERY AND MARTIN COLE
We believe this to be the most comprehensive book on the subject ever written. The joint authors have international reputations as experts on sex education. The illustrations are quite remarkable.

(*T.L.S.* 30 July 1971)

Meanwhile in the editorial department of *The Times* films which ten years since would have been generally thought obscene are classifiable as 'some harmless Continental sex-romp' (6 August 1971) and the genial tolerance of smut comes out in such paragraphs as this:

And what about that incest and all? Like the other matters in the film which seem in principle liable to give offence, it is dealt with, as it were, glancingly, in passing: it is not, ultimately, such an important matter for either of the participants – a tipsy extension of a Fourteenth of July celebration – and will leave no Oedipal trauma in its wake. Indeed, thus initiated, the first thing the lad does is to hurry off to try his new-found powers on an obliging girl nearer his own age. All part, you might say, of life's rich fabric, no more and no less.   (20 August 1971)

'Sir, you *may* say so.' My immediate point isn't to make judgments on this situation but to remark that, for instance, that paragraph would have been impossible in *The Times* of 1960.

What I want to ask is whether this new state of affairs threatens anybody, and if so how. I do myself feel threatened by pornography. When I look into *She* or *Cosmopolitan* I get in an acuter form the feeling I have just by glancing along the magazine-racks on the station, that I don't know anything any more and that if this is the world, I live somewhere else. It is my world that feels threatened, my orientations – and of course that could be a good thing, a jolt out of complacency. If I can show why pornography is the kind of threat that is the reverse of a good thing I shall have got further than the predominant enlightenment which preaches that pornography is either harmless or positively beneficial.

The Arts Council working party based its view of the harmlessness of pornography on the undeniable truth that there is no causal connection between indulging in erotica and committing sexual offences, and the debate is always conducted in these terms:

pornography is always thought of as causing (or not) some future action by which it must be judged. This is one of the unfortunate results of modern legislation. 'Before the 1959 Act,' said Lord Wilberforce (delivering a judgment 19 July 1972) 'the words "deprave and corrupt" had in fact been largely disregarded: the courts had simply considered whether a publication was obscene, and the tendency to deprave and corrupt was presumed.' But the Act's attempt at accurate definition, 'an article shall be deemed to be obscene if its effect . . . is, if taken as a whole, such as to tend to deprave and corrupt persons who are likely . . . to read, see or hear the matter', naturally puts the onus on the prosecution to demonstrate the depraved consequences. When no such causal connection is observable, pornography is found not guilty and people who feel threatened by it are nonplussed.

One of the more than usually ill-argued passages of *Pornography: The Longford Report* (1972) seeks to maintain this causal connection between pornography and depravity. 'We do not believe that any definition of the nature of pornography can exclude some account of its effects,' they say (p. 410) and 'Pornography clearly must have some effect' (p. 413). After the latter brave statement they have to admit at once that 'Only in very rare cases can a causal connection between pornography and anti-social behaviour be conclusively proved.' Despite which 'we repudiate the deduction that such a connection may not exist'. What can the repudiation be, in the terms of their own discussion, but a declaration of superstitious faith? 'No one can confidently deny that a connection between pornography and behaviour, whether promiscuous, deviant or aggressive, can sometimes be demonstrated.' I do confidently deny that any such connection is causal, until the demonstration appears. (The *Report*'s Section 1.6, to which it refers me here, contains a number of stories of different degrees of tallness, none of which could be useful to any kind of scientist or treated by any historian as reliable evidence.) But when a demonstration does appear the causal connection of pornography *and depravity* may still be to seek, unless depravity is agreed to be the same as what is 'deemed obscene' by 'the average person, applying contemporary community standards' (p. 408). For is anti-social behaviour, promiscuity, deviant or aggressive behaviour *depraved*? We don't prosecute them, anyway, unless the aggressive behaviour breaks the law.

The persistent attempt to treat the matter in a consistently frustrated way need not, however, establish the harmlessness of pornography. It may more reasonably suggest that to consider pornography within some scheme of cause-and-effect is to place it in the wrong category. It is a positive mania at the present day to judge everything by its consequences and to deny that anything whose consequences, if any, are undemonstrable, can be judged at all; a mania that affects not merely newspapers and ordinary folk but princes of the Church. So it was that when Cardinal Heenan denounced pornography his effort was to show that unbridled pornography will lead to anarchy. For instance the Cardinal is reported to have said more generally of sexual morality, 'It was true that the church had often reserved its most severe denunciation for sexual sins. They had often been singled out for especially trenchant condemnation because they so often led to the breakdown of the social order.'[5] We are living in odd times when a Cardinal is against sin not because it is sinful but because it may do social damage. 'It is opportune to remark,' he said, 'that it is not puritanical to deplore the determined efforts of a small group of writers and impressarios to remove all restraint imposed by modesty and decency.' But if modesty and decency were not realistically seen as bulwarks against anarchy, the Cardinal would have had to make an undisguisedly moral statement, which would, though it took him into territory where he could offer to speak with authority, have branded him as 'puritanical', and was therefore not to be thought of. The Responsible Society identically insists in the second edition of its Prospectus that its opposition to immorality is not on moral grounds. Its 'primary aim' is to educate and inform the public about 'the real consequences of irresponsibility' and a lesser one 'to prevent distress caused by irresponsible sexual behaviour'. It seems to follow that if we could have the irresponsibility without the distress that would be all right.

The Times too (the leader of the opposition to pornography – on those pages, at least, where it isn't offering pornography of its own) is similarly imprisoned within the prudential. 'Some parents see what they regard as a total dissolution of intellectual and moral standards, and naturally fear the consequences,' said one leader following the paper's usual line (29 April 1971). The consequences are feared, not the dissolution itself.

If one begins by agreeing that there are no causes and effects

[5] *The Times*, 18 November 1970.

in the places searched, that does not deny all connection between pornography and the rest of life. The connections between the flood of pornography, the increase in venereal diseases, and the achievement by promiscuity of a status halfway between fashion and respectability, would seem obvious enough; and it is not a convincing objection to a view of the way things belong together in an age (the contemporaneity, shall we say, of pornography, 'pop' and 'pot' which seems more than alliterative) to say that pornography and the pox are not to one another as cause to effect. If, therefore, I can remove the discussion from the factual plane, that doesn't mean I shall be disconnecting the discussion of pornography from conduct and action. It does mean that pornography will have to be judged in a way proper to its mode of existence.

The cause-and-effect talk commits the very basic mistake of trying to judge what happens in the imagination by some factual yardstick or other. What happens in the imagination has very important bearings on conduct, but does not *cause* conduct – and even if it did the chain of cause-and-effect could not be demonstrated. Lawyers called upon to judge questions about depravity and corruption naturally want to keep to tangible proofs, but that need not make us admit that what happens in the imagination is of no importance. With due respect to the Bible there is a great difference between looking on a woman to lust after her and committing adultery, and one aspect of it is that you cannot be had up in any imaginable court for the former. But yet it can certainly matter (and could conceivably matter more than adultery) when a man commits adultery 'in his heart' (Matthew 5: 28).

My most obvious remark then – so obvious that were it not for the terms of the contemporary 'debate' about pornography I would not trouble to make it – is that any judgment of pornography involves questions about values. For even if pornography could be caught causing events, the question whether the events are instances of depravity and corruption could not be answered by the events themselves *qua* events (if that is imaginable). What is and what is not depravity depends not on what happens but on what it means, on the place of events within some scheme of values. If we say that the Moors murderers Brady and Hindley were corrupt and depraved, we are judging their actions within the set of values according to which it is wicked to delight in murder. Within that set of values, but only within it, the murders are seen as proofs of depravity. And these values are established not by courts of law but by our common life as expressed in our language. I am not saying that murder isn't *really* wrong. Wrongness may be intrinsic to an act, and the act of murder is always wrong. But to say so is to see the action in a certain way – to see it as it is naturally seen in our language, which here provides the standards by which an act may be, in itself, intrinsically, right or wrong.

If pornography is a threat it is not because any man reading Mr David Storey's novel *Radcliffe* is likely to develop a taste for being orally homosexually assaulted – though he might – and not because any woman reading Mr Adrian Mitchell's latest, *The Bodyguard*, is likely to make for the nearest bar, there to enjoy fellatio – though that is imaginable too – but because pornography works on, affects and changes the common language of sex and love. It is the common language which pornography tends to deprave and corrupt.

It is possible to distinguish between understanding a work of art and responding to it: one may respond inappropriately for a variety of personal reasons and yet in a sense have understood. But it is also true that a kind of response is part of understanding. Works of art like sentences exist only in re-creation, and individual involvement is a necessary part of the re-creation that makes a poem. In that sense there is no reading a poem without being implicated by it: we do not read neutrally, objectively or disinterestedly. While we are reading we are understanding in the language of the poem; it is, for the duration, our language. Then perhaps we feel one of the vast varieties of inner protests or admirations that are the beginning of criticism: but that can only come from participation in the poem.

To read and understand pornography is to understand sex in the language of pornography. To do so habitually and with delight is to demonstrate that one's passions find their home in the language of pornography. 'It is an entirely clever picture . . . but it is also an entirely base and evil picture. It is an expression of delight in the prolonged contemplation of a vile thing, and delight in that is an "unmannered" or "immoral" quality. It is "bad taste" in the profoundest sense – it is the taste of the devils.'[6] Without the depraved, participating response (whatever we are to

[6] J. Ruskin, *The Crown of Wild Olive*, para. 56.

mean by that) pornography is not itself. It is not possible, for instance, for young children to read pornography as adults would; to the pure all things are pure.

Ruskin's very strong argument that his taste tells you the nature of a man is relevant here. 'The first, and last, and closest trial to any living creature is, "What do you like?" Tell me what you like and I'll tell you what you are.'[7] If one likes pornography that shows all too clearly what one is.

The case against pornography is therefore confused by the cause-and-effect talk. Pornography doesn't *cause* depravity and corruption, it *is* depravity and corruption: the tendency to corrupt and deprave is internally related to pornography; and the depravity and corruption occurs in whatever allows pornography to be itself. 'An article could not be considered obscene in itself; it could only be so in relation to its likely readers,' said Lord Wilberforce, trying valiantly to make sense of the 1959 Act. Lord Wilberforce is just a little confusing the issue here by a mild form of the fallacy of the typing monkeys, the old fancy that given an infinity of time a collection of monkeys taught to play with a typewriter would hit off the works of Shakespeare. So they might, but only for the reader, assuming he could retain his sanity, appointed to look over their shoulders. Only for him would the words of Shakespeare *be* that; just so pornography is only itself in relation to its readers, without which it does not exist.

If so the question what is and what is not pornography falls within literary criticism, and is therefore unlikely to be dealt with well in a court of law. This clears up the old confusions about a writer's intentions. Many an honest legal penny has been turned by counsel's demonstrating that a writer's intention was innocent enough though his work has an unfortunately guilty air. But in literary criticism we say that the real intention is the one that gets expressed, and intention is therefore the same as expression. Unless an author is a failure his work intends to say what it does say. Therefore the defence that he didn't mean to do it can at least not be offered if the author is also using the argument that his work deserves the immunity of 'literary merit'.[8]

---

[7] *Ibid.*, para. 54.

[8] Another fallacy which ought to be put painlessly out of its misery is that the words 'pornography' and 'obscenity' are really of very wide application and have been maliciously restricted by Lord Longford to sexual matters. The ploy was fallen for by *T.L.S.* when a writer said 'Of course

If, however, the definition of pornography must be left to the courts the important dialogues ought at least to go differently. At present the ordinary thing is for the defence to discomfit prosecution witnesses by asking them whether they personally have been depraved and corrupted by the work in question. Since witnesses may be expected to deny that they have, the case against the book is weakened. Or perhaps someone will say (as Sir Basil Blackwell very courageously did) that he *has* been corrupted – but then the question *how?* which naturally follows will still be embarrassing to answer. Instead it should go:

Question: Has it corrupted YOU?
Answer: Yes.
Question: How?
Answer: Look how it works *here* and *here*. This is depraved isn't it?

The discussion can now be continued of the book, not of the witness's possibly abnormal psychology; and if *The Times* wants to find 'disintegration' the place to look is in the pornography itself. But this is difficult in court, where neither criticism nor the language of sex is much at home. The questions we have to ask, though not quite the ones the 1959 Act forbids, are too much like them: 'Is the thing in front of us shocking, outrageous or offensive to decent feeling?' From the point of view of the lawyer the trouble is that really 'the thing' is not in front of us, it is within us. But in turn that is why pornography is legitimately a trouble to the moralist.

---

pornography should never be treated as if only its sexual aspects mattered – that is, as if no other kind of stimulus offered by the written word could be as socially or ethically significant...' (7 January 1972, p. 12), and by Mr Ben Whitaker when he objected to the House of Commons suddenly filling for a pornography debate with M.P.'s 'unseen before or since who had been invisible during the debates on real obscenities such as unemployment or Vietnam' (*The Times*, 11 December 1971). To call a political event obscene is to use a figure of speech, as when Mrs Shirley Williams used the word of the Aldershot bomb outrage. However, it is one thing to use a figure of speech, another to insist that the figurative use is ordinary. As an observation about English it is simply untrue to say that 'pornography' ordinarily refers to writings that have nothing to do with sex. The language might go that way, but it hasn't yet; and if the unemployment figures are obscene and pornographic one may ask how many M.P.s they provoke to unseemly sexual stimulation. Pornography is a perfectly precise word and there is no harm at all in defining something by using it.

The Longford Report's attempt to anchor its opposition to pornography on an appeal to 'contemporary standards of decency or humanity accepted by the public at large' fails in its last clause. Pornography is indeed judged by standards, but *they* are not established by a head-count. 'But, if enough people want it, is it right to call it pornography?' retorted the *Daily Mail*'s literary editor (20 September 1972) – reasonably enough, for the answer to that could not be supplied by the Longford argument. The answer is, nevertheless, *yes*, whatever people want; pornography is correctly so called if it *can* be so called, if the word remains meaningful. The Longford Report seems to suggest that in our democratic society majority prejudices should be enforced by law. Even less promising for our present discussion is the apparent belief that words could be defined by a Gallup Poll.

Because we have to do here with the language of sex, all readers are corrupted by whatever is corrupting in pornography to the degree of their reading, and non-readers to the degree of the impact of pornography upon the common language. So all those elegantly uninvolved essays by mildly disapproving liberals[9] are off the point. Even if one accepts a writer's imperviousness to pornographical stimulation, which I myself envy and make no claim to possess, he cannot escape the involvement of both the particular and the general kinds we have discussed. He who creates in his imagination a depraved and corrupt thing is to that extent depraved and corrupted, and he does general damage to the extent that his language of sex is affected.

How, though, to decide what is and what is not pornographic? How to recognize the true tokens of depravity? The identification of a pornographic work depends, like any other judgment in literary criticism, on the agreement of competent judges (not 'experts'), and competence depends here on things like experience of reading and thinking about the kinds of work in question. That sounds vague; and I shall try to make a few of the possible sharper distinctions: but it is important to see the need for vagueness here. All literary talk is vague when put beside anything as demonstrable as causes and effects; to say so, however, is not to say that judgments of pornography are either impossible or merely private, but to reiterate that they are questions concerning

---

[9] E.g. Gore Vidal, 'Straight Sex', *The New York Review of Books*, 4 June 1970.

values and language. It is, indeed, easier to recognize a pornographic poem than a great poem, yet there is pretty general agreement – necessarily based in individual experience and commitment – about who the great poets are. If there is no corresponding
agreement about who are the pornographers, that says more
about the state of our language of sex and about the complementary feebleness of criticism in our time, than about the difficulty of judgment.

He showed a group of children, aged between 11 and 18, films depicting
violence and sex, including one called *491* which showed a girl being raped
by a group of intoxicated louts and forced to have intercourse with a dog.
None of the children were frightened either during or after the film . . .
Curiously enough two adults, who saw the experiment, one a grandmother
and the other a mother, were so upset that they needed psychological treatment for a month afterwards! In 30 years' experience of treating patients
I have never seen anyone who proved to have been corrupted by pornography.

Letter to *New Statesman*, 10 July 1970

The writer has 'never seen' because he doesn't know corruption
when he sees it; the shock to the women suggests they were far
better judges than he was.

I can, however, on the strength of the foregoing discussion,
make some general distinctions between what is and what is not
pornographic. A work whose sexual content is left deliberately
uncontrolled by the artist is pornographic. Nude love-making
on stage or screen is always necessarily pornographic because the
expression – the understanding of the audience – cannot be controlled as part of the work. Nude love-making immediately breaks
the art of the play and instead thrusts real voyeurism upon the
audience. It doesn't weaken this contention to admit that at other
times and in other places it need not apply. The Etruscans,
perhaps, took sex seriously by making a public display of it. Two
apparently contradictory actions may have the same sense, but
only in two different languages; and if public sex couldn't be for
us anything but a low exhibition, that simply displays the strength
of our language. If there have been times and places where an
audience would not be unartistically engaged by stage sex, we do
not live in one. We are used to modesty and privacy, and in our
language of sex the response to nude love-making is not to the play
but to the real (or not) actions. We want to know how far they're
really going and what they feel like doing it. And are they really

doing IT? (How, by the way, can a fully frontal male nude *simulate* an erection?) Do not retort that any erotic gesture or pose of an actor or actress's might provoke similar unseemly questions. There will be doubt in some cases whether some gestures or poses point what a play says, but there are many cases where there is no doubt. The bare-bottomed bouncings, grapplings, wide-eyed oohings and aaahings, the long-drawn gasps and sudden grabs now almost *de rigueur* in plays on B.B.C. television are no more art than a brothel's exibeesh is. It is appropriate that the groups who specialize in stage copulation – reintroduced for the first time since the days of Heliogabalus – should also wish to do away with proscenium arch, the final development of the 'circumstances' of drama, when they cross it in order to lay the audience. This is a straightforward attack on the language of the art, a determination to destroy the art in favour of 'real life' – the real life in question being, again, strictly that of a brothel.

To emphasize that works of art control the events they depict, in order to make the sense the work of art is, defends many great stories and plays against charges of pornography. It doesn't follow that if a work makes fun of sex it is pornographic; it is on the contrary arguable that part of our present loss of control results from the determination of the Christian tradition to suppress anything like satyr plays or Aristophanic comedy. The belief that if sex is serious it cannot be 'the olde daunce' is itself an impoverishment of the language of sex, for it is not obviously part of the nature of sex, and so of any significance we find in it, to be in some of its aspects a pretty funny business? But a real work of literature will force us to take even obscenity seriously (how that could be is one of my subjects in the next chapter); hence one can distinguish between pornography and obscenity. Chaucer's Miller is obscene, but his obscenity (which I am not attributing to Chaucer in his own voice) is very far from pornographic. Perhaps the extreme case is Chaucer's Merchant, who makes a malign attack on all significance in sex, which could almost be offered as a definition of pornography. But even there one can distinguish between an attack on meaning shown by the poet as such, defined by the rich context of the rest of the Canterbury Tales, and the true, the unblushful reductiveness of the real thing.

The 'hard core pornography' that which, according to a Q.C. and member of the Arts Council, there can be nothing more innocent, works, at its simplest, by trying to disconnect sexual response from whatever significance it has in our lives. The ideal pornography would work directly upon the sex organs, using eyes and mind only as untouched intermediaries. The ideal is quite unattainable; and it is because pornography has to work through, in and on language that it can be seen as a threat to that language. The attempt to ignore values is itself an attack upon them and upon the belief that other works can create values. Pornographic novels and poems offer images and their language as much as any other work of literature: the defining characteristic of pornography is its determination to set off the strength of our sexuality without engaging whatever it is that makes it ours.

The bearings and possible consequences of pornography, then, are serious enough, but the worst thing about it is the thing as in itself it really is, an attack on the significance of sex. Pornography is identifiable as that which uses imaginative language for purposes of low stimulation (whereas literature might use stimulation for its imaginative purpose). It is because pornography speaks the imaginative language of real poetry, real novels, that one can see it as an indecent assault upon the kind of seriousness which real literature makes possible.

If one offers something like 'hatred of significance in sex' as the mark of true pornography, that takes care of the absurdity of the present British law which allows pornographic works to be published if they are of sufficient literary merit. Without arguing in favour of censorship one can say that a hatred of significance is the extreme opposite of merit in a work of literature, and that therefore, simply enough, a work of pornography, a work whose tendency is to deprive sex of significance, can have no literary merit. (The word 'literary' is in any case bound to confuse the issue: if an imaginative work has merit nothing is added by calling the merit literary.) It is one of the more fantastic signs of the times that attempts should be made to treat the higher pornography specialized in by Calder & Boyars and a few others as if it were literary art.

III

Pornography is then not the comic, the obscene or even the malign treatment of sex, it is the unserious treatment – 'unserious' in that it tries to deny the significance of sex in human life and to convert it into entertainment. (I shall go on to argue in the next chapter that real poetry is therefore never pornographic even when its tendency is to corrupt and deprave, for the depravity possible to real art is not of this unserious kind.) By this definition some things are pornography which generally pass as respectable, not to say sacrosanct. Much 'sex-education' is pornography; so is much work in sexology for which higher degrees have been awarded. And I find it hard to distinguish the Family Doctor booklet (published by the British Medical Association), *Getting Married*, from *Vanity Fair*'s 'Guide to the New Sexual Etiquette'. In their not very different ways they are all preaching that sex is a controllable pleasure which we need not take seriously. They are all so close to *She* or *Couples* or such serious-minded pro-pornography demonstrations as *Oh! Calcutta* as to be convincingly seen as branches springing from the same root.

I may have been unfortunate in the examples I have come across; but sex education seems to be an attempt in primary schools to talk about sex, without using any language of sex, to children who are in any case biologically incapable of understanding what is said. The result can only be to bewilder and frighten children. And what is this sex education supposed to teach? Not what used to be called 'the facts of life'; it is not offered as a lesson in human biology. Sex education gives a child factual, insignificant and functional images as a language of sex to store up and misuse at the right moment.

'Particular effects of the programme were found to include an overall gain in vocabulary, and a clear shift away from vernacular language to the "Latinate" words' – this was offered as a measure of the *success* of the B.B.C. sex education film *Merry Go Round*. Others were that it had 'reduced emotional attitudes' and that there had been 'a considerable reduction in errors of fact and emotional exaggerations in essays on "How babies are made and how they come into the world".'[10] It would be interesting to know by what standard an emotional exaggeration of sex is measured there, but in any case the measure would surely rule out The Song of Songs or Shakespeare's Sonnets as immoderate, abnormal, and overheated. No, on this showing Lawrence got it quite right in the passage of *Fantasia of the Unconscious* where he says 'The mass of mankind should *never* be acquainted with the scientific biological facts of sex, *never*' (chapter 9). One can only

[10] *The Times*, 3 April 1971.

have faith in the culture of the playground and look forward to the revenge the children will take in the next volume of *The Lore and Language of Schoolchildren*. The educators should have on their conscience that they are inflicting valueless sex upon little children, a particularly revolting form of obscenity, and not made less so by its self-righteousness.

For adolescents there is the Institute for Sex Education and Research (surely the coming true in the University of Aston of the late Labour government's dream that each university should be allowed to develop a few areas of special academic devotion) where Dr Martin Cole produced his once famous film *Growing Up*, described by the *Daily Mail* as 'a film of a naked couple making love' which is 'to be offered to schools throughout Britain in a drive for better sex education'. Its 'intercourse shots', according to the same authority, are a 'fifteen-second sequence, most unerotic'. Children will thus be stimulated and horrified by what in the course of a normal sexual life they may hope never to see – other people's unerotic sex – and will be educated, if into anything, into the delights of the voyeur. Another sex educator, 'went further and said he was in favour of some sort of sexual adventure playgrounds, where young people could make love in comfort, privacy and hygienic conditions'.[11] The period touch there is surely the word 'hygienic', and it is also the link with the science of sex which I shall next mention. The ambition is to make sex safe, clean, hygienic, and the proper activity for a playground – to deprive it, that is, of its significance in our life, to destroy its nature. Sex becomes the unique technique which has no point beyond itself.

Then there is the other, more humane pain-killer of a sex education which tries to tell children about the value of inter-personal relationships and such mouthfilling things. This is a misunderstanding of how language is learned. (By a strange co-incidence I have never heard of a programme of sex education which explains to children that one normal state of marriage is as living hell.) Real 'sex education', which could hardly be so called, is the interaction of individual experience and a language of sex: it consists of growing up in a community, learning its words and ways and trying – perhaps desperately and with agony – to see how they mean the strange things that befall one. School sex education makes that process of becoming fully human more

[11] *The Times*, 13 November 1970.

difficult, because it restricts the common language of sex to the coldly, warmly or solemnly trivial.

The popular manuals of sexual techniques which also offer, in their way, an education – in a sort of sexual acrobatics of which the elementary stages are presumably the 'sexercises for a happier love life' promised by an article in the October 1972 *She* – offer to teach what cannot be taught, and masquerade as practical advice though really, like all pornography, they are works of debased imagination.

Advice, information and new ideas are needed to create interest and stimulate one's own imagination ... America, bless her, has been the first to walk on the moon. But Europe has always and probably will always lead the world in sexual knowledge and enlightenment ... [This book] will be another weapon at your disposal in the battle for happiness and the war against sexual boredom and frustration ... If after reading this book, you and your partner are not enjoying new heights of sexual enjoyment and pleasure, simply return the book.

> Advertisement for *The Pictorial Guide to Sexual Intercourse* in *The New York Review of Books*, 18 June 1970[12]

The reader is given a synthetic fantasy which he may later, if he can find anyone to play with, play out with his 'partner': but the book itself exists as the fantasy not the results. One again objects that the language is debased – that the debasement is within the language, in the mind of the reader as part of the understanding, not in any later consequences with the 'partner'.

Another one, *Sexual Behavior*, makes my point for me by listing an editorial board consisting almost wholly of professors, doctors of medicine, divinity and philosophy, described in the blurb as 'America's leading authorities on sexual matters – from a variety of disciplines' and evoking from one Seward Hiltner Ph.D., D.D., the recommendation 'I welcome very much the kind of treatment of sex promised by this magazine. The distinguished Board of Editors guarantees both scientific accuracy and honest, socially conscious treatment of the subject.' The kind of treatment promised was of subjects listed in a kind of verse which began:

> Alcohol and sex · Blackmail and sex
> Cross-dressing · Child molesting

[12] This British dollar-earner promises 'Over 100 full color – full page photographs/For educational purposes, of a live man and a live woman,/ together engaged in sexual intercourse/positions with descriptive text.'

Coital frequency
Psychological castration
Depression and sex · Duration of intercourse
Sudden Death during sex

and went on through the alphabet to the nicely alliterative

Promiscuity · Petting · Rape · Ritualized sex
Sex in old age · Sadism · Sexual jokes
New York Review of Books, 12 August 1971

What a comfort to know on the authority of Rev. Dr Hiltner that one can indulge to one's heart's content in all this without doing anything worse than becoming socially conscious of the subject! The whole thing really belongs in the last quoted category – but the jokes aren't the kind Wittgenstein imagined philosophy could consist in.

Why is that sort of publication different in kind from the article 'How good a lover are you?' in the first *Cosmopolitan*, March 1972 ('turn to page 55 for an assessment of your lovemaking talents') which rewarded those who scored highly in a quiz with the praise 'you're a formidable competitor in the fields of love'? How is it different from the compliment paid by a woman in the same issue to one of her countless lovers, 'Jimmy enjoyed the role of expert tutor, and I was his not untalented pupil. Simple as that.'?

The attempt to restrict sex to a teachable 'performance' results naturally in a measure for sexual 'success' (itself a phrase which looks like a sign of the times) which is simply the intensity and extent of orgasm. 'For couples, orgasm instigated by manual stimulation may lead to better coition [better because more thoroughgoing] ... It is easy to make fun of the researchers ... but such research has led to the demolition of a lot of old beliefs and the discovery of simple procedures than can lead many people who think themselves sexual cripples into full enjoyment.'[13] This almost suggests that a diploma in sexual competence should be added to the growing list of courses to be followed at universities. (The results could be published according to the traditional formula, 'The following have satisfied the examiners.')

The consensus that all this technique and education is a reason-

---

[13] *T.L.S.*, 16 July 1970.

able way to talk of sex extends to writers as various as the late C. S. Lewis and Mr Michael Frayn. Lewis published this rather nasty little poem in *Essays in Criticism*:[14]

> TO MR. KINGSLEY AMIS ON HIS LATE VERSES
> Why is to fight (if such our fate)
> Less 'human' than to copulate,
> When Gib the cat, I'll take my oath,
> Wins higher marks than you for both?

There is the same pornographic belief that copulation is an activity for which an order of merit could be established, and quite independently of what the activity means in life. Lewis also, somewhere in one of his homiletic works, compares sex with plumbing – a question of keeping the pipes in order – and so reminds me of Mr Frayn. I mention *him* simply because he seems to me one of our most intelligent writers who should know better, but he didn't apparently intend to be ironical when he compared sex with driving cars (Mr Wilson's image for conducting the Labour Party) as a 'skilled technique'.[15]

Or, as Miss Mary Breasted wrote of the American deprived poor, in a book called *Oh! Sex Education!* (1970) 'their women are not frequently treated to the long foreplay that is helping middle-class women achieve more and better orgasms' (p. 293). More and better orgasms! is a sort of war-cry of modern liberalism. (The *Vanity Fair* booklet went one better and suggested a fitting prize for an especially impressive 'sexual performance' – a faked orgasm.) But if you think that more and better orgasms are guaranteed by the techniques which bring them on, you suffer from a deeper sexual crippling than the one compassionated with by the *T.L.S.* writer, for your language of sex has failed. 'More' orgasms may be arranged, but not that they shall be 'better'. Miss Germaine Greer showed her awareness of the unsatisfactoriness of measuring sexual success by intensity of orgasm when, discussing her lesbian encounters in a *Sunday Times* interview, she said they were first-rate 'from the orgasm point of view' – but boring.[16] It is possible for there to be a passionate sexual relationship between two people who never touch each other –

---

[14] Vol. IV (1954), p. 190.   [15] *The Day of the Dog* (1962), p. 82.
[16] If sex was ordained to be a great game and if extreme orgasm is the longest ladder, one consequence of the Masters–Johnson investigation,

'sexual' because it affects the deep passions and their sexual embodiment in one or both lives.

Challenged by this question Pierre raised his head and felt a need to express the thoughts that filled his mind. He began to explain that he understood love for a woman somewhat differently. He said that in all his life he had loved and still loved only one woman, and that she could never be his.

'*Tiens!*' said the captain.

Tolstoy, *War and Peace* (trans. Maude) book xi chapter xxix

The attempt to observe sex scientifically (unlike science itself a new development in our century) seems to me to be also a branch of pornography, for it too denies sex its proper significance and existence. Whatever else it may be sexology isn't science, anyway, unless a kind of bastard biology. Sexology tries to measure sexual behaviour, but in real physics measurements exist *vis-à-vis* the knowledge they provide. Physics is the way of looking at things proper to that science; it justifies itself in the physical understanding permitted by its methods. If sexologists did offer themselves as a kind of biologist, that would be all right but would carry with it the limitation on the sense of their study which in fact they deny.

But what is the sexologist observing? He rigorously excludes (or tells us he does) all personal subjective factors in himself and anything that is not physically observable in his subject, and seems to himself therefore to be observing only the real thing, that which is observable to others.

He is not observing sex, that is to say, except in its biological aspect. I argued that the sense, the reality of 'the same' sexual act varies with the language and context in which it takes place. This

to which we may look forward when their results have sunk into the general consciousness, is the total cessation of human sexual intercourse. For they demonstrate beyond contradiction (at least to anybody who believes that sexology is a science which can demonstrate things) that, at least for their subjects who were unusually interested in sexual performance, and especially in the case of women, the most intense and complete orgasms are achieved during masturbation. If so what need have the poor things of mere men? Not everybody will agree that such non-consummations are devoutly to be wished, final solution of the overpopulation problem though they may be – but that can only be because in general regard, in our language of sex, masturbation is the lowest rung of Jacob's ladder. The pursuit of women is therefore at least more basic to our language of sex than the pursuit of happiness.

is what the biologist *qua* biologist cannot observe. Meaning does inhere in particular acts and events, but the sexologists are up to the old trick of trying to get the event without the meaning, just like the old-fashioned linguists trying to understand languages by concentrating only on sound. The sexologist of the Masters–Johnson kind is denaturing sex just as much as the pornographer – and in much the same way. It is unnecessary to accord the respect due to science to those very self-righteous peeping-tomes, the works of American sexology.

The serious sexologist is therefore in an insoluble logical dilemma. If he doesn't see the sexual performances that are his subject for what they are, viz., exhibitions differing from those of the Danish stage only in that they are amateur and in some cases unpaid, he is not seeing what is there, i.e. not being a true scientist. (And if the law is put off from prosecuting these obscene performances because they are 'scientific' the law is even more of an ass than usual.) But if the sexologist *does* see what is there, he is merely assisting at an obscene entertainment and is no closer to being 'scientific' about sex – though he might learn a bit more.[17]

According to Masters and Johnson the subjects of their investigation were unusual only in their possession of 'a basic interest in and desire for effectiveness in sexual performance' (which might

---

[17] Another kind of scientism afflicts much of the Longford Report on Pornography. A 'research survey' reports Professor Eysenck's suggestion that 'writings can be graded on a dimension ranging from 0 (no mention of sex) to 100 (entirely concerned with sexual matters), independently of artistic merit, scientific value or historical interest' (p. 461). Perhaps they could, though 0 and 100 are both unimaginable. But what next? 'Construction of a rating table makes it possible, he says, "to measure with objectivity and reasonable accuracy the amount of 'pornography' contained in a passage of prose".' Only if you know what pornography is: as here reported, Professor Eysenck thinks it is the same as mentioning sex in speech, a position on which Queen Victoria could not have improved. The researcher concludes, 'In future work in this area, it is essential that stimuli and measures be standardized ... Sexual inventories ought to be used more widely by researchers; and differential aspects of pornography on individuals ... ought to be taken into account' (p. 497). That, as usual, could only make sense if the measure of pornography could be physical. Anything that rouses will be pornography to the physically measurable extent of the rousing; but what the physical *means* – and why sexual arousal isn't necessarily depravity – is as ever the essential begged question.

also be said for the Danish actors). The only happy aspect of the sexological misapplication of the jargon of science is that the common language is strong enough to make it appear at times what it is, howlingly funny. As a review in *The British Journal of Psychiatry*[18] said, '*Human Sexual Response* establishes a most important advance in the methodology of inquiry into sexual function and dysfunction, and an invaluable precedent for those investigators who need one.' We may then look forward to a great leap forward by the emboldened investigators hitherto held back by lack of a precedent. But it won't advance our knowledge of sex.

The *bona fides* of the scientific sexologist is in any case taken too easily for granted. Their brand of science does seem almost invincible in its obscurantism, but why should we believe so easily in its power to overcome the human nature of the scientist and the real nature of the thing investigated?

The author of this unusual study of 'homosexual encounters in public places' is a minister of religion turned sociologist currently Assistant Professor at the University of Southern Illinois. He does not attempt to test any hypothesis but is clearly influenced by Goffman. After a preliminary year of intensive observation he witnessed some 120 homosexual acts in 19 different lavatories in five parks of one city. He then concentrated on one particular park lavatory and by passing himself off as a deviant and acting as look-out man, made systematic observations on homosexual encounters there.

He was able to integrate his research sample into a much wider social health survey after identifying the subjects by tracing their car licence numbers. This enabled him to interview them personally and complete a questionnaire. The bulk of the book consists of a detailed analysis of 50 deviants (from an original sample of 134) and a matched control group obtained from the same health survey.

Review in *British Journal of Psychiatry*, no. 552, quoted in
Private Eye 3 December 1971

The scientist was, of course, quite untouched and uninfluenced by the games he joined in? Similarly we are asked to believe that the psychiatrists who 'have sex' with their patients do so out of the pure disinterested wish to analyse them more deeply. (For after all what knowledge goes deeper than the carnal knowledge?)

Other cases in the book concern a therapeutically successful homosexual 'affair' between a young civil servant and his older therapist, and a relationship between a young married couple and two male psychiatrists

[18] 1968, p. 160.

in which heterosexual, homosexual and group sex activity all took place. This was also a success.[19]

Let's hope the orgies were successful orgies, as well as therapy. I look forward to the day when the trend will spread to my profession (making it thus as respectable as the oldest) for I am sure that many unfortunate barriers of stiffness could be broken down, and close personal relationships satisfactorily commenced, if it were not still somewhat frowned on (in the stuffier redbrick universities, anyway – I am credibly informed that things have improved in the more progressive places) for tutors to seduce their pupils during tutorials. Ah! what group sex we in Redbrick have been missing for so many years, and what a deleterious effect that must have had on the class-lists!

I cannot see it as accidental that the area of overlap between pornography and these branches of sexual science is so wide, and that the latter are so easily annexed by the former. The high horses of righteousness are not, moreover, ridden only within the scientific enclosure. Much self-confessed pornography (if, at least, one credits the loud protestations of those who make a living by it) is propagated out of an 'undue sense of right' as determinedly held as that of any tract-distributing Victorian. Either the campaign is run in the name of the freedom of the press, or as 'educative'. Pornography is to do us good: to unfreeze the frigid, suggest ideas which the mere unaided imagination could never produce, and tempt us into unknown delights by telling tales of 'the most monstrous enormities committed in field and meadow, that made all ordinary naughtiness appear as child's play'. Even the January 1972 issue of *She* was following this immemorial line in answer to indignant readers' letters: 'But lots of people need help in learning about sex, conquering difficulties and beating that downward plunge of bad-sex, unhappy life, worse sex, misery. That's why we have one or two articles about sex in each issue. But only one or two...' (The last estimate is misleading: the trivially glamorous sex is very pervasive, not confined to articles about sex.) So I felt a little ironically about the letter that followed: 'Think of the thousands of people who read these articles and, although they profess to "know it all", are actually gaining very

[19] *Sunday Times* report, 28 November 1971. It ends with a list of 'guidelines – to help psychiatrists and patients decide whether they should embark on sex as a course of treatment' including, to the patient, 'If you are suffering more than you were before, break it off.'

knowledgeable advice, especially about contraception and V.D. These are a very necessary part of modern life.' Yes they are, and yes I do think about the thousands of people guided by *She* into a low and trivial picture of sex.

Pornography, sexology, sex education, manuals of good advice about marriage, can occasionally be seen to be all the same thing. 'Referring to a cartoon in *Oz 28* which depicted Rupert Bear having sexual intercourse with a character described as "gypsy granny", Dr Harvard said that he thought the message of the cartoon was to criticize the lack of dissemination of sexual education.[20] No doubt it was.

Getting Married, the B.M.A. booklet, is the worst example I know of the way advice, education and science all fall together into pornography. 'Sex Unlimited' and 'Variety is the Spice of Love' (pp. 13, 31) were both phrases I first met in one of those yellow-paper paperbacks that used to circulate clandestinely in the sixth form. 'No one's there to tell you you must or must not do this or that, it's up to you. If your sex life pleases you both it's a happy sex life' (p. 31). By this argument the advantage of marriage is that it prevents anyone from interfering with one's perhaps evil ways. There's no one to tell you – not even God or conscience; for here marriage is the perfect way of reducing sex to any kind of pleasure without reproach. (It is the doctrine of one of the nastiest characters in our literature, January in Chaucer's *Merchant's Tale,* except that he's realistic enough to dispense with his wife's approval.) The identical position is propagated (according to an advertisement in *The New York Review of Books,* 5 October 1972) by Dr Alex Comfort's *Joy of Sex, a Gourmet Guide to Love Making*: 'It's a book that proves [*sic*] that the whole joy of sex-with-love is that *there are no rules, as long as there is mutual pleasure.*' That is in itself a rule which might cause the mutual pleasure-seekers to feel guilt if pleasure for any reason is temporarily absent. The *Vanity Fair* booklet expresses the same idea more simply: 'There is nothing that can happen between two adults in bed that is wrong as long as they both want it' (p. 44). Not even if the adults are, e.g. father and son and their inclinations happen to be towards sadism-masochism ending in the killing of one partner and necrophilous enjoyment of the other? Another author, intelligently reviewed in *Marriage Guidance* (the reviews in that journal are so extremely mixed

[20] *The Times,* 3 July 1971.

as to suggest the editor needs guidance), also gaily asserted that
'as long as there is complete agreement and no embarrassment
about what you are doing, your sexual experiment will never
become "perverted" however peculiar'.[21] It is *infra dig.* to play
upon proper names, but I couldn't help being glad that this
gentleman's first one (we'd better not call it 'Christian') was Bent.
I remain more convinced by Professor Anscombe's view that 'To
marry is, not to enter into a pact of mutual complicity in no
matter what sexual activity upon one another's bodies.'[22] By
comparison with Bent and others the Pope has much more of an
air of knowing what he is talking about: he does at least realize
that we are the same people inside the marriage bed as out and
that those blankets cannot exclude our moral sense, if any.

'Sexessentials . . . Sex like other skills improves with practice
. . . Sex is very very pleasant . . . Wives make great mistresses . . .'
Which one, Family Doctor or *Vanity Fair*? As it happens all
those phrases are the former. The only way of knowing is the
reference to marriage, which for *Vanity Fair* is rather *vieux jeu*
and not quite proper. The greater naïveté of the doctors also
appears in the dictum 'No loving husband would want to cause
his wife pain' (p. 29). Not even if that's what she wants?

'People sometimes wonder if there are times when they
shouldn't make love. They wonder if sex is all right during
pregnancy. If you have any doubts, when that happy time comes,
then ask your doctor' (p. 32). Your doctor will of course then tell
you whether your health is likely to be damaged. That is all that
as a doctor he can tell you – granting him so much. And to that
question of happiness and health the 'should' has been reduced.
I would myself suppose that what is right here must vary from
time to time and couple to couple; I am not committed to the
position of Langland or Tolstoy, though Langland's reverence
for life, his feeling that the abstention of the breasts shows us a
reverence for the pregnant woman, is much more admirable than
the B.M.A.'s pursuit of pleasure. All I object to is the reduction
of a moral question to the calculation of what will give physical
satisfaction and what you can get away with, a reduction absolutely typical of pornography.

Getting Married, just like the B.B.C. or the White Paper on
the Common Market, appears to be disinterested, educative,

[21] May 1972, p. 95.
[22] *The Human World*, no. 7 (1972), p. 23.

scientific, while really it is propagating the new values of our changed and debauched language. It is suitably tabloid in format, and makes the common assumption that we are now incapable of reading plain prose. Instead it ends up with the question-and-answer form (so popular also in the last dark ages) to handle such matters as 'Should a woman "come" at every intercourse?' (the answer is *no*) and 'Can you tell me what is meant by "multiple orgasm"?' (p. 167). Yes, they can, and I hope it makes everybody happy. So back to the medical criterion of perversion: 'But as long as neither of you is harmed, or is making love in this particular way against your will, nobody has the right to censor you or make you feel guilty.' But why am I to pay more attention to the family doctors' opinion, for instance, than the Pope's? (And why, by the way, have they the right to censor [*sic*] us if we *are* harmed? Presumably because they are doctors: which again means that they are not particularly qualified as moral critics.) They can only be convincing through the quality of their argument, and by that I am not impressed.

The booklet seems, indeed, to have taken up a place pre-ordained for it in a Marxist picture of the world. It preaches the late capitalist ideology which will produce contented, decadent consumers of the products glossily advertised on most of the pages. It isn't a very convincing picture of human life or of the possible significance of sex.

We are here in exactly the same world as the heart-to-heart column of the *Sun*.

Dear Doctor Wendy: After 16 years' marriage and a happy and varied sex life with my wife, I find I'd sooner go to bed to sleep.
Even see-through nighties, bathing together, drinking before we make love, don't turn me on.
I am very worried. Do you think we're just too used to each other?
(22 December 1971)

If that was a real letter, not one cooked up in the office, the answer to it is that Mr G.M. has no problem – at least not in terms formulated. Marriage is not ordained as a perpetual turner-on or 'bureaucratized debauch'. We are all mortal and if the party lasted sixteen years that is long enough. Doctor Wendy, however, replied by recommending youth club work and carpentry, as a result of which 'you'll once again be more interested in making love instead of sleeping when you're in bed with your wife'. Then no doubt he'll write to complain to Doctor Wendy about insomnia and have to give up the carpentry.

Marriage itself has become for the *Sun* and the doctors the final consumer good. It is an arrangement to make sex pleasurable, to secure mutual happiness. This is – as well as wildly unrealistic – itself a pornographic opinion. 'Whatever you may think of the religious significance of the wedding service' – and, it's plainly implied, that won't be much – 'these ideas of mutual affection, respect, sympathy and help are the nitty-gritty of marriage.' That is the doctors' paraphrase of the Book of Common Prayer, in which, however, they will look in vain for their immediately following conclusion: 'Where they exist marriages are happy.' Indeed? A marriage with those qualities is perhaps more likely to be tolerable than one without; but it is not they which make it a marriage. A writer in *Marriage Guidance* was logical enough to conclude that such thinking does away with the need for marriage. 'As our fear that divorce is destroying family life is eliminated, we become much less concerned with marriage as the only form for expressing long-range commitments between persons. We can even encourage our public . . . to shop around outside wedlock.'[23] It is evidently not over-obvious to say that the one thing you won't find outside wedlock is marriage, and that if that journal needs to be told as much it's time it changed its name.

It is mere marriage that the Book of Common Prayer offers, and happiness is realistically there only as one of the possibilities. For richer or for poorer, in sickness or in health.

The general erosion of the idea of marriage *is* very alarming. Giving a brief account of the young manhood of D. H. Lawrence, Mr Keith Sagar mentions his woman friends and says 'But Lawrence was not able to bring any of these relationships on to a satisfactory sexual footing.'[24] The belief that sexual relations are of this arrangeable kind is worth mentioning, after all the other examples, only because of the oddity of the phrasing; what I notice more is that when Mr Sagar continues to another relationship of Lawrence's it is with Frieda Weekley, with whom he 'ran away to Germany together to begin a relationship which was to last the rest of Lawrence's life'. The word 'marriage' is not used at all; it isn't worth informing the reader, Mr Sagar assumes,

[23] January 1972, p. 5.
[24] Introduction to *The Mortal Coil and Other Stories* (1971), p. 8.

that Frieda became Lawrence's wife. What matters is that they put their relationship onto a satisfactory sexual footing.

'The object of marriage is to make each other happier. Isn't it?' I would like to draw towards a conclusion by showing why the answer to that rhetorical question from the B.M.A. must be a particular kind of firm NO, and why to answer it 'yes' convicts one of speaking the language of pornography. 'To make each other happier?' I would rather, though not a Christian, pin my colours to this:

Dearly beloved, we are gathered together here in the sight of God, and in the face of this Congregation, to join together this man and this woman in holy Matrimony; which is an honourable estate, instituted of God in the time of man's innocency ... and therefore is not by any to be enterprized, nor taken in hand, unadvisedly, lightly or wantonly, to satisfy men's carnal lusts and appetites, like brute beasts that have no understanding; but reverently, discreetly, advisedly, soberly, and in the fear of God; duly considering the causes for which Matrimony was ordained.

First, It was ordained for the procreation of children, to be brought up in the fear and nurture of the Lord, and to the praise of his holy Name.

Secondly, It was ordained for a remedy against sin, and to avoid fornication; that such persons as have not the gift of continency might marry, and keep themselves undefiled members of Christ's body.

Thirdly, It was ordained for the mutual society, help and comfort, that the one ought to have of the other, both in prosperity and adversity.

The difference is not merely that anything resembling the doctors' criteria of success in marriage comes third in the list, but that it follows from and is subordinated to the other reasons. Marriage can make people happier; I have come across cases of it. It is even true that the happiness may be taken as a sign of the reality of the marriage: the mutual society, help and comfort may suggest to man and wife that they are not merely living together for mutual satisfaction. But 'mutual comfort' in adversity – or even adversity without it – may be an equally good sign of the reality of a marriage, and may make a sense wholly beyond the reach of the family doctors, *Vanity Fair* or the other pornographers.

In *The First Circle* Solzhenitsyn presents, with the truthfulness to life one had thought to have died out of Russian literature with Tolstoy, several cases of marriages that are desperately unhappy, in every imaginable sense, because the husband is in a labour camp for periods that can be indefinitely extended at the whim of a tyrannical state. What could be more natural than for a prisoner in that condition to get what happiness he can? Sologdin does so, and is successful and happy. But the unforgettable thing is the story of Gleb Nerzhin and his wife Nadya, who keep their marriage and resist their temptations. The positively heroic and tragic value of their bond is expressed in the suffering itself – the suffering, also, of those other people who have the misfortune to love them. Anguish is not an ideal, but it is better than the indifferent judgment of everything by 'happiness'. The case could be made more strongly, but at what would have to be greater length, in a discussion of Wordsworth's great tale of Margaret in Book I of *The Excursion*.

Even Jane Austen, not usually thought of as an austere life-denier (Mr Harold Macmillan records that he read *Pride and Prejudice* the morning he was waiting to be invited to become Prime Minister and found it 'soothing') makes Anne Elliot several times reflect like this: 'I should have suffered more in continuing the engagement than I did even in giving it up, because I should have suffered in my conscience.'[25] That 'more' isn't some appeal to a quantification of happiness; it is an absolute statement of a value by which happiness may be judged.

I am not holding unhappy marriages up as a norm or ideal. We must hope that marriage *can* make for happiness. All I am objecting to is the B.M.A. style of seeing their idea of happiness as the 'object' of marriage, and thereby reducing marriage to a technique with a further end, which may be judged to have failed if the end is not attained.

The possibility of a more serious standard of judgment is lacking in *Getting Married* as in all pornography; and there is a direct link here between the possibility of seriousness in sex and in life generally. It is natural for us to take sex seriously but it is also mystical, in the same way that funerals are a perfectly natural part of life but also the mystical addition to putting corpses into the ground. You could imagine a life in which corpses were merely collected with the dustbins and sex was no more than blowing one's nose or picking mushrooms, but it wouldn't be a human life. I will quote the unspeakable *She* for the last time. In the January 1972 issue Mr Peter Fonda said in an interview:

The beasts of the fields and the forests have no problem. When the trees die they fall to the ground and become part of the earth again. But when man dies he puts himself in a box and hopes not to return to the earth.

25 *Persuasion*, chapter XXIII.

These actions are violent to me. A burial is a violent action. It violates the very nature of life in the world to which we owe everything. I can only conclude that man must dislike the world.

The nostalgic wish to return to the life of the animals, to the innocence of the trees, is the same whether it comes out in seeing funerals as an assault on nature, or in seeing sex as insignificant. The 'happiness' the doctors offer, even if one manages to believe in it, looks so trivial if you put it beside the idea of marriage in the Prayer Book.

In the end any significance is better than none; tortured or guilty sex (though, again, not a norm or an ideal) is much better than trivial sex. Even if sexology were right about masturbation as the supreme sexual pleasure, D. H. Lawrence would still be far more convincing, though he is far from maturely judicious on the subject.

'Masturbation is not just something we can make less fuss about; it is a necessary exploration for the ultimate discovery of full adult sexuality.'[26] That is itself verging on pornography: it is talking of sex in a low, meaningless way. I could make the objection by saying that the writer gives no grounds for thinking 'full adult sexuality' more valuable than adolescent masturbation. Both sound deadly dull. Miss Breasted commends somebody for dealing 'with masturbation in a matter-of-fact fashion'.[27] That is only appropriate if masturbation is a matter of fact. If on the other hand it is a matter of human sexuality, to treat it as a matter of fact is to debase human sexuality.

Is masturbation so harmless, though? Is it even comparatively pure and harmless? Not to my thinking. In the young, a certain amount of masturbation is inevitable, but not therefore natural. I think, there is no boy or girl who masturbates without feeling a sense of shame, anger, and futility. Following the excitement comes the shame, anger, humiliation, and the sense of futility. This sense of futility and humiliation deepens as the years go on, into a suppressed range, because of the impossibility of escape.

D. H. Lawrence, 'Pornography and Obscenity', *Phoenix*, p. 179

Lawrence is perhaps overheated here: at any rate he writes on the same subject more calmly and perhaps more convincingly in chapter 9 of *Fantasia of the Unconscious*. Perhaps Tolstoy is overheated too when he talks of adolescent sexuality as a 'fall':

I fell because, in the set around me, what was really a fall was regarded by some as a most legitimate function good for one's health, and by others

26 *T.L.S.*, 16 July 1970.   27 *Oh! Sex Education!* p. 293.

as a very natural and not only excusable but even innocent amusement for a young man. I did not understand that it was a fall, but simply indulged in that half-pleasure, half-need, which, as was suggested to me, was natural at a certain age. I began to indulge in debauchery as I began to drink and to smoke. Yet in that first fall there was something special and pathetic. I remember that at once, on the spot before I left the room, I felt sad, so sad that I wanted to cry – to cry for the loss of my innocence . . .

The Kreutzer Sonata, chapter 7

Overheated? Mr John Bayley, an expert on both Tolstoy and love, thinks so. 'In the sexual guilt that tormented Tolstoy we no longer perceive a problem. It has been taken care of by contraception.'[28] We are being asked that is, as usual, to see a technical development as the answer to a moral question. Mr Bayley on this point thinks he has presented evidence of 'how local and historicall conditioned' were *Tolstoy*'s problems.

Tolstoy's horror and terror are not the experience of sex I would wish for myself or my friends, but they are reliable signs of the extreme significance he found in sex. Without the possibilities of such extremes there is no reason why sex should matter more than blowing one's nose (as indeed it often doesn't in the novels of Mr Bayley's wife). The wish to make sex calm and rational, and the belief that technical devices can remove guilt, necessary as the former sometimes is, so easily become the modern programme of changing the nature of sex, by de-fusing it – just as Dr Coggan's jibbing at calling lusty people 'frail and trembling sheep' was a de-fusing of religion, a removal of God in the interests of humanity. Tolstoy's character's belief that he had sinned and fallen short of the glory of God is, at least, a view of something that mattered terribly in his whole life.

So I am with Lawrence not in offering opinions about masturbation (or about his idea of nature, which is no more attempted science than his 'no boy or girl' is attempted statistics) but in recognizing that he is discussing something very important, found to be so in life. This is the sense that Lawrence and Tolstoy, but not the enlightened and the pornographic, can bring to the matter. Lawrence is truer to life, whether we actually agree with his opinion or not, because he is using with conviction a real language of sex.

And generally speaking I think Lawrence, in his unmatchedly

[28] *The New York Review of Books*, 30 December 1971.

pure and direct way, says all that need be said to define
pornography:

> Pornography is the attempt to insult sex, to do dirt on it. This is unpar-
> donable. Take the very lowest instance,[29] the picture post-cards sold ...
> in most cities. What I have seen of them have been of an ugliness to make
> you cry. The insult to the human body, the insult to a vital human relation-
> ship! Ugly and cheap they make the human nudity, ugly and degraded
> they make the sexual act, trivial and cheap and nasty.
>
>   'Pornography and Obscenity', *Phoenix*, p. 175

– but any uglier, any more degraded, any more cheap and nasty
than a hundred west-end films, every other new fashionable play
and a large proportion of what the B.B.C. offers as family entertainment? No uglier, cheaper and nastier, at any rate, than the
T.L.S. writer on masturbation.

    In the first quotation from D. H. Lawrence the word 'guilty'
is in the background, not stated. It is at least a sign of coherence
on the part of the enlightened that they should wish to do away
with guilt. 'Solid research such as supports the writing of this
book can do much to mitigate the guilt and shame often associated with divorce.'[30] Similarly Miss Germaine Greer exhorts one
group of her disciples to 'Choose lesbianism in an honourable,
clear-eyed fashion, rejecting shame and inferiority feelings as a
matter of principle, whether such feelings exist or not'.[31] The aim
of the aforementioned film of Dr Cole's was – like his earlier
classes in hard-core pornography for Aston undergraduates – 'to
dispel the sense of guilt and shame that surrounds the subject'.
'Anything that can be done to alleviate the guilt complex about
sex is good', said Mr George Melly, defending the notorious *Oz*.
He went on naturally enough, 'We are learning to accept ourselves as animal creatures with needs, desires and fantasies. The
more open sexuality there is, the less feeling of guilt and the less
misery.'[32] (The same report quoted the martyred Neville as saying
that 'the general purpose [of *Oz*] was to elevate and enlighten'.)
Yes, we could abolish guilt if we could lose our humanity and be
animals – or, as Mr Fonda imagined, trees.

[29] Lawrence was writing many years before the modern development
which allows an official of the National Theatre to turn himself into a
pornographic impresario.

[30] *Publishers' Weekly*, quoted in an advertisement in *The New York
Review of Books*, 22 October 1970.

[31] *The Female Eunuch* (1970), p. 294.

[32] *The Times*, 29 June 1971.

Anything rather than face the facts that sex belongs in human life, that it is there subject to all our ways of organizing life, including morality, and that the removal of the possibility of guilt is the removal of the possibility of significance.

It is because marriage guarantees the possibility of significance – because it makes possible, that is, a certain splendour of life as well as the ghastly human muddles we see around us – that marriage is and must remain central to the grammar of sex. That I learn from the Prayer Book, or from observing life, but not from the modern advisers, guides and counsellors, and not from *She* and the rest. Marriage, living hell as it often is (and as it must possibly be if it is to have a chance of being the other thing) and full of guilt and fear as it makes life, is yet the sure sign that our sex is more than 'hot flesh straining on a bed' even when it seems to be just that. We have to retain our judgment; and marriage is the great guarantee that judgment is possible.

Another guarantee is the opposite end from pornography of the imaginative language of sex: the great love poems and novels, The Song of Songs (which now surely sounds much less like a book about sex than *The Encyclopaedia of Adult Relationships*), *Troilus and Criseyde*, *Antony and Cleopatra*, *Macbeth* (*sic*), *Phèdre*, *Le Rouge et le Noir*, *Anna Karenina*, *Women in Love*. To the question how they can be a guarantee, and precisely of what, we must now turn.

6

Notes on the Language of Love:
II, Where have all the Demons Gone?

> The God of Love, a! benedicitee!
> How myghty and how greet a lord is he!
>> Chaucer

> The word has a mild sound; it is used sweetly in poetry and is sung romantically in hymns; it is also uttered affectionately in dark lanes behind trees, and sometimes at street corners; but it appears, for all its mildness, to have something in it very forcible and violent.
>> T. F. Powys

I

What can make sex serious? And what allows us in some cases but not others to dignify the relations between the sexes by the name of love? How do we know that we are serious about sex and what could the evidence be? These may seem strange questions. We know by experience, you might retort, and there's an end on't. I do not deny the force of the retort; it is true at least in the sense that if we are not serious about sex in our own experience we shan't be anywhere else. But we can still ask what experience, or what about it, counts as seriousness.

Could one say, for instance, that the institutions of marriage and the family make sex serious? It is notoriously possible to get married, in church, in a kind of fit of abstraction, and for the ensuing changes in one's life not to matter much. Domestic and sexual arrangements change; perhaps domestic comfort is damaged by the appearance of children. But what makes that serious? – what makes it more than a series of comforts/discomforts, to be talked of happily in terms of success measured by happiness, or mistakes to be rearranged?

Would it make a marriage serious if it were solemnized according to the Anglican rite of 1662 in the Book of Common Prayer? Again I don't think one can say more than it *can* – not that it need. If *N* and *N* do take each other for better or for worse, in those terms, they are doing something serious; but the seriousness still lies in 'well discerning' the sense of what they do.

I *N* take thee *N* to my wedded husband, to have and to hold from this day forward, for better for worse, for richer for poorer, in sickness and in health, to love, cherish, and to obey, till death us do part, according to God's holy ordinance; and thereto I give thee my troth.

That is a guarantee of seriousness whatever happens to the subsequent marriage, but only if it is properly understood, if the 'I will' they also say is sincere.

Here, for once, is a definintion. Love poetry is the creation of sexual passion in language. Poetry is some demon or other uttering himself in common speech; in love poetry the demon belongs to the not wholly respectable family of Venus and Cupid. By this definition anyone who manages to be passionate in language is a poet. I accept the conclusion and heartily concur in the line of thought from Vico to Collingwood which sees poetry as original language and makes us, in that sense, all poets.

Here's another definition: love is the concentration, with delight, upon one object.

What would come of it all he did not know and did not even consider. He felt that all his powers, hitherto dissipated and wasted, were now concentrated and bent with fearful energy on a single blissful goal. And this made him happy. He knew only that he had told her the truth: that he had come where she was, that the whole happiness and meaning of life for him now lay in seeing and hearing her.
Anna Karenina, transl. Rosemary Edmonds, part one, chapter 31

Hate is the same, but with repulsion. Love or hate may define the object loved or hated: thus it is possible to love English Literature, or God, as well as one particular member of the opposite sex.

Though we are all primitive poets it is not given to many to express the demonic, potentially to all the speakers of a language, in writing. Love can be created and published in poems or novels, but when that happens the relation between the love and the whole language is not an ordinary one.

The only thing wrong with pornography is that it is (in a phrase of Mr David Sims's) the demonic by arrangement. Pornography subordinates the passionate to the pleasurable, whereas love poetry need be no more than pure passion – in language. But 'Passion running unrefined/May ruin what the masters taught': if love poetry is *simply* the creation of passion in language, doesn't that mean it is very dangerous? Ought it not to be properly safeguarded and kept from the young?

My definition certainly offers no guarantee that love poetry will always be moral, improving or worthy of imitation in life.

Love poetry may well be both immoral and destructive; Vronsky's is, amongst many other things, both. What can be said for love poetry is that it is always serious because of the relation it makes between passion and language; that is where the guarantee of its seriousness resides. The expression of passion in verbal language already involves a kind of criticism, for the poet (or each of us as primitive poet) has to make his passion a possibility of the language. Doing so is his guarantee that he isn't suffering some merely private and personal derangement (not all lovers are mad, as Aquinas concedes), and when others read it the *poetry* is the guarantee of the seriousness of the feeling. (How do we know the poetry is serious? is naturally the next question, which I shall try to answer in the next chapter by seeing that kind of judgment as a definition of life.) Though there is plenty of bad or trivial verse we call it 'poetry' only by mistimed courtesy. If we judge something to be poetry we also judge it to be serious. The seriousness of love poetry is then the relation it makes of the poet's impulse to his language.

To call something 'love' is to make a judgment of its seriousness. But how is the seriousness shown? How do we know what is true love? For instance can people prove the seriousness of their love by dying for it?

> For with my deeth the trouthe shall be seen

says Chaucer. Will it? Only if the 'trouthe' is already there. (In 'Merciles Beaute' Chaucer doesn't in fact depict himself as dying: he ends up so fat that he counts love not a bean.) Cleopatra tries to prove her love by dying for it, bringing in for good measure (of all things) marriage:

> Husband, I come:
> Now to that Name, my Courage prove my Title.

Does her courage prove her title? That is answered not from the fact of the ensuing death, but from its context after what she has already said. There, perhaps, the death does show that earlier appearances were deceptive and she was serious in her love. But Cleopatra's seriousness is in what she says before she dies, or nowhere.

Does it prove the seriousness of your love for Ireland if you get shot, throwing a nail-bomb in Belfast? Again, it might, but I don't think it need. The concentration upon one object may be there without the poetry. It may be that no terrible beauty is born. 'Perhaps to you,' an editor objects, 'a terrible beauty wasn't born in 1916. Much the same situation, though. Same issue, same death, same folly if you see it all like that.' Leaving aside objections to the politics, my retort to that is: but not the same or comparable *poetry*. I have my doubts about 1916, but not about the seriousness of Yeats's poem, for the 'terrible beauty' is there in its lines for all to read.

'Greater love hath no man than this, that a man lay down his life for his friends.' But it is even possible to lay down your life for your friends in a moment of trivial abandon or despair. You do not *prove* your great love by laying down your life for your friends. Christ's words are nonetheless deep – not because of anything verifiable in them, anything you could prove by experiments with events (which isn't to say that they are not about life) but because the great love is there, if at all, in the words.

II

It seems very natural, indeed obvious to the point of tautology to say that love poets write about love; and the naturalness (which says something about our ideas since the late seventeenth century about thinking and expression) has led to shelvesfull of books expounding, e.g., Donne's doctrines of love, as if the love were something outside his work on which he is writing a verse commentary. The first sign that there is something wrong with this is the dullness of the critical upshot. Every year I examine all too many scripts in which bright and interested young people are led away from poetry by what they see as their duty to write seriously and critically – that is, to discuss a poet's doctrines. This is always a way of losing interest in his poetry. It seems to me, trying to follow out a line of Rush Rhees's thought, that poets don't talk about love, they speak the language of love. If a rather odd phrase can be permitted I'll say poets don't write *about* love, they write love.

Evidently none can write about love. Gifted writers don't try. (Stendhal – but has anyone else?) When anyone does, the result is commonplace and boring. Not because love is boring. It is the theme of poems and plays and stories more frequently, perhaps, than any other. And a new portrayal of it by any real writer will always hold us. But if he starts to tell us *about* love, we stop reading.
     Rush Rhees, 'The Tree of Nebuchadnezzar', *The Human World*,
                                                           no. 4 (1971), p. 24

Love poets create their love in what they write. Love poetry is more like ending a letter 'with love' (a phrase of very various force) or saying 'give my love to', than discussing ideas of love.

Mr Adrian Mitchell, one of our more talented contemporaries, I think, despite his recent stage travesty of Blake, has a poem with a chorus-line

> Making good love, making good good love.

This is *almost* what love poets always do in their verses. They make love. Whether it's good love or not is, however, another question. Whether Mitchell is in fact making love depends on the movement of his verses. I suspect he is closer in that poem to making gooey sentiment, making gooey, gooey sentiment; but that will only be established by critical discussion.

This is why Dame Helen Gardner's way of discussing the matter is so misleading.

> We cannot assume that the best love poets were the best lovers; and there must be many persons capable of passionate and exalted love who either could not, or in most cases had not the slightest desire to, write poetry about their feelings. There does not seem any particular reason why we should assume that there are more inarticulate and poetically inept persons among those with whom religion is a powerful emotion than among those who feel other emotions strongly.
>
> *Religion and Literature* (1971), p. 127

But is poetry writing about – describing, that is, or reporting – separately existing feelings? Has it not more to do with something that could not exist without expression? It is not as if the object, love, is shivering naked in the poet's mind waiting to be clothed with words. If poets express love in some especially telling way they have created love beyond the common (though through the possibility of making it a common possession). So it may well be that in that sense the great poets are the great lovers – though that wouldn't be a reason for recommending girls to take up with them. (And Wordsworth is a greater love poet than Byron.) Dame Helen defines religious poetry as a man writing of truths 'which are not presented as personal discoveries, values that are not his individual values' (p. 135). This is a contradiction in terms. To accept a 'truth' if the acceptance is sincere or goes deep, is to make it one's own; and the poets are personally discovering truths even if the truths are already known to others. The love poems and the religious poems are respectively the truth of love and of religion as the poetry shows the poet to understand them. A poet who satisfies himself that he has expressed his religion, or his love, in a sentimental, shallow poem is judging his religion or his love to be sentimental or shallow.

What was love for Dryden? His lyrics show his love as a matter of strong, jolly but rather trivial lusts, called 'fires', which lead to one of two states, like a primitive finite-state language:

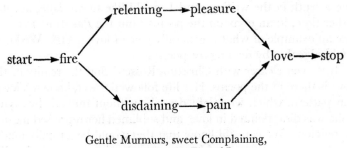

> Gentle Murmurs, sweet Complaining,
>   Sighs that blow the Fire of Love;
> Soft Repulses, kind Disdaining,
>   Shall be all the Pains you prove.
> Ev'ry Swain shall pay his Duty,
>   Grateful ev'ry Nymph shall prove;
> And as these Excel in Beauty,
>   Those shall be Renown'd for Love.

If love is in this way reduced to pleasure and/or pain, it is coarse yet tame. The fires are not fires anyone has had to pass through; they are furnaces stoked under the boilers. ''Tis love that has warm'd us/In spight of cold weather/He's brought us together . . .' Dryden is therefore not a love poet, though he has enough sexiness to give a hint to Purcell, who certainly is, wonderfully, a speaker of love, when he turns such stuff into beautiful and passionate music.

If a poet's love is in what he writes or nowhere, we have in love poetry love available for criticism.

Hardy's *Poems of 1912–13* are a fumbling, sincere exploration which eventually creates the poet's love for his wife, there in the poetry. Did Hardy love her? To read the scholars one would think the question could be settled by an appeal to his letters or the memoirs of other people – which generally say 'No, after the first infatuation he didn't love her.'

> but was there ever
> A time of such quality, since or before
> In that hill's story?

The poetry answers the question; the poetry gives the quality to the time and creates the love. These poems could not have been written except by the man who had Hardy's particular life behind him. But the question what was real in what had really happened in Hardy's life is settled by the poetry itself. I instance this case because it is a peculiarly clear one of the poet's discovering a truth *in* the writing (and I would like to say *how*, at some other time, in an essay on the poems); but the *Poems of 1912–13* are an example of what is generally true of love poetry. We know and judge that by reading the poetry.

It is even clearer with Christina Rossetti that the reality of the love is there in the poems. Her life followed a well-known Victorian pattern, which we might describe without untruth by saying 'She was disappointed in love, and sublimed her repressed passion in religion'. We can still know that that would be a totally inadequate account, because of her poetry: the significance in her life not translatable into that formula is the poetry of renunciation itself. That was her fate, rather than any events that occurred. (W. M. Rossetti's edition, if its dates are accurate, shows that many of the best poems were written before Christina Rossetti said her first 'no': she found her fate in poetry before living it.)

If sex is not serious for us we shall not get much out of love poetry, but it is also true, and more startling, that if there is no love poetry there is no seriousness in the relations between the sexes. In the wide sense in which we are all primitive poets, this may perhaps be allowed. Love poetry in this primitive sense is itself the seriousness of love, dependent, as I argued last chapter, on a common language as well as the individual life. But I also mean the proposition to apply to love poetry in the more ordinary sense of the treatment of love in the verbal language and particularly in its imaginative literature. Love poetry is the guarantee that love can be taken seriously in the common language.

He who writes real love poetry is *eo ipso* making what seriousness he can of sex; and if anyone reads the poem the language is shown to be one in which passion can be expressed. I quote from an unpublished essay by Mr David Sims:

Without a love poetry of some kind in our own language ... there will be no longer any interest in sexuality. There will be, of course, sexual activity. No one will be any less eager to pursue, flee and grapple, than they are now. I am not even imagining an absence of language, insofar as speaking a language can be, in this case, wholly a matter of knowing what verbal devices one should use to obtain sexual gratification and of accompanying such gratification – or frustration – with verbal substitutes for cries. All I say is that to go through such hoops so blindly is to retreat towards the bestial wilderness Vico speaks of.

Making sex serious is not the same as making love good.

Clown: Would you have a love-song, or a song of good life?
Sir Toby: A love-song, a love-song.
Sir Andrew: Ay, ay, I care not for good life.

Twelfth Night (II. iii)

(When it comes it *is* a love-song: it is 'O Mistress Mine'.) Mr Mitchell's line might have been better if it had run

Making serious love, making serious, serious love,

and better still

Making love serious, making love serious, serious.

That is what love poets always do. I hope it is clear that I don't mean love poetry cannot be comic: on the contrary there is something wrong with a totally uncomic love poetry. (I am thinking of the limitations of Wordsworth's achievement, going on to the crippling of Tennyson by mellifluous solemnity.) Donne at his best, at his scarce moments of greatness, creates an immoral love which is always on the edge of falling into the comically absurd, or of dissolving into uninteresting lust. He is a great love poet nevertheless simply because his poetry (and nothing else) shows him capable of making something serious of what in Restoration writers is simply, and frivolously, the hunt for women. (Cf. David Sims in *The Human World* no. 6 (1972), reviewing Wilbur Sanders).

It goes deep with us to see love as good; and let us hope some sense can be made of the feeling. But Mr David Holbrook is quite right[1] to see he must turn against D. H. Lawrence if he is to go on believing that love is reparative, good, creative and not their opposites, for Lawrence (who laboured incessantly and with genius to make the sex-relationship 'valid and precious') won't let him; nor will any other great writer. Real love poetry is as likely to make life unbearable as to have a therapeutic effect. '*Intolerable* music falls . . .' To insist that love is always good when it is itself is to give up hope of taking it seriously.

[1] In *Human Hope and the Death Instinct* (1971).

On the contrary, poets are often most serious, convincing and true to life when they show the destructiveness of love.[2] It goes deeply against our grain, and in some ways rightly, to admit that love can really be

Vénus toute entière à sa proie attachée

as Racine characterizes the love of Phèdre (and as Jane Austen, I have heard it convincingly said, might well have characterized the love of Fanny Price with Fanny as Venus and Edmund as the prey). But that is love, though not, thank God, the only variety, and it has to be so called; Racine shows in the power of his words in that play that this is one true picture of love. Another is the wish to torment and bully which Tolstoy shows the old Prince Bolkónsky unrestrainedly practising on his daughter the Princess Mary. It is also very possible to be (as Rush Rhees translated a phrase of Wittgenstein's) 'broken up by love' – though also to find in it the 'grete worthyness' of life.

Shakespeare is the greatest poet of destructive love; I shall work back to our modern failure to appreciate that. I mean not only the relevant sonnets, but also *Othello, Antony and Cleopatra, Hamlet, King Lear* and *Macbeth*. Hamlet's love of Ophelia is unmanning and destructive – and couldn't be anything else, given their respective characters and situations; yet that and the feeling of Claudius for Gertrude are the two convincing instances of love in the play.

The extreme case here is the Macbeths, almost the only lovingly married couple in Shakespeare, whose love for each other is *the same* as their monstrous creativity in murder. Lady Macbeth is *femme inspiratrice*, and the concentration of Macbeth's love upon her is his only source of inspiration for the artistic slaughter which is what he wants of the world. Macbeth *wants* the bloody horrors of the end of the play, but it takes his love to allow him to realize his ambition.

[2] Cf. 'A man who killed the woman he loved because she was dying from cancer was sent to a mental hospital for an indefinite period ... The judge told Searby: "... She was enduring terrible physical misery but she had a right to live. Her misery could well have been discounted by your love. I will not accept that you killed her out of affection. Love doesn't kill life, it supports and sustains it." ' – the *Daily Telegraph*, 25 March 1972. No, in that case love evidently didn't sustain life. The woman certainly had a right to live, but the man was apparently sent to a madhouse instead of a gaol in order to sustain the judge's untenable idea of love.

Act III scene iii, for instance, is a love-passage between Macbeth and Lady Macbeth. At the beginning of the scene, having accomplished the murder of Duncan and the 'election' of Macbeth to the throne, they are both finding life very weary, flat, stale and unprofitable. They are trying to view their situation from a sensible political point of view, and at the beginning of the scene any love there is is a kind of tenderness, much mixed with nostalgia and regret. Lady Macbeth says (and her figure of speech is worth noticing):

> Nought's had, all's spent
> Where our desire is got without content:
> 'Tis safer, to be that which we destroy,
> Then by destruction dwell in doubtfull joy.

The appeal to 'safer' is the appeal to commonsense. Yet it is the *doubtful* joy (the *dredeful* joy of the first stanza of Chaucer's *Parliament of Fowls*) of murderous love which is their salvation from the regrets of the opening of the scene. Macbeth comes in and even envies Duncan. 'After lifes fitfull Fever, he sleepes well;' and Macbeth seems too to want the sleep of death. Lady Macbeth's reply is again tender, loving and melancholy. 'Gentle my Lord' she calls him and her 'sleeke o'er your rugged Lookes' surely contains a stage direction for her tenderly to caress him. The alternative is the fitful fever of love. Macbeth and Lady Macbeth come to life again, and change the character of their love into what is for them the real thing, when Macbeth abandons commonsense and surrenders himself to the truly creative impulse of his 'violent love' (the phrase he has used, truthfully, to describe the murder of the grooms):

> O full of Scorpions is my Minde, deare Wife:
> Thou know'st, that *Banquo* and his *Fleans* lives.

Are these scorpions in his mind hurting Macbeth? Or (or even if they are) may they not be the stirrings of the inspiration he really wants? The last line, at any rate, is Lady Macbeth's cue to go right over from tender melancholy and nostalgia to new life, inspiration, and the arousal of sexual love.

> *Lady*: But in them, Natures Coppie's not eterne.
> *Macb*: There's comfort yet, they are assaileable,
>   Then be thou jocund: ere the Bat hath flown
>   His Cloyster'd flight, ere to black *Heccats* summons
>   The shard-borne Beetle, with his drowsie hums,

> Hath rung Nights yawning Peale,
> There shall be done a deed of dreadful note.

We then come to perhaps the most horrible line in English, in which Macbeth's perfectly genuine endearment is the same as his artistic inspiration for the next 'terrible feat', realized in the next scene.

> Be innocent of the knowledge, dearest Chuck,
> Till thou applaud the deed.

The scene that began in dejection ends in the triumphant arousing in Macbeth of night's black agents – that is, the arousing of his active passion for his wife, and of his murderous creativity. The two are, throughout the play, quite inseparable.

That is one way of taking love seriously, but not of making it good. It may be said that *Macbeth* shows the monstrousness of that love, shows it for what it is, and thereby perhaps vindicates other, better love. But this works both ways. Macbeth and Lady Macbeth love each other; and if there is good love to be made there is theirs too, for it has to be called by the same name.

It seems to me that the *very* great writers, the people who show in the depth of their grasp of life how far humanity can go, unanimously show *both* sides of love (and that is the only doctrine to be had of them). There might be a sincere lyric poet who showed only love's destructiveness but he would be comparatively minor. In the great people love is good and evil, splendid and ridiculous. (The last is one of the words applied to love by Biron, the first of Shakespeare's characters also to show its splendour; and Catullus made love a *res ridicula* in the same poetry which celebrates its beauty.) Chaucer puts the lines promising the fulfilment of 'al good aventure' above *the same* gate into the garden of love which also leads, in *The Parliament of Fowls*, to 'the sorowful weir/There as the fish in prison is al drye.' All these things are love, they all meet in Chaucer's images of Venus, where you can't have one side without the other.

I cannot contend then (though, since I too live in our century in English, I would dearly like to) that the love made by the poets is always good, only that it is always 'anything but trivial', and that its being so in our reading guarantees the seriousness, though not the goodness, of that part of our lives. If love poetry is life-enhancing it is necessarily so only in that sense: it shows that we take love seriously, or it may shock us into doing so.

But this also saves us from the complementary trap of dismissing love poetry when it is immoral. If it is real and true, though immoral, we have to take it seriously. What do Paolo and Francesca find in that book by the wicked Galeotto? Sex! Fornication! Dante would say, and he enforces his opinion and gets rid of the pair by putting them in hell. This is a wrong and too easy way of judging which begs the question of the seriousness they have created. For what Dante's poetry shows, with the 'final certitude of speech/Which hell itself cannot unlock' is that what Paolo and Francesca find, *tutto tremante*, is not something easily to be dismissed as carnal sin, but love. Galeotto lets the God of Love into their lives; and that is what love poetry always does, whether the God of Love comes from hell or heaven. And the reader has more of a problem than Dante will allow.

III

I know of hardly any serious creation of love in imaginative literature published in Britain since Lawrence and Yeats, the absence of love being the yawning gap in T. S. Eliot's *oeuvre*. This may simply be due to my ignorance; when there is no serious reviewing one is lucky to know if anything real is coming out. It is, at any rate, indisputable that no contemporary English writer has achieved general recognition or even general attention as a poet or novelist of love.

I am not suggesting that if we go for forty years without a great love poet that need in itself be a matter for great concern. What worries me is that there seems something about our language which rules out love poetry; and if so we lose not only the possibility of new love poetry, but also the possibility of reading the love poets we have (the feebleness of criticism in this area is a later theme) and with that the guarantee that our sexual experience can be serious.

Love is strangely absent from highly-thought-of modern novels. Miss Iris Murdoch's characters, to be sure, fall in and out of love with the frequency and nonsensicality with which other people when in a run-down condition catch colds. Some symptoms appear, *A* is said to be in love with *B*, then the symptoms go away and all is as it was. The failure of *The Middle Age of Mrs Eliot* to treat love other than soppily is the limit of Mr Angus Wilson's genuine talent. Mr David Storey can give us something of the male comradeship which is also important in the Anglo-Saxon poems with which he has a certain affinity, but when sex comes he seems to me to be brutal rather than passionate. At all events, to the best of my knowledge we have no novelist who can present love so unaffectedly – so free from the wish to be clever, perverse, or art – with the natural importance it has in life, as Solzhenitsyn: one somehow can't imagine an English or American novelist publishing anything so straightforward and deep as the relationship of Kostoglotov and Vera Gangart in *Cancer Ward*.

As for formal poetry, one might mention the work of Professor F. T. Prince, which seems to me not quite love poetry, in being elegant (need I say I do not mean that term pejoratively?) but not, to my mind, passionate. 'Soldiers Bathing' is (I think rightly) his best-known poem, and representative of what he can do; and there the *poetry* is in phrases like 'all's pathos now' and 'the sweetness of his nakedness' – in contrast with which

> for so few
> Can suffer all the terror of that love

is writing *about*, pointing to something outside the poem. Mr Prince is not himself one of those so few, and in his later verse his elegance seems to me to run to prettiness. I don't think the real love poets are ever pretty writers.[3]

[3] A serious admirer of Professor Prince's work tells me that the dramatic monologues are the real thing, but I cannot see that they alter the picture. 'The Old Age of Michelangelo', for instance, is still, for me, writing *about* the old man's love, and the thing created *in* the poem is the elegiac feeling of looking at the love which is not itself there. Not to turn this into a discourse, I'll only say I think the address to Messer Thomas Cavaliere at lines 84–95 is the characterizing instance of the poem's elegiac response to love:

> Cold, burning with sorrow,
> I am naked in that sea and know
> The sad foam of the restless flood
> Which floats the soul or kills, and I have swum there
> These fifty years and more,
> And never have I burned and frozen
> More than I have for you,
> Messer Tommaso.

The speaker is still only, sadly, saying what he knows, looking at himself in that plight, and showing us not the plight itself but his resultant meditation. Perhaps this is the poet's intention; if so my point still stands. Prince is anything but a foolish passionate man.

I like, too, Mr David Holbrook's poems: they are so decent and so unafraid of being decent ('Unholy Marriage', for instance): but that again points to the limitation on poetry I am trying to discuss, for who would ever use 'decent' as a word of praise for one of the great poets of passion? It is a word that would separate Herbert from Donne, Gower from Chaucer – and David Holbrook from D. H. Lawrence. (On the other hand 'decent' supplies a sufficient criterion for judging adversely the work of Sylvia Plath, and Mr Holbrook's judgment is made as forcibly by putting his poems next to hers as in his critical writings.) But the poetry I am discussing can be positively devilish, and is always demonic.

Mr Adrian Mitchell has to his credit at least one genuine love poem, called 'All Fools' Day':

> A man sits counting the days of spring,
> His hands may tremble but his mind won't stir,
> And one thought runs through all his watching:
> 'I would have burnt my heart for her.
>
> 'If she had recognized my face
> As I knew hers, and listened to me sing,
> I would have left the careless human race
> For one hour of her careful loving.
>
> 'When spring swings round again, and I am here,
> I will forget the terrors of her voice –
> But I would stay with terror at my ear
> And burn my heart, if I had any choice.'

I call this genuine because it moves me; it commands tone and feeling. But in the end it is obscure, not in the sense that one doesn't understand the meaning, but that the meaning itself is vague. I feel the violence of the emotion in the image 'burn my heart', but indefinite violence of feeling is *all* I feel. 'Terror' is certainly one of the necessary words, and Mitchell has done enough work in the movement of these verses to justify his using it; but it remains such a vague terror. The poem does, in a way, 'tremble'; but Mitchell doesn't know well enough what he feels (the real self-knowledge here) because he can't say it exactly enough.

The only fully and finally successful love poems nowadays express the impossibility of expression.

> TALKING IN BED
> Talking in bed ought to be easiest,
> Lying together there goes back so far,

An emblem of two people being honest.
Yet more and more time passes silently.
Outside, the wind's incomplete unrest
Builds and disperses clouds about the sky.

And dark towns heap upon the horizon.
None of this cares for us. Nothing shows why
At this unique distance from isolation
It becomes still more difficult to find
Words at once true and kind,
Or not untrue and not unkind.

Philip Larkin, *The Whitsun Weddings*

To show the success of this poem one would only have to point to
the way defeat is so well expressed in the nostalgia for iambic
pentameter, the near approach to traditional regularity of metre
which in the end lapses, with the effect of resignation (not
patience) into octosyllabics. The last two lines also wearily abandon the great ambition of love, substituting a decency and nice-
ness ('true and kind') so unpassionate and unsustaining as to run
easily enough, elsewhere in the poet's work, to an equally unpassionate and weary nastiness ('If, My Darling'). But this is the
end for love poetry. Anything that follows has either to be
pastiche (of Lawrence in 'Wedding Wind' and 'Wants', of Eliot
at the end of 'The Whitsun Weddings') or completely unemotional. Ronald Duncan's little poem has gone the further step:

Words are a net,
Feeling, the water escapes through the meshes
I fish for silence.

Here the presence or absence of feeling doesn't seem to matter
much: he is as calm as any other fisherman. But are the fishes
there?

When we descend to the pop- and circus-poets of the last few
years we find them all in this state of *belle indifférence*. The verses
in the jauntily-titled anthology *Love, Love, Love*,[4] the love poems
of the age of sexology, sex manuals, sex education and pornography, are absolutely unemotional. Their theme too is often
failure of expression, which appears not expressing itself as in
Larkin's poem, but as Duncan's next stage.

I wanted to say
I love you

[4] Edited P. Roche (1967).

> In fourteen different languages
> But most of all (most
> Difficult of all) in English
>
> I wanted to say a lot of things,
> But they all seem to have lost themselves
> Somewhere on the way; and now I'm here
> There's nothing I can say except
> Hello, and
> Yes, I'd like some coffee, and
> What shall we find to talk about
> Before the night burns out?

That starts promisingly, but there is nothing in the second stanza to bear out the poet's statement that he wants to say something. He seems not to want anything much, including her. Donne makes an interesting comparison. He is not in difficulties about what to talk about: he has only one subject, and not all that much time to treat it, since he is more interested in action. (Not to dreame all my dreame, let's act the rest.)

> Sometimes the line's died
> Between our eyes.
> What's the matter?
> You've said.
> Nothing
> I've replied.

Nothing will come of nothing. Donne, once he gets his eyebeams twisted with the girl's, won't leave off so easily. But these people seem so unconcerned about their boredom – which is what it amounts to.

> You rose
> and suddenly there was so much
> I wanted to say
> But I couldn't.

What makes the poet so sure then that he wanted to say anything? There seems no point in naming the authors of these indistinguishable verses.

These poets, and the ones in the Penguin anthology *Children of Albion*[5] seem for the most part tired to death, as if, having outlived their language and emotions, they have nothing left but to sink into eternal sleep.

> I was tired and lass-
> itude lay over me as I

[5] Edited Michael Horovitz (1969).

> lay on the bed. What got me up
> and to the table
> was to write this. Enough
> to get me on my feet, to sit here
> with damp hair and wanting to go to sleep.

Was it *really* enough to get him on his feet? Why not follow the natural inclination? 'Tis perhaps a good dullness, about which like Miranda he has no choice. But he will be writing.

The characteristic love of these tired people is

> a woman to love, if not exclusively,
> at least with some claims to continuity.

These lines do at least express the tiredness. 'The flesh goes tired on one's bones' reading them, and I am strongly reminded of Mr George Melly's definition of love as 'a steady sexual liaison'. What a bore! Demons are at least never boring.

When these poets do attempt feeling, the resultant sentimentality, of an old-fashioned literary kind, can be surprising. I used to be taught at school that Eliot and Pound had succeeded the Georgians in the twenties: here is Mr Adrian Henri in 1967:

> REMEMBER
>
> And somewhere
> It will always be Whitsun and summer
> with sandals to keep the rain from your sunburnt feet
> And you will have just given me a bunch of artificial flowers
> lilies-of-the-valley made of cloth with stiff glossy leaves
> And turn and wave goodbye smiling
> hair over your eyes caught in sunlight by the windowframe
> ... Remember?

The possibility that the cliché of the last two lines is deliberate, done for some ironical reminiscence of the attitudes of past poets and Victorian painters, will not survive a reading of the rest of Mr Henri's work. He is, young acquaintances inform me, a great poet, and he certainly appears in all the anthologies.

The death of emotion and the failure of expression may not be so surprising: what is likely to startle more (though it fits my case equally well) is that the poems in both *Love, Love, Love,* and *Children of Albion* are devoid of sexuality.

> Maybe things could have been better.
> We are unable to make more than love.

But are they able to make that? Even when in bed (in these poems as much the venue as the May-morning-green-mead in the medieval poets, and as conventionalized) they are so nonchalant. The usual praise of a girl is that she is an animal:

> When my woman moves
> she does not
> break into a thousand pieces
> into air.
> Her body is of earth
> upright on beautiful
> animal legs
> like a creature of forests will stand
> among trees
> quite silent
> one of them.

It is good to know the girl can move without breaking into a thousand pieces, but the lapse from even the animal to the vegetable is quite right, for though these girls may be as inarticulate as animals, they seem not to rise to the animal level of vigour. There's nothing in the least like

> Though we cannot make our sun
> Stand still, yet we will make him run.

Instead,

> You are a creature
> that is beautiful that can sing,
> You're a wood anemone ...

(See graceless Venus to a virgin turn'd! (*Dunciad* III. 110))

How sweet! But is that all she can do? It wouldn't have been enough for John Donne. He wouldn't have been satisfied to go to bed with a wood-anemone. What happens in those beds? One isn't in any similar doubts about Donne's. What happened there was sexual intercourse, often of an unsweet and un-nice kind, but manically pursued by Donne with the poetic seriousness of his lines.

> Or *snorted* we in the seven sleepers den?
> 'Twas so. But THIS, all pleasures fancies bee.
> If ever any beauty I did see
> Which I desired, and *got*, 'twas but a dreame of thee.
> (my italics)

Donne writes as one who has really lusted after girls, whose sex includes smells and stickiness, not to be prettified away by any glory his verse may make of it. But

> Here's to the girl who stands up straight
> and lies down so
> no faiths no fears no promises
> we come and we go.

With things like faith and fears has gone sex. No love no sex no nastiness either; and he seems to come and go without doing anything in between.

The absence of anything passionate – of, that is to say, love and sex – makes these poems so nice, pretty and boring. *Love, Love, Love,* ought to have been called *Nice, Nice, Nice.* Love is supposed to be blind, but in the real poets he seems to me clairvoyant. Here everything is a nice vague mush; nothing shocks, interests, or makes the reader see newly.

The Children of Albion have almost lost the idea that poets *write.* With the new status of poetry as live popular entertainment the words of the poem have changed from something like scores for the reader to perform to something more like programme notes, which make no sense without the performance. (Another best-selling collection was called *The Mersey Sound.*) These texts belong more to the sermon tradition than to poetry. I don't refer to the rather clogging didacticism with which many of them order us to make love, but the difficulty of knowing how to read them. Why are almost all old sermons so dull and musty? Not because of the nature of sermons, which were for hundreds of years the liveliest entertainment of our ancestors, but because a sermon demands virtuoso performance. The changes of pace and tone, the mimicry, the use of the body for expressive attitudes, are supplied by the preacher not by the text, and the text is therefore not quite a self-sufficient literary form. When a sermon becomes literature these remarks no longer apply: Chaucer gives us all the preacher's parts of the sermon usually missing from the text when he writes the Pardoner, though not when he writes his own sermon, *The Parson's Tale.* The difference between written poetry and the sermon is particularly striking in the case of Donne, whose sermons seem so jerky and disproportionate because we need Donne to perform them, but whose verse contains the instructions for performance within itself, so that Donne's control of the speaking voice in his verse is a commonplace of criticism.

The *Children of Albion* writers (with the almost unique exception of John Arden, who seems to be there by mistake) are writing texts like sermons, which get any life they may have in professional performance, but on the page are quite inert, giving the reader no hint about how they should be read. Perhaps love is there in the performance; but if it isn't there in the poems one can't call them love poems.

> In the cracking up
>   of my body
>   my organs are being sorted
>   by master eyes;
> as a shadow walks into life
>   and purple colours.
>
>   I move
>   cold as a fish in hell
>   shaking my body.
>
>
>   And again, the boy
>   combing my body
>   with an electric comb.
>
>   (p. 153)

What explanation *could* there be for that layout, except as some sort of esoteric instruction to a performer?

Of course not quite all the Children of Albion are so feeble. I think if they were, and if it became general, the world would stop. Mr Gael Turnbull seems a civilized writer in strange company, and Mr Bernard Kops has just one poem ('The Sad Boys') in which he succeeds in controlling his nostalgia and making it charming. But as a bloc, which they unmistakably are, these writers are worse than others because they should have known better. They see themselves as the heirs of English literature and they claim centrality. They have in some cases gone through the motions of reading some of the English poets – though it can't be said that they have understood them – and the attack on poetry seems willed and deliberate. It is as if they are trying to make sure that the language of Donne and Shakespeare and Blake *cannot* now express passion. They won't have it. Yet they will try to speak for Blake and impose themselves as the present day Blakean poetic.

What their works have done to Blake is an epitome of their feeble literariness[6] and of what *that* has done to the possibility of

---

[6] The Children of Albion are often more literary than the writers of the *New Lines* they execrate. One poem called 'I have considered consider-

the demonic in our English. The word for it is perhaps emascu-
lation. Blake becomes a patron of intellectual fuzziness and of
the death of emotion. That is the way Mr Adrian Mitchell seems
to have gone since he was capable of writing the love poem I
quoted. His 'Lullaby for William Blake' gently lays Blake to sleep
– not the real Blake available in the libraries, but the patron of
the emasculated.

> Blakehead, babyhead,
> Your head is full of light...

– the light defined as babyish. The poem ends

> Blakehead, babyhead,
> Accept this mug of crude red wine –
> I love you.

This 'love' is, by my argument, defined in what the poem does.
Love is here feeble literary sentiment. (And Blake's poetry provides one great standard for making the judgment.) My point is
that there are no tygers amongst the writings of the Children of
Albion, and couldn't imaginably be. The effort of all these nice,
sentimental, and rather feeble-minded boys and girls seems on the
contrary to be to fix the tigers and make them tame.

Mr Mitchell seems to me the saddest case, because as I tried
to show he has a certain poetic gift; he is now so given over to the
present situation as to have gone quite soft.[7]

> Peace is milk
> War is acid
> The elephant dreams of bathing in lakes of milk.
> Acid blood
> Beats through the veins
> Of the monstrous, vulture-weight fly,
> Shaking, rocking his framework.

ably' begins 'I have considered considerably./There's not much object
in that sentence.' (It was John Wain, that old-style professional, who
contributed to several anthologies a poem called 'Poem without a Main
Verb'.)

[7] In politics, too. His puppet-play *Punch and Judas* was one of the last
signs of life from C.N.D., really sharp and well done; and his attack on
the then Lord Home for saying we are willing to die for Berlin was
at the least a lively piece of rhetoric. But the more recent moans about
Vietnam ring very hollow to me: the sentimentality of a man telling
himself what he ought to be feeling. Vietnam has become a sort of opium
of the people to Mr Mitchell.

Pausing to observe only the childish simplicity of this symbolism, so unlike the deliberate restrictions of *Songs of Innocence* made by 'a man who knew he had it within him to write "The Tiger"', I merely observe that this boils down to 'Love is pap, war is nasty.'

> Let the pot-smokers blossom into milk-coloured mental petals.

By all means, if they can. But why worry?

> We all need to be breast-fed
> And start again,

Pap! Love is nice, war is nasty. It isn't even true: love is anything but nice. Being weaned is the first step along the path to seeing as much.

> For al be that / I knowe nat Love in dede
> Ne wot how that / he quiteth folk here hyre
> Yit happeth me ful ofte / in bokes rede
> Of his myrakles / and his crewel yre
> Ther rede I wel / he wol be lord and syre
> I dar nat seyn / his strokes been so sore
> But 'God save swich a lord' / I can no moore.

You won't read of Love's miracles or cruel ire in Adrian Mitchell's recent work, or find there anything of Chaucer's terror and awe.

> Make love well, generously, deeply.
> There's nothing simpler in the savage world,
> Making good love, making good good love.

Or, there's nothing nicer in the nasty world. It isn't true. Poetry is here the antidote to passion, the remedy of love 'Drink more milk.' Or, a pinta of love a day does a body good. Meanwhile, as Chaucer elsewhere wrote,

> the God of Love anon
> Beteth his winges and farwel, he is gone.

And so Mr Mitchell even falls into the technology of love I discussed last chapter.

> STUNTED SONNET
> Love is like a cigarette –
> The bigger the drag, the more you get.

No, that isn't true either. Mr Mitchell has ended up agreeing with C. S. Lewis.

Impossible to take love seriously? If these poets were the whole language one would say so: as it is perhaps all I mean is

'impossible to get published if you do', which is, as far as 'the age'
goes, pretty much the same. But I do suspect the change in language goes deeper and that it is connected for instance, with the
great embarrassment we feel at the unironic expression of emotion.
The English are notoriously reticent, and that isn't what I mean,
or the necessary criticism which can object to too naked feeling.
But in the novels of the supposedly repressed Victorian age men
and women do manage to make their consuming passions clear
to one another – in *Anna Karenina*, or *Daniel Deronda*, for
instance. Can we? And if we can't does that mean that we cannot
even *experience* anything passionate? That, at any rate, seems to
be the testimony of our literature, since Lawrence and Yeats.

Moreover, it seems as difficult for critics to recognize the demonic
as for poets to create it. I am not making the claim that they can't
and I can, and I say so not out of ill-timed modesty but to record
the feeling of bafflement which I share with the other critics and
which I think is the state of the language. I think I see some of
the things wrong with criticism but it is part of my observation
that as soon as I think I'm getting there the 'there' vanishes. I
feel, as May persuades January when he has got the use of his
eyes back inconveniently soon, that I have a glimpsing but no
certain sight.

How should a critic praise a love poem? Critical talk is necessary but dangerous. The language of health and sickness is used
by both F. R. Leavis and the Book of Common Prayer, and this
can be convincing so long as we realize it is metaphorical.
(Healthy sex, sex as exercise or, as it might be put, physical jerks,
is another matter which I don't think could ever be made convincing.) Love itself can be thought of convincingly as a disease
('the loveris maladye/of Ereos', or in Biron's image the plague)
and that is perhaps less of a metaphor than to speak of the health
of love. It is not enlightening to draw an analogy between goodness in love and having a healthy appetite or bowel-movements.
The critics who do so seem to be casting around for something
they can recognize and feel at home with. Another result is to try
to recognize as love any decent relations to which the words 'normal' or 'normative' can be applied. They don't seem much more
true to life or much more of a compliment to 'Cupid our Lord'
than 'decent'. We might say something is downright *abnormal*,
but to use 'normal' of love is rather like talking about 'normal'

poems. How could 'normal' not judge love by some statistical rule of thumb? – most likely an economic one.

One of the many ways in which *Mr. Weston's Good Wine* is a great work is in its offer as central and in a sense 'normal' of a love which defeats all normative preoccupations and occurs only by a miracle. The ordinary love that keeps life going in that novel, the light wine of life, is Luke Bird's for Jenny Bunce. But Luke Bird isn't far off mad (converting Squire Mumby's bull and the vicarage geese to Christianity) and his love becomes 'normative' only when, in a passage of splendid revelation mentioned below, Mr. Weston turns his well-water into wine:

I have reason to think,' said Luke, in a very low tone, 'that Jenny is a young woman.'

Landlord Bunce laughed loudly.

Luke led him to the well. Luke slowly raised the cover. He reached down and filled the jug.

The jug had only touched the water when a wonderful odour of rare wine new-tapped, but of an old and ripe vintage, scented the damp evening air.

Mr. Bunce asked for the jug; he raised it to his lips, and took a very long draught. Luke slipped the jug into the well again – the well was full of wine . . .

Luke placed the wine upon the table, and after doing so he went to Mr. Weston and kissed him. The wine merchant returned the embrace.

'A good tradesman loves a grateful customer,' he said.

Mr. Weston's Good Wine, chapter 35

I shall recur in my final chapter to this centrally important question of how we judge love. The critic's first duty, however, is to see the love that is in the poem. And that is what seems so much more difficult for us even than for the Victorians.

The first F. R. Leavis Lecturer, Mr H. A. Mason, whose book on the early Tudor writers is by far the best thing in its field, and who has done good work on the idea and practice of translation, recently published a book, *Shakespeare's Tragedies of Love*, in which, despite his unfailing flow of words, he seems all but speechless about love. The climax of the book is an essay on *Antony and Cleopatra* which finally abandons the love in the play. 'When has anything corresponding to a god been present in the play?' Mr Mason asks. *All the time* is the answer to that one, and if a critic can't see the God of Love in that play, he may as well give up. The love of Antony and Cleopatra is *not*, according to Mr

Mason, 'a valuable love with all its attendant stresses as it conflicts with the normal judgment of decent men'. I suppose he must
make the same judgment on Donne. Must the love be without
value because it also fits well the opening account of a gypsy's
lust for a strumpet's fool?

Of course the love of Antony and Cleopatra isn't to be
approved and certainly not to be imitated. The proper attitude to
hope for is a subtle problem for the critic: I am not advocating
Dover Wilson's drooling over the pair. But this critical problem
follows from seeing what is there, which Mr Mason can't do because he is blind to the demonic.

If we go along (as we can't help) with Professor Leavis, we are bound to
feel when we hear 'The Windes were Loue-sicke', that the winds really
were more than what the meteorologists might tell us. We do not think
of ordinary river or sea-water but of a new non-material [why?] liquid
endued with feeling. In short, we feel ourselves in a world where fancy
has out-worked Nature. (p. 246)

This is used as an adverse judgment on Shakespeare's attempt to
bind us with verbal spells rather than do a dramatist's proper
work of giving us the real.

But 'ordinary river water', what is that? If love is to be judged
by the standards of meteorology, Mr Mason is right. He is bend-
ing his eye on vacancy because he believes river water is always
and only what it is to commonsense, and that we never transcend
the weather-forecast. He can't see the spirit of the play, the terror
of the God of Love as he transforms something otherwise as petty
and tricky as Cleopatra. Mr Mason goes on to say that the
'nereides and mermaides' of that passage can't be the company
we have met in the second scene of the play. It seems to me on
the contrary particularly right that they should be, that they
should go on to die for Cleopatra in act v, and that *her* suicide is
deliberately sexy and voluptuous. I believe the barge does burn
on the water, and I am glad that even in that passage there are
risqué puns and images. (And I believe also in *Mr. Weston's Good
Wine* that Luke Bird's well is brimming over with the light wine
of love, also that when the commonsensical Landlord Bunce
plunges in he gets soaked with ordinary well-water.) The winds
in *Antony and Cleopatra* simply *are* love-sick.

It is, predictably, worse when we get to *Othello*. Professor John
Danby, who in his enthusiastic *Spectator* review of Mr Mason's

book[8] took care to agree about *Antony*, mildly demurs at Mr Mason's description of 'Othello, in the bedroom scene, "kissing and pawing and smelling and savouring the externals of the sleeping body".' That does seem to me a vile phrase, though not physiologically inaccurate. Othello does all these things: but to put it this way is to deny that they are the signs of his love for Desdemona. He is, apparently, only appreciating her as a kind of lecherous connoisseur.

But here Leavis himself is unsatisfactory: if that great man cannot see clearly what hope is there for the rest of us? I put it rather strongly here: Leavis on Othello hovers uneasily on the verge of missing the point without ever quite doing so. He is, however, *half*-mesmerized by the idea that love must be good, and that therefore Othello's love for Desdemona is not true love.

> Yet I'll not shed her blood,
> Nor scar that whiter skin of hers than snow
> And smooth as monumental alabaster.

Dr Leavis comments, 'Tenderness here quite clearly is that characteristic voluptuousness of Othello's which, since it is unassociated with any real interest in Desdemona as a person, slips so readily into possessive jealousy.'[9] I don't deny the truth of the remarks about Othello's possessive jealousy. But why doesn't what a person beautifully is in her person belong to her as a real person? 'Person' itself is otherwise limiting. Over the page Dr Leavis writes, 'When she is awake and so is no longer a mere body but a person . . .'. But has Othello been speaking of the sleeping Desdemona as a *mere* body? Is 'person' more convincing than the Desdemona he kisses? The line of comment in Dr Leavis's essay is, morally and psychologically, more or less unanswerable. But I still want to protest when in another essay he writes '*Othello*, on the other hand, it would not be misleading to describe as a character-study.'[10] Granting the truth of the moral comment and that there is plenty of character-study *in Othello*, *Othello* is still not primarily a moral fable or a character-study; it is a tragedy. Its status as such seems to me less securely based than in the case of *Lear* or *Macbeth*, and depends on a handful of speeches. But this is one of them. It is one of the signs that

[8] 3 April 1971.
[9] *The Common Pursuit* (1952), p. 149.
[10] *Ibid.*, p. 177.

Othello is more than a cautionary example, more than the kind of character who gets into the newspapers every week. The 'more' is, as ever, in the poetry, which if it is found in real life 'tragedies' is not reported in the press. Othello's poetry (I don't mean the limited beauty of his earlier poeticizings) makes of that characteristic voluptuousness, of his lethal stupidity (Emilia is right to call him 'as ignorant as dirt') and furious destructiveness that accompany it, love, and love of the most terrible and tragic kind. 'Voluptuousness' suggests something less. (Leavis on Blake, *The Human World*, no. 7 (1972), is not open to the same objection.) Othello is at least not negligible or unserious in his perverse passion.

All a love poet has to be is demonic. That is in itself rare; but on the other hand I am not suggesting that love poets are never anything else as well. Often, thank God, they are critical too. Macbeth is himself a demonic poet of love, so is Othello; but William Shakespeare criticizes their love by putting it in those plays. His creation is also the just description of the love. Yet it is the expression of the passion of love in language which defines the love poet, and in some cases that is all there is to it (Burns – the passion of regret and separation, Dante in the *Vita Nuova*, Donne).

Seeing passion in life, in its splendour, terror and ridiculousness, is taking love with the appropriate seriousness made possible by language and guaranteed by the great creative uses of the common language. Love poetry is in that way the possibility of glory and terror in love. The poet has done his work if he shows us the possibility of this wrath and grace in our world. But must not the critic (and all readers are critics) go further and commit himself to what is good in the poet's inspiration?

7

Anarchy and Criticism

yis quod she ther is liberte of fre wille. ne ther ne was neuer no nature
of resoun that it ne hadde liberte of fre wille. ¶ For euery thing that may
naturely vsen resoun. it hath doom by whiche it discernith and demith
euery thing. ¶ Than knoweth it by it self thinges that ben to fleen. and
things that ben to desiren.

Then said the other, Do you see yonder shining light? He said, I think I
do. Then said Evangelist, Keep that light in your eye . . . So I saw in my
Dream, that . . . the Man put his fingers in his Ears, and ran on crying,
Life, Life, Eternal Life.

I

All a poet *need* do is get his demon down on paper; and no more
criticism need be involved than enters into the coaxing of the
demon to speak our language. But it isn't equivalently true that
all the critic need do is get the demon up off the page – though,
of course, if he doesn't he can't do anything else. The literary
critic, i.e. the serious reader, has to digest the demon rather than
swallowing it whole: he has to respond, reflect, and ask himself
exactly how the poem matters. This asking is what, by the argument of my first chapter, defines in the way proper to criticism
the existence (the full meaning) of the poem, and until he knows
where he stands in relation to the poem (which one needn't after
reading and understanding) the critic's work is not complete. But
with a great poem the critic's work is never done, for he will
always be able to find more in it and so stand in a new relation
to it: his knowledge may be true, in a sense complete, and as unfailing as language, but will always be modifiable.

I want to suggest why criticism, the natural connection of the
passional with the whole of life, is so important (and not only with
regard to poetry) as to be the way of taking things that in allowing them their full existence also allows us ours.

Love poetry (to continue with the same example) is the poet's
making love seriously; but what *he* does is not the complete
seriousness. For that, the poem has to be read in the kind of
reading that makes the reader ask whether what he reads is true
and what difference it makes.

This criticism naturally has to be made by the critic alone with the poem and committed to nothing but his true response. I have not a word to say against D. H. Lawrence's well-known remarks at the beginning of his great Galsworthy essay:

> The touchstone is emotion, not reason. We judge a work of art by its effect on our sincere and vital emotion, and nothing else. All the critical twiddle-twaddle about style and form, all this pseudo-scientific classifying and analysing of books in an imitation-botanical fashion, is mere impertinence and mostly dull jargon.
>
> *Phoenix*, p. 539

I never read that without wanting to cheer, except when, as an academic critic, I take it as a rebuke. But earlier in the same paragraph Lawrence has called criticism 'a *reasoned* account of the feeling produced upon the critic' (my italics) and has said 'It is concerned with values that science ignores'; and in the next paragraph he speaks of the need for the critic to be 'emotionally educated'.

The critic has to speak his own response; he is offering it, however, not as a report of a private feeling but as something generally true. Whether it *is* generally true depends on the responses of other individuals to what he says – and on the belief that those responses are not merely private and personal, either. The critic's own response, that is to say, must be seen as a true judgment capable of belonging to others, i.e. at home in the common language. And if that seems paradoxical it is because of the misleading distinctions between individuality and what we have in common which we discussed in the first chapter. What I want to add to Lawrence can be 'unpacked' from an objection made to the position 'Art isn't a matter of *what* but of *how*' by a minor character in Solzhenitsyn's *One Day in the Life of Ivan Denisovich*: 'To bloody hell with your "how" if it doesn't arouse any good feelings in me.'

The dawning of wonder is the beginning of criticism as well as of poetry. Dr Leavis is convincing in the first chapter of *Nor Shall My Sword*, when, speaking of 'that creative lapse, or escape, from Eliotic habit, the unique and lovely "Marina"', he says, 'Wonder is the welcoming apprehension of the new ... It is the living response to life, the creative – the life of which the artist in his creativity is conscious of being a servant.' But there seems to me a certain incompleteness in the very important truth expressed there.

For Macbeth welcomes and wonders at the new as much as Pericles.

> that suggestion
> Whose horrid image doth unfix my hair
> And make my seated heart knock at my ribs

– that is wonder, too, but Macbeth is emphatically wrong, however creative, to welcome it. So is Conrad's Mr Kurtz to welcome the whisper, 'proved irresistibly fascinating', which came to him out of the heart of darkness.

What if the critic is a thoroughly depraved person, responding with sincere delight to the monstrosity he finds in art? Someone might show a quite deep understanding of *Macbeth* by embarking on a career of artistic slaughter. That could imaginably be the sign of having seen some of the things really in the play and of having responded to them strongly and sincerely. But I wouldn't want to call it criticism.

I don't pretend to be able to understand the force of *all* the objections to poetry in the Tenth Book of *The Republic*, but the 'most serious' does strike me as a convinced tribute to the power – and rightly to the potentially dangerous power – of art.

> When we listen to some hero in Homer or on the tragic stage moaning over his sorrows in a long tirade, or to a chorus beating their breasts as they chant a lament, you know how the best of us enjoy giving ourselves up to follow the performance with eager sympathy. The more a poet can move our feelings in this way, the better we think him. And yet when the sorrow is our own, we pride ourselves on being able to bear it quietly like a man, condemning the behaviour we admired in the theatre as womanish. Can it be right that the spectacle of a man behaving as one would scorn and blush to behave oneself should be admired and enjoyed, instead of filling us with disgust?
>
> x. 605, Cornford's translation

If anything as mechanical as pornography can capture our imagination and language, how much more can poetry, real passion in language, and how much more dangerous that it should! for we do indeed, if we are good readers, give ourselves up to follow the poetry with eager sympathy. The poet's power to play on the soul is indeed a terrible one. (All that solider Aristotle could do with that was to try to use the theatre as a way of getting safely rid of the emotions the poet arouses, in 'purging' them.) And I don't think it makes the artist's power less terrible if we remind ourselves that we are all primitive poets and that what

Shakespeare may do to us in *Macbeth* is only more deeply, strikingly and formally what we do to each other all the time in conversation. Plato is not wrong to be afraid that this poetic power on stage may 'corrupt the good, all but a few' by making them forget their goodness. Nor was Tolstoy simply wrong in *The Kreutzer Sonata* and elsewhere: his fear too springs from the power of his true response to art.

Ugh! Ugh! It is a terrible thing, that sonata. And especially that part. And in general music is a dreadful thing! ... How can one allow anyone who pleases to hypnotize another, or many others, and do what he likes with them? And especially that this hypnotist should be the first immoral man that turns up? It is a terrible instrument in the hands of any chance user!
The Kreutzer Sonata, chapter 23

One can indeed apply Tolstoy's ideas to his *Kreutzer Sonata* itself. Tolstoy thought he was showing the wickedness of sex and that 'eschewing is the only remedy'. One might conceivably be converted by the tale to that point of view. But it certainly works through its compelling picture of the lust to murder. Read by one whom blood allures, *The Kreutzer Sonata* could be a very dangerous story.

What can protect us against art, or generally against enslavement by language? Both Tolstoy and Plato lived before the days of 'O' level, which effectively cauterizes (I have never met a freshman at university who had any idea of the depth of evil in *Macbeth*); an academic training must then be counted as one effective safeguard. I would like to hope that real criticism is a better one. Criticism is the only defence against art that can yet allow art to be itself. If the reader is not simply mesmerized (a sub-critical response) or unaffected, the art can find its place in the critic's life only with his active co-operation. We are responsible for our responses even though we may not control them; and the responsibility, however it shows, is critical judgment.

In that passage of *The Republic* Plato has been offering as the central objection to art that it overwhelms what I am calling criticism. 'What encourages him to resist his grief is the lawful authority of reason, while the impulse to give way comes from the feeling itself; and, as we said, the presence of contradictory impulses proves that two distinct elements in his nature must be involved' (x. 603). Poetry, too, 'waters the growth of passions which should be allowed to wither away and sets them up in control, although the goodness and happiness of our lives depend on their being held in subjection' (x. 606). I am only unconvinced here in that the notion of self-responsibility, of the laws by which we judge and rule ourselves, seems to me too rigid. I would like a criticism that can submit itself to poetry and in a sense learn from it, without being either overwhelmed or, as Plato would have it, untouched – though simple outright resistance to a poet's power may sometimes be necessary. (Harold Macmillan would have been a better statesman if he had resisted his propensity to succumb to the siren-songs of Lloyd George.)

Criticism is as basic to human life as impulse, and as inspirational, though in a different way.

> In *Poets* as true Genius is but rare,
> True *Taste* as seldom is the Critick's Share;
> Both must alike from Heav'n derive their Light.
> Pope, An Essay on Criticism, 11–13

We can do nothing without impulse, and the instinctive energies and appetites which come from beyond the consciousness. They are God-given, necessary, and to be reverenced. But impulse is not absolute. Impulse is, in any case, never found untouched by criticism, to which expression necessarily subjects it in allowing it to be itself, except perhaps in certain psychotic conditions; and there is something wrong if we have bright ideas without asking ourselves in the very act of having them, whether they are true. (Whether I am writing about what P. B. Medawar and others call 'synergism' I know too little about science to guess: all I mean is that in thinking one can distinguish two parts – though I do not think they always need be in chronological order – which I am calling impulse and criticism, and that they are organically related – even if

> *Wit* and *Judgment* often are at strife,
> Tho' meant each other's Aid, like *Man* and *Wife*.
> An Essay on Criticism, 82–3)

But even when inspiration can be distinguished from finished expression, it is not necessarily to be followed or trusted, as in the case of Macbeth and Mr Kurtz.

We are critics when we make decisions. To fall in love, for instance, is not to make a decision; but if two people decide to marry on the basis of love they are criticising it, according it a certain value in life.

And to what are our important decisions responsible? By what standards do we make them? We may rightly make a decision by a kind of inspiration. Sometimes it is easy, as in Lawrence's imagined case:

> When I say to myself: 'I am wrong', knowing with sudden insight that I *am* wrong, then this is the whole self speaking, the Holy Ghost. It is no piece of mental inference. It is not just the soul sending forth a flash. It is my whole being speaking in one voice, soul and mind and psyche transfigured into oneness. This voice of my being I may *never* deny. When at last, in all my storms, my whole self speaks, then there is a pause. The soul collects itself into pure silence and isolation – perhaps after much pain. The mind suspends its knowledge, and waits. The psyche becomes strangely still. And then, after the pause, there is fresh beginning, a new life adjustment.

> *Fantasia of the Unconscious*, chapter XI

Yet even this seems to me not absolute. I can well imagine that Hitler might have had just such a new life adjustment before deciding on the final solution of the Jewish problem: it is still possible to be quite wrong. Criticism is still necessary, the responsibility to something not listed by Lawrence, and affecting the 'fresh beginning'.

For we may make as firm and right a decision if our feelings are crying out against it. One may leave home, renounce someone one loves, or cause onself anguish by joining the Conservative Party, because it is right to do so, though against some parts of one's very self. And how do we know what is right? By, in general, the sincere exercise of our critical faculties, and by inspiration: there can be nothing more definite even for those with the comfort of a dogmatic creed, for it will always have to be applied and interpreted.

Critical judgments (which Lawrence would sometimes deny[1]) are as dependent on the common language as poetry, by the axiom that the common language embodies in all its speakers a common set of assumptions and values. This is to see from a different point of view the earlier contention that the critic's personal judgment is not *merely* personal but belongs to the common language. We can demonstrate our sincere personal belief that murder is wrong merely by using the word ordinarily in English. (It isn't easy to make adultery or fornication right, either: you would have to begin by calling them other names.) To say 'he's a murderer' (or 'he's silly' or 'he's clever') is to exercise what I will

---

[1] Cf. my 'Note on D. H. Lawrence and English Prose', in *D. H. Lawrence*, ed. A. H. Gomme (1972).

call a common-language judgment, cf. above, p. 13. It may, of course, be a wrong judgment – he may not be a murderer etc. – but the possibility of judgment here is made available by our sincere use of ordinary speech. (Judgment and perception are not always separable.)

A related observation is that nobody actually puts up a notice-board reading 'So-and-so, So-and-so and Company, Estate Agents, Gazumpers and Crooks'. Even when more ordinary descriptions of a firm's activities are mere lip-service, the lip-service is paid. Similarly even the late Hitler never issued statements like 'the German army has crossed the such-and-such frontier agressively with the intention of extending the territory of the Third Reich and my power'. Common-language judgment forces the wolves for better or worse to wear sheep's clothing as understood in a particular language. And the standards to which people in public give their lip-service are the *critical* standards of the language.

To continue with the example of love poetry – some of the judgments we make are the merest commonsense, and none the worse for that. (For instance Tolstoy is wrong in *The Kreutzer Sonata* to take human sexuality as in itself an evil: it is possible to share his view but only by going wildly against commonsense.) The more interesting cases are when we make a judgment suggested by a common sense that isn't so obvious.

Think of the plight of Titania in *A Midsummer Night's Dream*, doomed by the power of the God of Love to fall for the first man she catches sight of. That isn't in itself incredible: people do get into a hypervulnerable state and fall for the strangest objects, not limited to the human race. (Poor T. H. White and J. R. Ackerley and their alsatians . . .) And people do fall in and out of love all day long, like the play's Athenians. The oddity of the play isn't the arbitrariness of impulse, but what the characters do with their impulses: the *donnée* is that people follow their impulses straight into action, without criticism. Grant the *donnée* and everything is perfectly natural. But the common-language comment is to say the play *is* a dream because in real life we have to turn into critics before the last act. That isn't to refuse to respond emotionally to a marvellous play, but to see that the sincere true response is itself an appeal to a common sense.

We make a complementary common-language judgment upon the love of *Pamela*. If Oberon's drug operates by suppressing the critical part of Titania's nature, Pamela's critical faculty controls her impulses far too neatly. The situation of the girl prudently saying 'no' to Squire Booby until he proposes, whereupon she finds herself able to say a sincere 'yes' is not necessarily untrue to life or reprehensible. It is perfectly clear in *Pamela*, true to that world, that Pamela's alternative to marriage or chastity is to be another Sally Godfrey and lose any tolerable place in the world; and it's also true, which we may find it harder to admit, that love is often controllable, that you *can* make people fall in love by throwing them together in the right way. (The *mechanism* of sex is an idea that goes against our grain; but it remains true that almost any man can be roused, in the right circumstances, by almost any woman.) *Pamela* is still far too easy. It seems to me that the real common-language judgment, a little teased out, is that Richardson is untrue to life not in arranging the falling in love and not even in making it happen at the prudentially appropriate moment, but in trying to fix in advance the sense of the fall. That is substituting criticism for poetry.

Yet it *is* possible for the common language to supply reasons for loving or hating. (We have, for instance, the words 'lovable' and 'hateful'.) These come into literature rather with the novel than with love poetry. If Dickens had been a lyric poet he might have written David Copperfield's clichés to Dora, and later his frustration; but being a novelist Dickens shows us that love criticized by the whole life of the novel. We make as we read the novel the common-language criticism that David's love for Dora is an insufficient reason for marriage.[2] Another example of Dickens's use of the novel to make a common-language judgment is *Hard Times* – as a whole, perhaps, in its criticism of the language of utilitarianism, but I think particularly of the moment where Louisa (and the common language) demolishes Mr Gradgrind by asking if she is expected to *love* Mr Bounderby.

These 'common-language judgments' are made as we find ourselves able (which not everyone can) sincerely and naturally to speak the common language.

Commonsense is a great bulwark of criticism, though eroding, but we need more than that. A healthily-working civilization generates its standards and values at its centres and they are then lived and modified into commonsense by all its people. At present the situation often seems to have been reversed, with the centres

[2] Cf. Q. D. Leavis's perceptive essay in *Dickens the Novelist* (1970).

restrained from utter madness and breakdown only by common-sense: if that happens commonsense is itself in danger.

In the more difficult cases the critic has (in his different way) to be as creative and exploratory as the poet, *discovering* what judgment can belong to the common language. And how to do that? It must, anyway, in accordance with Lawrence's axioms be asking what is true to the life we can only know by living it.

Criticism has to take *everything* into account – into evaluation, that is to say – including all those bits of experience which it would have been irrelevant for me to mention but which have significance in life: it is not my intention to deny that we judge by experience. If only it were a possible English phrase I would say that the critic has to bear everything in language. He has to judge by the best life of the language, as he knows it in experience. The critic's search is for the good new life of the language, which he recognizes by its consistency (in its newness) with the best he knows. 'Change is not only compatible with consistency. It makes no sense to talk of consistency where there is no change. For consistency describes a manner of changing. What distinguishes the consistent man is that when he changes he feels obliged somehow to fit the new together with the old . . .'[3]

For the critic (for us all as critics or for formal criticism) there must be identity between the 'reason' I mentioned in the first chapter and this fitting the new together with old that is consistent with the best of the common language. I have been using 'meaning' and 'value' together not because they are always the same but to suggest that the place where they become the same is that activity of the whole man which I am calling criticism. It is to every man as critic that nought is but as 'tis valued. As critics we define what things are as we ask what they mean and (inseparably) how they matter to us, what they are worth.

Arnold's position seems to me, then, obviously right: that (paraphrasing into the terms of my present discussion) a critic is responsible to, and derives his standard from, the best he knows – including, firstly, what he has learned by experience. There is no split between this view and Lawrence's emphasis on the finality of sincere emotional response. The kind of response Lawrence is discussing is the way our knowledge speaks, when we are granted

---

[3] Shirley Robin Letwin, 'Against Tolerance', *The Human World*, no. 8 (1972).

the grace to be good critics: this is the sense of the earlier contention that the sincerity the critic must aim at has to be the statement of the whole truth of his own feeling *as generally valid*.

By 'the grace to be good critics' I mean that the power to be a good critic is not self-dependent or self-derived. If I were confining this discussion to the subject of my second chapter I would here quote the hundred and twenty-first psalm; I also remember that judging by the best one knows is, often enough, an invitation to oneself to repent. In the terminology in which I was brought up and which comes most natural to me, I am merely saying that we are all responsible to the Holy Spirit and that our appointed struggle is to know God's will and to do it. The failure to be a critic – the failure to go on trying to recognize the good – would in this sense if it were quite final and unalterable be the sin against the Holy Ghost, which cannot be forgiven because it precludes the wish for repentance. But the alternative condition (and there are only two, either/or), the recognition and service of the good, is a gift of grace to those who ask.

I do indeed believe that it is as what I have been calling critics that we can come to judgment (it seems to follow from the axiom that every judgment measures the critic as much as the thing criticized) for by 'taking everything into language' and allowing everything a particular significance within a whole we are coming dangerously close to that seeing life as a whole in which the soul may define itself. The judgments we come to, like the ones we make, are not, except in the stories told about us by others after our death, last judgments, but the successive, changing judgments that make up, in this context, the life in question and in which the soul pictures, in the direction of its will, life as a whole. (The whole is a little one, perhaps, necessarily limited by individuality, for we cannot all be magnanimous, but a whole nonetheless, from which the parts derive.) The common language enters so deeply into us that it becomes part of the material of which the soul is made; conversely, when we manage to speak from the soul we make the common language.

Not all souls are saved: we might see from a point of view like Macbeth's and construct a devil's-eye view of the world, whole and consistent. But the judgment by which one says so is itself critical (the witches could not make it) and from the point of view of the best. We *are* responsible, as critics, for not surrendering the language to devils.

The guarantee of the sanity of the world can only be in the common part of true judgment, the critic's reliance on the language which is not merely his private possession. The judgments we may be granted as critics fructify (to paraphrase Eliot) in the continuance of the best of the language in other lives. (If our judgments are wrong or devilish they may have corresponding consequences but not *critical* ones except in the resistance of others.) The sense that one person finds is criticized, renewed, made again differently by others equally responsible to consistency with the best, to the maintenance of the standards of the common language.

The judgments we make as critics can be infallible (but not unmodifiable) in the sense I discussed at the end of the first chapter: they can define our new life and take on its substantiality. If a critic's judgment becomes current he has also defined the part of the life of the whole community he is treating – in other people's acceptance of his judgment as they speak his language. But because the acceptance is in individual lives. necessarily in Leavis's form 'yes but . . .' the continuing discussion modifies the judgment and life. The continuing discussion is the continuing definition of the values and standards by which it lives, and that is the same as the unfailing life of language.

II

Formal criticism – the comment on different aspects of life which appears in the dailies and weeklies, in all the humane academic disciplines, even in published literary essays – is to the necessary human activity what Donne's poems are to the kind of primitive poetry we all express. Formal criticism guarantees the criticism there must be in every life in the same way that love poetry guarantees the seriousness of sex. Unfortunately 'criticism', unlike 'poetry', carries with it no necessary implication of seriousness; on the contrary it is pretty common for people to think that criticism is frivolous.

Yet the formation of opinion is one of our cornerstones, in our private lives and generally in civilization. I am talking generally of just judgment, which has never been more necessary and never more generally misunderstood. (I discussed some of the ways in previous chapters.)

A common fallacy amongst even the most intelligent and

serious of my pupils is that any opinion is as good as any other. 'Of course, that's only my personal opinion' – the *only* and *personal* indicate a central confusion about how opinion matters and how it is generated. Oddly enough this often goes with a determination to stick to one's only personal opinion even if it is shown to be erroneous, because we all have a right to our own opinions. As far as I know people don't extend these beliefs to their doctors ('Henry will very soon be dead, but of course that's only my personal opinion') or their solicitors ('you are sure to lose a hundred thousand pounds in damages in this case, but of course that's only my personal opinion'), presumably because *their* opinions are thought to be somehow 'scientific'. Often the incommunicability of opinion about what is right or wrong is also believed in (I have more than once heard it maintained with attempted seriousness that Hitler was *right* to exterminate the German Jews, that it was right 'for him' because in his opinion it was right) but I doubt whether this extends very far into practice. In practice we mostly know what is right and wrong – and as always with critical matters our knowledge has to do with the sincere use of a common language.

Perhaps it is now more generally recognized than it used to be that the phrase 'creative writing' conceals a trap if it implies that other writing, particularly criticism, is destructive – though I still have pupils who, having concentrated their intelligence and seriousness upon evaluating a writer who matters to them, will refer to their work as mere criticism, as against the real creative thing, the formless verses they toss off at idle moments; and though I did recently read in *T.L.S.*[4] an account of English studies at an ancient university which reported as a students' attitude 'Judgment was widely thought to be the enemy of spontaneity'. In the latter case I'm afraid I wasn't surprised when the report continued, 'At an open faculty meeting the other day, one student put the problem succinctly: "My supervisor says I have to study Pope. Why should I study Pope when I want to study comics?"' Why indeed? (That last question was meant to be rhetorical, but I came across a practical answer to it in what is probably our best critical journal:

The old classical approaches are almost moribund. No longer is literature a handing down of tradition, the best of what has been thought or spoken,

[4] 25 February 1972.

the precious life-blood of a master-spirit. In the English lesson ... our emphasis is upon the present moment and its value, irrespective of the past or the values of the past.

> B. Hollingworth, 'Existentialism Writ Small', *The Use of English*,
> vol. XXI, no. 2

– i.e. abolish literature and criticism. We are not told in that case where the value of the present moment might come from or how it might be recognized.)

Criticism is traditionally distinct from poetry and poets traditionally hate carping critics, by which they intend, when not merely being bloody-minded, what I call academic criticism. In the sense I am using the term, however, criticism has always been part of imaginative literature. Wordsworth denounces the 'false secondary power' (=, I think, 'academic criticism') which in his terminology is to criticism what poems of the fancy are to poems of the imagination. But Wordsworth seems to me to be describing criticism when he writes

For our continued influxes of feeling are modified and directed by our thoughts, which are indeed the representatives of all our past feelings; and, as by contemplating the relation of these general representatives to each other, we discover what is really important to men, so, by the repetition and continuance of this act, our feelings will be connected with important subjects ...

It is as critic of life that the poet may be 'the rock of defence for human nature; an upholder and preserver, carrying everywhere with him relationship and love'.[5] Shelley, a wild untutor'd phoenix in his verses if ever there was one, is yet upholding criticism as much as passion when he says in the excellent *Defence of Poetry* 'Poetry strengthens the faculty which is the organ of the moral nature of man, in the same manner as exercise strengthens a limb.' This is true, but only for the critical reader.

III

The great work of art surprises one, makes one think, 'Good God! the world can be like that!' But there is also another and, it seems to me, higher art, which says to the beholder, 'The world is like

---

[5] Preface to second edition of *Lyrical Ballads*.

this, isn't it?' Readers are in that case necessarily critics, having to answer 'Yes, but . . .'

It is a commonplace, though not a very clear one, that a novelist can create a 'world' and that the reader enters and imagines within that world. Because of the difference between imagined and real situations the world of a novel can be very potent and can make us imagine styles of life and systems of value we could not live. A novelist can even upset the things we take so much for granted that to question them would be crazy. If a girl has gap-teeth she is not necessarily more inclined to lechery than the rest of us, as we all know perfectly well; but I take the Wife of Bath's gap-teeth without murmuring as a mark of St Venus's seal. That in its way is saying 'Good God! the world can be like that!' – though the force of the art is to make us not exclaim at all.

Something radically new and different came into the world with the nineteenth-century novel, the acceptance by the artist of the criticism of life as his prime responsibility. I don't mean there was no criticism of life in art before that. Homer is surely at work on values, so too Pope and Blake – and Mozart, and Rembrandt. Even the new thing I mean, the presentment of the artist's world as *the* world, has plenty of forerunners: in English *The Canterbury Tales*, for instance and, above all, *Hamlet*, that splendid and nearly perfect play.

But in the nineteenth century we do find for the first time a dominant artistic tradition aiming at 'the world is so, isn't it?' The creative energy in George Eliot, Dickens, Tolstoy, Stendhal is concentrated on criticism of the age. Like their predecessors they are, of course, fascinated by individual human beings and their tragedies, but the fascination is of that kind. How is our world changing? they ask, and their novels answer the question in the way proper to fiction. Criticism of life became an attempt to see, as well as be, 'the age'; and this involved novelists in a new kind of responsibility to language.

Does any writer in the traditional modes of imaginative literature show *our* age to us? If we were considering the U.S.S.R. I would answer 'Solzhenitsyn': the tradition of Tolstoy survives miraculously in him. It would even be possible to offer an equivocal answer in the U.S.A. by reservedly pointing to *Catch-22*. But in England the last writer fully capable of this kind of criticism of life died in 1930.

By saying so I intend no insult to any living writer. We have quite a number of talented people who deserve sympathy as well as respect. But the nature of literature is that the minor talents find their place in relation to the great writers. Mark Ruherford's work lives, but in the light of George Eliot's; E. M. Forster and T. F. Powys both make sense, in their own right, but as the contemporaries of T. S. Eliot and D. H. Lawrence. We have nobody now in any of the traditional modes to provide the standards by which the proportions of an admirable minor talent could be seen; and that is a disaster for the minor but real talents, for it means they are as lost as the rest of us.

I think here particularly of the poetry of Mr Ted Hughes. *Crow* marks Mr Hughes's effort to become the true heir of T. S. Eliot as critic of the age, and he has some of the necessary talents: he is surely one of the most accomplished writers of verse of the century, and he has that persistence of effort in his task which is one necessary and rare qualification for success. I don't think, all the same, that he has yet succeeded (and David Sims and I argue the case in an essay in *The Human World*, no. 9 (1972)). Mr Hughes's true poetic voice, we try to show there, is a Tennysonian one: like Tennyson, when he goes beyond gentle melancholy he is 'crying in the night,/And with no language but a cry.' He is a poet of nostalgia and regret, and when he tries to turn into the voice of the critic of the age who can lead us through (and how can one not sympathize with the ambition? – aren't we *all* tempted?) he is not true to his real but limited inspiration. In the end *Crow*'s survival seems so trivial; the blood and death produce diminishing returns; one surfeits – and goes on living as before, not very much touched. Willy-nilly we find ourselves confronting again the question of sincerity: is *Crow* really the poet getting his new passion and criticism into the English language? or is it the poet convincing himself (and many of his critics) rather too easily that he has progressed beyond poignant wistfulness into a sort of *vita nuova*? Mr Hughes would have been less likely to have confused his real talent by taking himself, and by being too easily taken, as the great writer of the age, if there had been any obvious competition.

If we *had* a great living poet or novelist it is unlikely that he would get published or, if published, reviewed and read. It is at least apparent that George Eliot's position in her own day – or even Tennyson's – is not *mutatis mutandis* a possibility for a present writer, which is a depressing factor on the work of some of the best.[6]

And yet criticism of life is not dead in English, and that is the one great hopeful thing about the present state of our language. The life of English literature, which in the nineteenth century expressed itself in the novel and the novel's criticism of life has, in our time, flowed (somewhat attenuated) into formal criticism.

This may seem a wild thing to say, since my whole book has been documenting various failures of criticism. I take it, too, that the absence from our contemporary scene of a serious literary-critical journal is too notorious a fact to need demonstration. As ever, I don't intend an all-inclusive insult: *Essays in Criticism* has published some good things, so, even, has *The Critical Quarterly*. (Challenged by the editor of another journal to substantiate this statement I found three.) But there is no reliable upholder of standards of criticism. *Scrutiny* is succeeded by *The Cambridge Quarterly*, whereby the standards of criticism are badly let down. We discussed at length the very similar incoherence of *The Times Literary Supplement* in a review in *The Human World*, no. 7, 1972.

I don't intend, either, to accept the explanation of contemporary barrenness fashionable a few years ago, when it used to be said that English literature was undergoing a 'period of consolidation', one of the critical fruits of the growth of the university study of English, and entering an age of criticism for which we should be grateful. 'Consolidation' reminds me more of a famous trial more or less contemporary with its heyday. The word better fits the deceased in that case (who later turned out to have died a natural death). She had been a lady who expired before the war

---

[6] In two years' editing a quarterly review I have come across the work of one genuine novelist (M. B. Mencher) and one outright genius (Roy Kerridge) neither of whom can get published, for the good old reason that they offend modern expectations. Mencher dare still write of the spiritual problems of love and marriage. As for Kerridge, his *Tales of Black London* (which seem to me a real criticism of life) commit the crime for which this decade reserves the feelings the thirties applied to pornography: his villain is a black man, which is unthinkable – and beside that, Kerridge's *love* and sharp perception of immigrants counts as nothing. He is too shocking to print. It also goes against him that his stories are extremely funny, well-observed and full of twists of plot, so that they are a pleasure to read and therefore can't possibly be 'serious art'.

suddenly, and in the absence of a post-mortem examination, inexplicably. Her landlady, fearing she would be suspected of murder, sealed up the corpse, together with a quantity of fly-papers, in a cupboard on the stairs, where it remained for twenty years, the landlady meanwhile drawing the deceased's pension. During this time the corpse, instead of rotting in the ordinary way, was undergoing a period of consolidation. When the cupboard was at length opened it was found to contain not a skeleton but a mummy; the dead lady had attained to such a degree of consolidation that the autopsy before the coroner's inquest had to be performed with a hammer and chisel. Just so did English literature, after a long and chequered career, and living quietly in retirement off a pension granted by the readers of the world, perish with mysterious suddenness. The landlady, afraid that foul play would be suspected, went on drawing the pension of esteem and royalties, and now the post-mortem is in full swing from the hammer and chisel of academic criticism. The certification of death, however, is known to be of increasing difficulty to medical as well as literary practitioners (death used to 'occur' at a precise moment but now – a locution I first saw used of the late Prime Minister of India, Lal Bahadur Shastri – it is said to 'set in') and it is likely to be some years yet before life in the mummy is acknowledged to be extinct.

I am not arguing, then, that we live in an age of a galaxy of shining criticism, or that critical standards are generally upheld. Though criticism goes on necessarily, like speech, it is often enough in despite of the views of the professional critics. I won't descend to the Sunday papers for an example: this is a Professor of English literature:

Sociology offers to provide what used to be mediated by the novel. Open shelves are replaced by data-retrieval machinery . . . It is idle to suppose that this is a passing phase and that the old literary programme will come in again to occupy its old station. The whole technical and productive organization of the modern world is moving in the other direction.
In this new cultural situation criticism can no longer expect to have the scope and authority that it once claimed. Arnold's conception of a largely literary culture, refining and fertilizing the life of its time, may survive as a pious formula, but it only commands the allegiance of those past middle age. It has little to do with the pressure of the world as it is. It is easy to relapse into an Arnoldian attitude and see this development as a substitution of 'machinery' for the life of the spirit. But this will not really do. Culture has always depended on the productive and social

machinery of its age. Until fairly recently that machinery was largely controlled by verbal and linguistic processes – processes, that is to say, which
have some obvious affinity with literature and an obvious connection with
literary culture. That is no longer the case.

Graham Hough, 'Criticism as a Humanist Discipline', *Contemporary
Criticism*, Stratford-upon-Avon Studies 12 (1970), pp. 45–6

This is an abandonment of human nature. It couldn't be *said*
except within a context of criticism that renders it untrue – unless,
that is, 'machinery' is still controlled by language. Culture
'depends' on productive machinery only in the sense that we all
depend on food; it isn't food, however, that produces humanity
nor the consumption of consumer durables that makes us cultured.
Surely it is an emblem of the age when a Professor of English
should be ready to abandon criticism to data-processing and to
abdicate, unasked, in favour of the young. Perhaps I count as the
latter, not yet being past middle age; but to me the Arnoldian
position seems not so much a pious formula which fails to command my allegiance as a self-evident truth about the place of
criticism in language and life.

If criticism does collapse (and I cannot distinguish here between
formal criticism and the necessarily critical part of all our lives)
values, opinion, judgment, the direction of life, are all handed
over to the new anticultural machines, and centres of culture
become in the ways I have illustrated the mouthpiece of gross
inferiority, with the resulting cheapening of life. The pop world,
the growth-worshippers, and the manipulators become the meek
inheritors of English – which we have to go on speaking and
living in.

I am far from being as hopeless as Professor Hough, however,
and that is what I had in mind when I asserted that in our age
the life of literature has flowed into formal criticism. I mean
principally one writer: it is in any case rare for several great men
to be producing at once, and if there is one that is enough.

F. R. Leavis is a *great* writer because of the passion of his
devotion to criticism and to the creative part it must play at the
present time in our literature and our life. This has been decisively
established by his work of the last ten years, a splendid development for a man at an age when anyone less determined and inspired would have been ready to rest on very well-earned laurels.

Dr Leavis has never been an inmate of the academic ivory
tower. He could not have been a literary critic of stature if his

interests had ever been confined to literature, and the purity of his concern for what matters in life has always been the mark of his distinction as literary critic; but in fact his direct concern for the state of civilization has always been explicit. Leavis began with the social comment of *Mass Civilization and Minority Culture*; and in this early pamphlet one is struck (as well as by the attractive and obviously genuine earnestness) by the crudity of some of the formulations about health in society, satisfactory living etc., and by the number of unsubstantiated *offers* to analyze such-and-such a work. Dr Leavis needed his intense preoccupation with imaginative literature as a condition for a convincing commentary on the age. One is also struck in early Leavis by a Shelleyan fervour, an afflatus which it has taken the discipline of a lifetime's literary criticism to convert, in the recent lectures, into something more like art. The phase initiated by the Richmond Lecture on Snow (and equally on the modern world) has united his love of literature and his concern for civilization into a new whole whose parts could not now be separate. Understanding Leavis's Clark Lectures or the lectures in *Nor Shall My Sword* is understanding the depth and generality of his concern for the place of criticism in language and life.

The phrase 'the third realm' is Leavis's means of making his step from the great particular example, the existence of a poem, to a general truth about the nature of language:

The implicit form of a judgement is: This is so, isn't it? The question is an appeal for confirmation that the thing *is* so; implicitly that, though expecting, characteristically, an answer in the form, 'yes, but –', the 'but' standing for qualifications, reserves, corrections. Here we have a diagram of the collaborative–creative process in which the poem comes to be established as something 'out there', of common access in what is in some sense a public world. It gives us, too, the nature of the existence of English literature, a living whole that can have its life only in the living present, in the creative response of individuals, who collaboratively renew and perpetuate what they participate in – a cultural community or consciousness. More, it gives us the nature in general of what I have called the 'third realm' to which all that makes us human belongs.

Nor Shall My Sword, p. 62

This in turn becomes Leavis's widening literary criticism into a criticism of life. He has done it through an increasingly assured and convincing sense of language in its relation to the individual's critical activity by which we live. Literary criticism has thus in Leavis's hands become the means of making the essential judgments on our age as surely as Dickens could through the novel. In exploring 'the third realm' to find a place in it for literature Leavis is necessarily at work, in his different way as much as a novelist, on exploring humanity and asking what it is that makes us human.

Dr Leavis's most important literary judgment is 'that our time, in literature, may fairly be called the age of D. H. Lawrence and T. S. Eliot: the two, in creative pre-eminence, I think, though Lawrence appears to me so immensely the greater genius, will be seen in retrospect to dominate the age together'.[7] This view of the literature of the first half of our century is, however, the product not of that age but of the present age that has followed it. Sensibility, in Eliot's famous dictum, alters in us all from age to age, whether we will or no; if 'expression' has been changed to allow us to see the age thus, the man of genius responsible is Leavis himself. The present age of English literature is the age of Dr Leavis; the power of our imaginative literature to show us the seriousness and the shape of our lives survives in his work, though necessarily, since he is a critic, with less assurance and fecundity than in some ages. Leavis's prose (and I am on record calling Leavis a great master of English prose) succeeds Lawrence's, and English literature retires into the university. The *great* achievement is to maintain the life of literature in that not very promising climate.

Leavis's work shows that there is still a most important place for imaginative literature in our world: it also shows with obvious clarity that that cannot be distinct from the place of criticism. It is thus the peculiarity of the present age of our literature that its great man should be a critic rather than a practitioner of any of the traditionally creative modes. The prejudice against criticism is strong enough to make this very hard for some people to stomach.

Yet it is not unprecedented for English literature to be dominated for a while by a critic. Dr Leavis's position has of late been comparable with Dr Johnson's at the end of the eighteenth century, except that Leavis has yet to attain Johnson's general recognition (which itself says something of the place of imaginative literature and criticism in our world). Temperamentally and in style of thought the two writers are, of course, very different. Yet Leavis's Clark Lectures and the ones in *Nor Shall My Sword*

[7] *D. H. Lawrence, Novelist* (1955), p. 303.

put me strongly in mind of the Johnson of *The Vanity of Human Wishes,* as well as the Pope of the *Moral Essays* and *Dunciad.* Leavis is like Johnson or Pope in his capacity, very rare at the present time, to make strong general statements about human nature and to go on from them to the lively examples that display their truth. His work has something of the poetic-fictional strength of Pope's picture of Sir Balaam or Johnson's of the Young Enthusiast. In all these cases the life of the poetic imagination flows into criticism.

Leavis has a demon if ever a poet had – the 'depth of vital consciousness' in his work is his claim to greatness as much as any poet's – and we are lucky in that it drives him to what I have been calling 'criticism of life'. Leavis's genius is that of Wordsworth's 'upholder and preserver'. But with that 'lucky' I come, perhaps paradoxically, to the part of Leavis's critical position I cannot agree with. With his own 'creative *nisus*' Leavis cannot but believe that 'to be creative in the artist's way is implicitly to assert responsibility'.[8] In his own creative life that naturally follows from the words about the 'essential human creativity that is human responsibility'[9] I used as an epigraph, and which are the best definition of criticism I know. But the consequence is not inevitable: there can be evil geniuses. Baudelaire was creative in the artist's way without being critically responsible.

If what Leavis says of Blake, that he was the 'vindicator of the creativity of life as, in man, responsibility' is generally true of poets, that is a critical feat, not explicable by the nature of poetry itself. If our literature since the great novelists has been 'creativity ... as ... responsibility', that is its peculiar character, not the necessary character of creativity; it is something that could imaginably be lost without the death of poetry. Here is another of Leavis's definitions of criticism:

Our time faces us with a new necessity of conscious provision: we have to make provision for keeping alive, potent and developing that full human consciousness of ends and values and human nature that comes to us (or should) out of the long creative continuity of our culture.

English Literature in our Time and the University (1969), p. 2

Yes indeed, and Leavis's career shows how that need can only be supplied by passional, creative newness of life. But the other way round it doesn't *necessarily* work: new, passional life is not neces-

[8] *Nor Shall My Sword,* p. 14.
[9] *Ibid.,* p. 19.

sarily expressed in responsibility. That Leavis's creativity should
be of the kind I have been calling critical is a gift of grace, for
which we can only be grateful.

The weaker things in his recent work seem to me to flow from
this belief that all true creativity is critical. He insists too much
on the word 'positive' – is less positive than usual when doing so[10]
and is sometimes too close for comfort to the edge of the pit in
which he so clearly sees Blake. Leavis has no illusions about the
possibility of building an actual, physically demonstrable and
complete Jerusalem in England's green and pleasant land, and
his account of Blake's failings that naturally followed from his
belief that *he* could, is fully convincing. And yet Leavis himself,
in the great essay on Blake I had the privilege of publishing[11] can't
resist, in a minor way, the attempt to get things neatly and finally
tied up, by an enthusiastic endorsement of the campaign of
Professor Marjorie Grene. I too have learned things from Professor Grene's work, and especially from some of her associates',
and don't wish to sound ungrateful; but the effort to see her group
as having successfully initiated a philosophical revolution is not
only unconvincing in itself, it is falling into the Blakean trap of
thinking that revolutions in philosophy *can* be directed and
managed in the service of a *telos* – which could only be a modern
variant of a finished Jerusalem.

We await Leavis's treatment of the *Four Quartets*, which must
at all events be a landmark in English letters. But I am afraid from
the hints in other recent work that he is going to attack Eliot for
not being positive enough. The remark to that effect in the opening chapter of *Nor Shall My Sword* is one of the unconvincing
things:

... the astonishingly rendered continence of affirmation – through *Four
Quartets* to the word 'Incarnation' in 'The Dry Salvages'. It mustn't be
taken as implying that what Eliot offers as an apprehension of the trans-
cendent spiritual reality satisfies. It seems to me that, for all his slowness
to affirm and his subtly elaborate technique of exploration and definition,
he plays false with the *ahnung* and fails to protect the nisus against the
promptings of the selfhood. The failure is a failure of the courage of self-
knowledge – that is, a weakness of the disinterested 'identity', and the
consequence manifests itself in the poem as a basic stultifying contradiction.

(pp. 25–6)

[10] Cf. *Nor Shall My Sword*, p. 30.
[11] *The Human World*, no. 7 (1972).

We wait, as I said, the demonstration of that. As it stands, the bent to the 'positive' seems to me not there creative: Leavis is belabouring Eliot with what amounts to jargon; for all the work done on the words earlier in the essay, *ahnung, nisus* and selfhood come out a little pat, and the inverted commas will hardly rescue 'identity' for the common language.

A cognate flaw, as it seems to me, is Leavis's use of 'need'. He writes often, sometimes movingly, of 'human need'; but 'need' is bound to demand the kind of satisfaction that can be prescribed. And that is not the kind that can be offered by the great poet or critic – as Leavis, most of the time, is well aware. Jerusalem is always to be built: we always have to pray 'Thy Kingdom come' until death, until the crack of doom. We have to go on praying that, but not actually to expect its arrival. (The Israelites' mistake, not made by Moses, was surely to enter the promised land.) Even Bunyan could only let the pilgrims catch a glimpse of the celestial city from the land of Beulah, and quite rightly showed the way back to hell after that. Leavis seems to me sometimes to err on the side of optimism when distinguishing the battles that can and must be won from the war which is eternal, as long as life. The kind of need which the poets and critics deal in is the need for grace, and it is perpetual in human life. The *Four Quartets* seem to me a deep recognition of that truth.

Nor Shall My Sword is, for all these minor criticisms, the great creative work of our generation, and the account in the first chapter of its mode of composition is the great account in our time of the nature of poetic inspiration, imaginative thought and the struggle for values – for creativity as human responsibility, for what I have been trying to point to as the necessary critical condition of human life. Leavis's work is therefore the great example for our time of the convinced embodiment of standards of criticism which, as much as any other standards in art, have to do with the concentration of the whole language – the whole man – upon the great problems of human nature, and are recognized in the conviction of others. The criticism in *Nor Shall My Sword* is as much the sincere achievement of a new point in our literature and sensibility as *Four Quartets*. There can still be inspired criticism in our age, and that ought to give us a kind of hope.

IV

My opinions in this book about the state of our language and life may have seemed crashingly obvious: I hope so, though one of my reasons for having written it is that the position is not often publicly sustained. Yet what could be more obvious than that our present problems in Britain result from certain easily-seen historical changes which may also be seen in different forms elsewhere in the world?

Is it hard to see that in this country our traditional value-forming élite has broken up and we are looking for a replacement? The cohesion of the British ruling classes, right down to 1914, must be a source of wonderment to the observer after the deluge. We had, for better or worse, a still confident aristocracy, whose 'society' still really functioned as a forcing-house of critical judgment capable of recognizing a range of talent; we had a dominant middle class small enough to be catered for by two libraries but big enough to support several very good newspapers and reviews; and in 1914 we still had a literature – on the verge, indeed, of one of its greatest ages.

Then came our modern world. The twilight of the Victorian gods was the triumph of the idea of equality. For all the self-security of the Victorian élite, they had uneasy feelings that in a free country all heads must be counted equal, and so granted universal manhood suffrage well in advance of any irresistible demand for it, and decreed compulsory literacy by the act of 1870.

Henceforth, anyway, in the modern world, we were to be masterless. Now, since all societies need language, values and government, the vacuum caused by the abdication of a whole class has been filled – grossly by the popular press, I.T.V., the crude life of 'pop' idols dispensing what they take to be morality, etc., less obviously but more significantly by the low new languages of the centre which have been my theme.

Yet criticism, the survival of the formal activity and the guarantee it gives to the individual life, offers a kind of hope. D. H. Lawrence, in one of those cataclysmic imaginings of which he was a little too self-indulgently fond, says 'Supposing a bomb were put under the whole scheme of things, what would we be, after? What feelings do we want to carry through into the next epoch? What feelings will carry us through?'[12] Lawrence assumes

[12] 'Surgery for the Novel – or a Bomb', *Phoenix*, p. 520.

so calmly that after this bomb has exploded our scheme of things we shall still be there, ourselves, in the next world! That which makes us ourselves, in his image, is a certain kind of feelings. Is it so? (And what would it be like to carry these feelings through without our language and without our critical faculties?) Mr Ted Hughes writes even more briskly about the end of the world, and sees Crow as 'what manages to drag himself out' of 'the complete abolition of everything that's been up to this point'.[13]

Lawrence's 'great bomb' *has* been put under the whole scheme of things: one might call it in shorthand the industrial revolution and the disappearance or corruption of the old value-forming centres which that has led to. The bomb is a slow one, but we are now used to ecological time-scales. Is Crow, or even what Lawrence offers, sufficient to take us through the explosion?

The necessary kind of hope I find in the idea of criticism – and the reason I think Dr Leavis a more hopeful writer than Mr Hughes – is the possibility it gives of continuing true description and real standards, the possibility of seeing something steadily and whole even if what we see is monstrous or the destruction of what we cannot afford to lose. If we see something as it really is that in itself improves the situation and shows we have not lost the power to perceive and to judge. That is the hope that the good life of our language can continue and renew itself in change, however threatened and derided it may be, and however frail its survival. After all, though present threats are new, it is the nature of the human world – and doesn't detract from the marvellous dependability of language – that it should always be threatened.

I have not been writing about *how* to be a critic. 'The rest/Is prayer, observance, discipline, thought and action.' Whether we manage the criticism that is necessary to life is between each one of us and his or her conscience, not a question for me to discuss in public. All I have hoped to show is that criticism is the continuing possibility of a serious language – of the possibility of salvation, or love, or Jerusalem, in a life recognizably human.

It is not generally realized (as I know from the experience of discussion groups) that D. H. Lawrence's poem of great triumph, 'The Song of a Man who has come through' is a hymn to criticism.

What is the knocking?

[13] Interview in *The London Magazine* (January 1971), p. 19.

What is the knocking at the door in the night?

It is someone wants to do us harm.

No, no, it is three strange angels.
Admit them, admit them.

That, I think, is one for Plato and in favour of Leavis on 'wonder'. If 'admit them' is right, it is true criticism of impulse, and that itself is inspiration, and new life.

Literary criticism has to start with new life, with the apprehension of the work of art that wonders at it and enjoys it. We have to try to be faithful to the best we know, come what may; literary criticism is one great sign that faith is not unrewarded, for the knowledge of great poems cannot but be its own reward, since the 'knowledge' is the same as the delight in which we recognize the poetry. 'It is impossible to feel them without becoming a portion of that beauty which we contemplate,' Shelley says.

The force of the paradox in Chaucer's great poem 'Trouthe' is this recognition that new life comes out of faithfulness to the old. The poem is a beautiful account of what I have been calling criticism in human life. To the modern eye the penultimate line of the first stanza looks contradictory, but I don't think it is:

Hold the high way, and let thy ghost thee lead.

But what if my spirit leads me off the high road? Chaucer is right: we must have faith in the creativity of our great language, faith that we can, by grace, make our souls within it, by extending the path. Criticism is holding the high way and letting thy ghost lead thee. The reward Chaucer promises is what we all as critics have to believe in:

And trouthe shal delivere, it is no drede

Faithfulness to the best we know, a kind of bondage, will yet set us free. That is a faith we can and must hold on to, whatever else we lose.

Coda: One Language or,
The Renascence is not Dead[1]

This quarterly review is the offspring of the marriage of two ambitions. One of them is to treat with seriousness and between one pair of wrappers a wide variety of subjects normally left to specialists, browsing undisturbed in their fields. We wish to follow the great Victorian reviews in dealing wth politics, art, literature, philosophy, etc., and at a level of accomplishment which one anticipates (often in vain) from a periodical of the kind that sells only to university libraries and is read, if at all, only by the people who write it.

Anyone who sympathizes with this ambition will know that it is

> of a birth as rare
> As 'tis for object strange and high

but he may well want to continue the quotation:

> It was begotten by despair
> Upon Impossibility.

A few words may therefore usefully be given to suggesting why what we want to do is not merely possible, but necessary – for the well-being of (*inter alia*) the specialisms.

A cultured man in the Renascence – so runs the commonplace belief of our century – could possibly acquire the sum of human knowledge; but, thanks to science, the sum of human knowledge is now so vast that no one man can possess more than a tiny fragment of it: so the intellectual world now consists of specialists talking each about his own specialism to his fellow-specialists. One belief behind this publication is that, on the contrary, our modern modesty has little to do with the sum of human knowledge, and much with the present condition of our civilization.

[1] The prospectus for *The Human World*, issued in 1970.

243

'The sum of human knowledge' is not, as the phrase suggests, an aggregating pile; it is not an arithmetical sum in addition; neither is it a sum of intellectual money accumulating at compound boredom in the libraries of the world. Knowledge is not contained in books or computers: the only object capable of harbouring that doubtful guest is the individual human mind.

But each branch of knowledge, each 'subject', has its own discipline. Few people undergo more than one discipline; hence few are competent outside one discipline, and only others within it can judge their work. This has a certain kind of truth; but the way in which these reasonable-looking ideas are used to cut off the humane disciplines from the human world is the centre of our concern.

Scholarship is not distinct from humanity: all scholars have been human beings before they become scholars, and some even remain so, afterwards. The humane disciplines on which we centre – philosophy, history, criticism of literature and the arts, politics, economics, theology – all have their characteristic modes of thought, in the understanding of which the subject consists. All these subjects make use of special weightings of language; in them words take on meanings they do not possess in, for instance, 'ordinary speech'. Nevertheless, it is important to remember that works in these subjects are, at their best, written in a common language. We go further and say that at bottom they are written *for* a common language. In these central cases the link between the language of the specialism and the common language is so strong that anything really thought about, let us say, religion, politics, the life of society present and past, has to be written in the common language. If what a subject has to say is translated into the common language from a specialist jargon there is something wrong not with the common language but with thought in the specialism. (Translation is more likely to be *into* a jargon, to satisfy the demands of specialist journals.)

Is history written for historians and philosophy for philosophers? On the contrary, scholars extend the language in this or that direction without its being any the less the common language; which means that, to a measure, others outside the specialism may follow it – the measure of seeing some of its bearings upon their life and their specialism. It is the bearings of the subjects on each other and on other things within a language that makes culture possible. The cultured man is the man potentially or actually capable of thought about these things, in his own language – though of course not 'capable' without a great effort which will modify his language as it is moulded by the language of a specialism. If we do succeed in providing a centre where ('speaking in English', as Gillie Potter used to say) the academic specialisms can meet, they will be in our debt, for we shall have reminded them of one of the conditions of their existence: that they speak the language of men. This would be a sign of the continued existence of our civilization.

This brings us to our second ambition, also well within the tradition of the Victorian general reviews: we wish to offer thoughtful criticism of the state of English civilization. Our contention is that as the 'subjects' only exist as the inter-related parts of a common language, the 'subjects', our civilization, and the individual, stand or fall together.

It is as true now as in the Renascence that a man is human by virtue of taking his place in the human world, and that *that* consists, in large measure, of his finding himself in his native language. Standard English, the language we all understand, is the place where we can know politics, novels, newspapers, letters, railway timetables, conversations, religion, learned works – all polite discourse, that is, except the exact sciences and the technologies. (And the latter depend on the common language.) The former vast range of activities are all found in the various styles of one language, in our case English; and the written language is their mode of thought, by means of which they can meet in the individual mind. It is not necessary for everyone to be proficient in every style, just as scholars need not master each humane discipline. But none of these styles, none of these subjects, is separate: all are found only as they bear on each other within one language, that is to say, within a particular civilization and, potentially, within the individual mind that speaks the language. As we once read in (*mirabile dictu*) *The Observer*, 'Ideas, scientific or otherwise, can only be born and flourish and be recognized as important where men talk a common language in which such ideas can be discussed and evaluated.'

If the relations of the common language go, we no longer have the possibility of a civilization: we become some different, post-human creature that cannot have a name. When the centre cannot hold mere anarchy is *necessarily* loosed upon the world. Languages and civilizations can decline, and that cannot be distinct from the impoverishment of individual lives. Civilizations can also improve, of course. In either case the dialogue, the creation of language across the range of what we call the human world, *is* the particular civilization. Our wish to ask questions about 'the state of English civilization' is the natural partner of our contention that the specialisms belong to the common language. Perversity, it may be objected, has made strange bedfellows: is not this 'state of English civilization' just the kind of phrase that cannot be made to mean anything precise enough to be discussed? We share the fear, but hope to put salt on that phrase's tail by resolving it into 'how people write and talk, what they are doing to the language'. If we can quote the ways people write – the ways they organize their world – we may escape the obvious dangers of prophesying and/or waffling. And again, this attempt is a thoroughly traditional object for a review.

These remarks will, we anticipate, be taken as little-England-ism, provincialism, élitism, paternalism, patriotism or worse. We hope to carry a French Commentary; in number 2 we shall be taking the Prime Minister *et al.* to task for their failure to understand the meaning of 'Europe': but we do recognize that 'home is where one starts from' and that English is our language. And, though we are resolved not to print much academic literary criticism, we shall be keeping in mind that our language is the language of Shakespeare, and that in the possession, in our language, of the most splendid tradition of creative writing there has ever been, we have at once a goad and a guarantee – as well as what must be for us the prime example of thought in a common language. As to 'élitism' – if we show ourselves to be an *élite* we shall think ourselves lucky.

How to have a human civilization in a world of academic specialism? One answer of our century has been: journalism – which offers creation of and comment on a human world, but only by making a common language which is incapable of expressing thought. Increasingly our civilization holds itself together within the thought-forms of journalism. Our centres of national consciousness have never been so uncivilized. The press (see our review of *The Times*), broadcasting, parliament, the churches, the universities (was it not a professor, and an expert on semantics at that, who recently wrote that 'the potential of the computer in the world of thought is perhaps as great, if not greater, than that of the human being'?[2]) – all the places that should be 'rocks of defence for human nature', are becoming the no-man's-land left by the decay of language. The principal target of our comment will be the disastrous unwisdom of the prevailing climate of our 'technologico-Benthamite' enlightenment which controls all three parties, the daily and weekly press, and all the television channels. If their English is 'the state of our civilization' there is certainly a place for a criticism we do not find in our contemporaries and, in a world where decisions (or failure to see the need for decisions) have such overwhelming consequences, there is a great *need* for the criticism that is possible to a common language.

So we like to think of ourselves as competing with our very successful rival, the *News of the World*. We too must be able to say, almost, 'All Human Life Is There.' It is by covering the range of the humanities that we hope to be working on a sense of what human life – *our* human life, where 'history is now and England' – is, and must be.

[2] F. H. George, 'Man and the Computer', *Progress* (1969), p. 179.